Phalcon Cookbook

Master Phalcon by implementing hands-on recipes using
industry best practices with the Web and CLI interfaces

David Schissler

Serghei Iakovlev

BIRMINGHAM - MUMBAI

Phalcon Cookbook

Copyright © 2016 Packt Publishing

First published: November 2016

Production reference: 1281116

Published by Packt Publishing Ltd.
Livery Place
35 Livery Street
Birmingham B3 2PB, UK.

ISBN 978-1-78439-688-6

www.packtpub.com

Credits

Authors
David Schissler

Serghei Iakovlev

Reviewer
Nikolaos Dimopoulos

Acquisition Editor
Reshma Raman

Content Development Editor
Parshva Sheth

Technical Editor
Rutuja Vaze

Copy Editor
Safis Editing

Project Coordinator
Ritika Manoj

Proofreaders
Safis Editing

Indexer
Tejal Daruwale Soni

Production Coordinator
Aparna Bhagat

Cover Work
Aparna Bhagat

About the Authors

David Schissler was born and raised in Northern California. He received a significant portion of his education from Santa Rosa Junior College, Chico State University, and ultimately received a Bachelor of Computer Science from Sonoma State University.

David started his career as a programmer working with VB.net before transitioning solely into web development. He is a longtime Linux user and is an avid supporter and user of completely open source development platforms, including, the firmware, operating system, programming languages, and text editors.

David is a world traveler who has lived on three different continents for extended periods of time. He is quite comfortable living out of a single bag while developing web software, writing books, and traveling the world.

I would like to thank Bill Wiggins for sharing our dreams and for my profound cafe experiences in many parts of the world. I would like to thank John Gudgeon for giving me that necessary kick and helping me evacuate my apartment so that I could jump onto that fateful sail boat heading south , and my father Jim Schissler for writing puzzle games for the TRS-80 that we hooked up to the living room television. I'd also like to thank everyone that has been supportive of my education and adventures.

Serghei Iakovlev has been working as a Ruby/PHP developer for over 7 years and has been specializing in web application development. As a supporter and advocate of Behavior Driven Development (BDD), he is also a member of the Codeception team.

Serghei can be found neck deep in innovative technologies, which introduced him to Phalcon. He is responsible for the coordination of bug fixes, testing, developer tools, incubator, and supports other Phalcon-related projects.

When he's not working, Serghei enjoys watching documentaries, science fiction movies, and sometimes plays Mahjong or Go.

I'd like to thank my wife, Yaroslava, for her patience, encouragement, and assistance in translation of my part of the book. I'd also like to thank my technical leader, Andres Gutierrez, for creating such a wonderful framework, and my team mate, Nikolaos Dimopoulos, for his assistance in technical details and for all his recommendations. These people helped me get this book finished.

About the Reviewer

Nikolaos (Nikos) Dimopoulos has over 20 years of progressive experience in designing and developing applications. He is currently serving as a Senior Developer/Analyst for ITWorks Inc. Nikolaos has always been passionate about quality, testability, and good design. Throughout his career, he has been everywhere, from leading the Technical Cooperation Project Monitoring and Management System (TCPMMS) at the UN/International Atomic Energy Agency in Vienna, to being a main catalyst in the growth of a widely popular online community.

He is constantly curious about new technologies and finds ways to increase the performance of his applications. This led him to discover PhalconPHP a few years back. With his contributions, it was not long before he became a member of the core team, helping with documentation, tests, and other duties.

In his free time, he enjoys time with his family, contributes to open source, writes his thoughts on his blog, and tries to keep up to speed with technology.

> I would like to thank my family for all the support they have given me throughout the review of this book. Without it, I would have never made it.

www.PacktPub.com

eBooks, discount offers, and more

Did you know that Packt offers eBook versions of every book published, with PDF and ePub files available? You can upgrade to the eBook version at www.PacktPub.com and as a print book customer, you are entitled to a discount on the eBook copy. Get in touch with us at customercare@packtpub.com for more details.

At www.PacktPub.com, you can also read a collection of free technical articles, sign up for a range of free newsletters and receive exclusive discounts and offers on Packt books and eBooks.

https://www.packtpub.com/mapt

Get the most in-demand software skills with Mapt. Mapt gives you full access to all Packt books and video courses, as well as industry-leading tools to help you plan your personal development and advance your career.

Why Subscribe?

- ▸ Fully searchable across every book published by Packt
- ▸ Copy and paste, print, and bookmark content
- ▸ On demand and accessible via a web browser

Table of Contents

Preface

Phalcon was created to maximize the performance of PHP applications. Along the way, Phalcon adopted many industry best practices and became a model of what a modern PHP application should look like.

In the beginning, Phalcon was written purely in C language, and this made it difficult for many types of developers to contribute to the project. Starting with version 2.0, the project was rewritten in a new PHP resembling language called Zephir, which allowed many more people to contribute. Recently, with the release of Phalcon 3.0, the framework has begun its first period of long-term support and adherence to semantic versioning.

What this book covers

Chapter 1, *Getting Used to Phalcon*, demonstrates how to start a Phalcon project, configure your IDE to make your work on the project easier, and brings to light the main principles you must understand while dealing with the Phalcon Framework.

Chapter 2, *Structuring Your projects*, covers the project structure. This chapter demonstrates one of the optional versions of the project structure and helps configuring routing and introduces how to use middlewares in your project.

Chapter 3, *Processing Requests*, takes you through the process of a normal web request as well as explores the Websockets and EventSource request models.

Chapter 4, *Dealing with Data*, teaches you to the skills to deal with real data using relations, PHQL, or raw SQL and how to use customized database adapters.

Chapter 5, *Presenting Your Application*, introduces Views. It covers aspects such as using HTML fragments, working with layout structure, viewing snippets, as well as working with Volt Template Engine.

Chapter 6, *Making Use of Advanced Features*, covers the strong points of Phalcon Framework, such as dependency injection, validation, working with sessions, event management, complex routing, and so on.

Chapter 7, *Debugging and Profiling*, demonstrates how to handle the unusual and troublesome aspects of a project.

Chapter 8, *Fine Tuning and Optimizing*, talks about how to optimize a project for high throughput and reliability.

Chapter 9, *High Performance Applications with Phalcon*, covers the work with high load projects. You will learn how to work with the message queues and caching. This chapter also introduces Zephir language. It covers the main principles of creating extensions in Zephir and the Phalcon Framework enhancement.

Chapter 10, *Securing Your Applications*, avoids common attacks and implement an ACL with password hashing.

What you need for this book

This book requires PHP 5.5 or later, a web server, database server, and command line access. Although any web and database server can be used in this book, the reader will have a much easier time with Apache and MySQL. This book makes extensive use of the Phalcon Developer Tools to create projects, and this will require command line usage. Some recipes in this book will require specific PHP extensions and so the reader will need to have the ability to install these extensions on their machine as well as the ability to restart the web and database server, to read the web server logs and many other things that require administrator access. Windows, Mac, and Linux are all supported environments.

Who this book is for

If you are a beginner-to-intermediate Phalcon developer who wants to level up, or an advanced user who is seeking some new techniques and insight, then this book is perfect for you. This book will be relevant to you over a long period of time due to the mixed nature of this book in providing both abstract comprehension as well as specific examples meant to be usable in your projects. You will be able to experiment with each new aspect of integration in prebuilt recipes meant to best illustrate each specific feature. This will save you lots of time getting up to speed before attempting to integrate into a real application.

Sections

In this book, you will find several headings that appear frequently (Getting ready, How to do it, How it works, There's more, and See also).

To give clear instructions on how to complete a recipe, we use these sections as follows:

Getting ready

This section tells you what to expect in the recipe, and describes how to set up any software or any preliminary settings required for the recipe.

How to do it...

This section contains the steps required to follow the recipe.

How it works...

This section usually consists of a detailed explanation of what happened in the previous section.

There's more...

This section consists of additional information about the recipe in order to make the reader more knowledgeable about the recipe.

See also

This section provides helpful links to other useful information for the recipe.

Conventions

In this book, you will find a number of text styles that distinguish between different kinds of information. Here are some examples of these styles and an explanation of their meaning.

Code words in text, database table names, folder names, filenames, file extensions, pathnames, dummy URLs, user input, and Twitter handles are shown as follows: "The stubs are located in the phalcon-devtools repository you just cloned under the /ide subfolder"

A block of code is set as follows:

```php
<?php

class Hats extends Phalcon\Mvc\Model
{
}
```

Any command-line input or output is written as follows:

```
$phql = "SELECT Hats.* FROM Hats JOIN Colors WHERE Colors.name = 'red'";
```

New terms and **important words** are shown in bold. Words that you see on the screen, for example, in menus or dialog boxes, appear in the text like this: "Create a user by entering the user name and password and clicking the **Create a User** button"

 Warnings or important notes appear in a box like this.

 Tips and tricks appear like this.

Reader feedback

Feedback from our readers is always welcome. Let us know what you think about this book—what you liked or disliked. Reader feedback is important for us as it helps us develop titles that you will really get the most out of.

To send us general feedback, simply e-mail feedback@packtpub.com, and mention the book's title in the subject of your message.

If there is a topic that you have expertise in and you are interested in either writing or contributing to a book, see our author guide at www.packtpub.com/authors.

Customer support

Now that you are the proud owner of a Packt book, we have a number of things to help you to get the most from your purchase.

Downloading the example code

You can download the example code files for this book from your account at http://www.packtpub.com. If you purchased this book elsewhere, you can visit http://www.packtpub.com/support and register to have the files e-mailed directly to you.

You can download the code files by following these steps:

1. Log in or register to our website using your e-mail address and password.
2. Hover the mouse pointer on the **SUPPORT** tab at the top.
3. Click on **Code Downloads & Errata**.
4. Enter the name of the book in the **Search** box.
5. Select the book for which you're looking to download the code files.
6. Choose from the drop-down menu where you purchased this book from.
7. Click on **Code Download**.

You can also download the code files by clicking on the **Code Files** button on the book's webpage at the Packt Publishing website. This page can be accessed by entering the book's name in the **Search** box. Please note that you need to be logged in to your Packt account.

Once the file is downloaded, please make sure that you unzip or extract the folder using the latest version of:

- ▸ WinRAR / 7-Zip for Windows
- ▸ Zipeg / iZip / UnRarX for Mac
- ▸ 7-Zip / PeaZip for Linux

The code bundle for the book is also hosted on GitHub at `https://github.com/PacktPublishing/Phalcon-Cookbook`.We also have other code bundles from our rich catalog of books and videos available at `https://github.com/PacktPublishing/`. Check them out!

Errata

Although we have taken every care to ensure the accuracy of our content, mistakes do happen. If you find a mistake in one of our books—maybe a mistake in the text or the code—we would be grateful if you could report this to us. By doing so, you can save other readers from frustration and help us improve subsequent versions of this book. If you find any errata, please report them by visiting `http://www.packtpub.com/submit-errata`, selecting your book, clicking on the **Errata Submission Form** link, and entering the details of your errata. Once your errata are verified, your submission will be accepted and the errata will be uploaded to our website or added to any list of existing errata under the Errata section of that title.

To view the previously submitted errata, go to `https://www.packtpub.com/books/content/support` and enter the name of the book in the search field. The required information will appear under the **Errata** section.

Piracy

Piracy of copyrighted material on the Internet is an ongoing problem across all media. At Packt, we take the protection of our copyright and licenses very seriously. If you come across any illegal copies of our works in any form on the Internet, please provide us with the location address or website name immediately so that we can pursue a remedy.

Please contact us at `copyright@packtpub.com` with a link to the suspected pirated material.

We appreciate your help in protecting our authors and our ability to bring you valuable content.

Questions

If you have a problem with any aspect of this book, you can contact us at `questions@packtpub.com`, and we will do our best to address the problem.

1
Getting Used to Phalcon

In this chapter, we will cover the following topics:

- Getting your IDE to work nicely with Phalcon
- Creating the application directory structure
- Setting up your request entry point
- Easily loading code on demand
- Initializing Phalcon to handle a request
- Understanding the request life cycle

Introduction

Despite the fact that **Phalcon** is a framework for **PHP** application development, it isn't itself *PHP*-based. Therefore, some difficulties may appear when using syntax highlighting or code autocompletion. In this chapter, we will try to study how to set up autocompletion in a modern **Integrated Development Environment** (**IDE**) and how to enable code autocompletion.

An essential step in the architecture process when developing an application is a clear understanding of the project directory structure and the role of each of the directories. We will use a variation of a Phalcon project directory structure, which is easy to deploy and upgrade. The directory structure, which we work with in this chapter, isn't a rule set in stone. In future you will, time after time, use different directory structures, which will be different than the one we will be using. That structure is only one of the options and a starting point for your needs, and it easily responds to changes caused by certain technical conditions.

Phalcon is not only the fastest framework in the world, it is one of the easiest frameworks. As a rule, you don't need any special knowledge or additional software. However, when developing an application with Phalcon, you will need to create a base system configuration and application skeleton. In this chapter, we will learn how to deploy an application with the use of Phalcon, how to make its base configuration, and how to create a flexible and efficient application skeleton, which you can use in future.

Any object-oriented PHP application needs classes. You have to tell your class autoloader where your classes are situated and which way they can be searched for. We will look at some possible options of class auto-loading in Phalcon and their usage methods.

Many developers, despite their experience, have difficulty when working with a `Request` component. Phalcon isn't an exception. We will discover how to make a base application configuration so that Phalcon starts handling requests. We will learn how Phalcon handles these requests and in what sequence they are executed. We will learn which components take part in a **request life cycle**, where it is possible to catch the request, how to specify its state, as well as how to take any suitable actions.

Getting your IDE to work nicely with Phalcon

Most IDEs have some form of code completion as part of the program. To enable auto-completion for Phalcon's namespaces, we will need to help the IDE recognize those namespaces. We will also see how to enable Volt syntax highlighting and Phalcon API auto-completion for major IDEs.

Getting ready

To get started, we should have **Git** installed. To enable auto-completion in your IDE, you need to get the Phalcon stubs. For these purposes, clone the `Phalcon Developer Tools` repository:

```
git clone git@github.com:phalcon/phalcon-devtools.git
```

How to do it...

The following are the steps needed to complete this recipe.

Ways to enable Phalcon API autocompletion in major IDEs

PhpStorm

1. Using the **Project Tool** window in **PhpStorm**, select **External Libraries**, right-click on the section, and select **Configure PHP Include Paths...** from the drop-down menu.

2. Then, using the **External Libraries** dialog box, click the **+** button. Next, select the **Specify Other...** option in the drop-down menu and specify the location of the Phalcon stubs. The stubs are located in the `phalcon-devtools` repository you just cloned under the `/ide` subfolder. You should specify the path `phalcon-devtools/ide/stubs/Phalcon` and click on **Apply**.

NetBeans

1. In NetBeans, you need to open the **Projects** window (*Ctrl + F1*) and select **Include Path**. Right-click on the section and select **Properties** from the drop-down menu.

2. Then, open the **Project Properties** window and click on the **Add Folder...** button. Next, specify the location of the Phalcon stubs. The stubs are located in the `phalcon-devtools` repository you just cloned under the `/ide` subfolder. You should specify the path `phalcon-devtools/ide/stubs/Phalcon` and click on the **OK** button.

Ways to enable Volt syntax highlighting in major IDEs

Netbeans

1. Click on the **Tools** menu entry and select **Options**.

2. In the opened window, select **Miscellaneous | Files**.

3. In the **File Associations** group box, click on the button **New...** next to the **File Extensions** option, enter the extension `volt`, and click on **OK**.

4. Select **TWIG (text/x-twig)** in the **Associated File Type (MIME)** drop-down menu.

PhpStorm

1. Open **File | Settings**. Next select **Editor | File Types**.

2. In the **Recognized File Types** group box, select **Twig** and add the extension `*.volt` into the **Registered Patterns** group box by pressing the **+** button.

Syntax highlighting for Sublime Text or TextMate

Installation via Package Control

If you have **Sublime Package Control**, you know what to do. If not, well, it's a package manager for **Sublime Text**, and it's awesome!

After installing Sublime Package Control and restarting the editor:

1. Open the **Command Palette** (*Ctrl* + *Shift* + *P* or *Cmd* + *Shift* + *P*).

2. Type `Install Package` and press *Enter*.

3. Find **Volt** and press *Enter*.

Manual installation

For manual installation, clone the `Volt` syntax highlight for the `Sublime Text 2/ Textmate` repository:

```
git@github.com:phalcon/volt-sublime-textmate.git
```

Depending on your OS, copy the `volt-sublime-textmate/Volt` directory to any of the following locations:

1. **Sublime Text 2**:
    1. Mac OS X:

        ```
        ~/Library/Application Support/Sublime Text 2/Packages
        ```

    2. Linux:

        ```
        ~/.Sublime Text 2/Packages
        ```

    3. Windows:

        ```
        %APPDATA%/Sublime Text 2/Packages/
        ```

2. **Sublime Text 3**:
    1. Mac OS X:

        ```
        ~/Library/Application Support/Sublime Text 3/Packages
        ```

    2. Linux:

        ```
        ~/.Sublime Text 3/Packages
        ```

    3. Windows:

        ```
        %APPDATA%/Sublime Text 3/Packages/
        ```

3. **TextMate**:

    ```
    /Library/Application Support/TextMate/Bundles
    ```

How it works...

Some IDEs need help understanding the framework syntax. To get the IDE to understand, we download a list of all the Phalcon stubs. Then, when we add it to the `include` path, NetBeans (or PhpStorm) will automatically check the file and show us the autocomplete options. To enable the `Volt` or `Zephir` syntax highlight, we have to configure our IDE or text editor accordingly.

Creating the application directory structure

In this recipe, we will take a brief look at the commonly used directory structure of a single module application. A structure of this type is aimed at providing a great starting point for different applications.

Getting ready

We don't need any special means to implement this recipe. We will create the project structure on site, at the development stage. Important points of this recipe are the names of directories and their location.

How to do it...

Follow these steps to complete this recipe:

1. Create a root directory for your project, where `myprojectname` is the name of your project:

    ```
    /var/www/myprojectname
    ```

2. Create three second-level directories in the root directory:

    ```
    /var/www/myprojectname/app
    /var/www/myprojectname/public
    /var/www/myprojectname/.phalcon
    ```

3. Create the following subdirectories in the `public` directory:

    ```
    /var/www/myprojectname/public/css
    /var/www/myprojectname/public/img
    /var/www/myprojectname/public/js
    ```

4. Create the following subdirectories in the `app` directory:

    ```
    /var/www/myprojectname/app/cache
    /var/www/myprojectname/app/config
    /var/www/myprojectname/app/controllers
    /var/www/myprojectname/app/library
    ```

```
/var/www/myprojectname/app/logs
/var/www/myprojectname/app/models
/var/www/myprojectname/app/tasks
/var/www/myprojectname/app/views
```

5. Create the following subdirectories in the `cache` directory:

```
/var/www/myprojectname/app/cache/annotations
/var/www/myprojectname/app/cache/data
/var/www/myprojectname/app/cache/metadata
/var/www/myprojectname/app/cache/volt
```

6. Make sure that the just created structure eventually appears as follows:

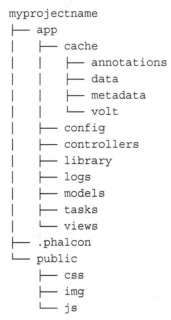

```
myprojectname
├── app
│   ├── cache
│   │   ├── annotations
│   │   ├── data
│   │   ├── metadata
│   │   └── volt
│   ├── config
│   ├── controllers
│   ├── library
│   ├── logs
│   ├── models
│   ├── tasks
│   └── views
├── .phalcon
└── public
    ├── css
    ├── img
    └── js
```

How it works...

The project root directory contains the following directories: `app`, `public`, and `.phalcon` (note that the last one has a point at the beginning of its name).

In the `app` directory, there will be, as you would expect, the main application code. We will describe this folder in detail shortly.

The `public` directory will contain the entry point of your application and directories for various static assets (JavaScript files, images, and CSS files).

The .phalcon directory will be used by the Phalcon developer tools for internal purposes (migration creation, code generation, and so on). This is the Phalcon system directory. There is no need to create something in it.

The app directory contains a subdirectory for controllers as well as their views and models. Additionally, there is the tasks directory, which is intended for **cli** tasks, the library directory for the general application components (plug-ins, helpers, and other custom classes), the logs directory, where we will store our log files, and the cache directory for storing cached data of different application components.

In the cache directory, there are the following directories: annotations to store the file cache of model annotations, data to store common file cache, metadata to store the model structure cache, and volt to store the view cache.

Note that we have created different directories to store screenshots. These directories are utilized when we are using the **File Cache**. If you will be using a cache adapter other than the File one, you don't need to create the directory structure here.

Setting up your request entry point

After installing Phalcon, we need to create a **Bootstrap** class in which we'll set about our application tuning. We will create a flexible yet robust Bootstrap file to receive requests for the application.

Getting ready

The first and most important file you need to create for the initial loading of your application is index.php. This is the file in which all your HTTP requests will be redirected. Create this file in the public directory of your project, if you haven't got one:

```
/var/www/myBlog/public/index.php
```

How to do it...

Follow these steps to complete this recipe:

1. Put the following code into the index.php file:

```php
<?php

define('APP_PATH', realpath(dirname(__DIR__)));

try {
  include APP_PATH . '/app/library/Bootstrap.php';
  $di = new \Phalcon\Di\FactoryDefault();
```

```php
    $bootstrap = new \MyBlog\Bootstrap($di);

    echo $application->run();
} catch (\Exception $e) {
    $logger = $di->getShared('logger');
    $logger->error($e->getMessage());
    $logger->error($e->getTraceAsString());
}
```

2. Create a `Bootstrap` class skeleton in your `app/library/Bootstrap.php` file:

```php
<?php

namespace MyBlog;

class Bootstrap extends \Phalcon\Mvc\Application
{
    protected $loaders = [
        'environment',
        'logger',
        'loader',
        'database',
        'views',
        // other loaders ...
    ];

    protected $config;

    public function __construct(\Phalcon\DiInterface $di =
null)
    {
        $di = $di ?: new \Phalcon\Di\FactoryDefault();
        $this->config = include APP_PATH . '/app/config/config.php';


        // Store config in the DI container
        $di->setShared('config', $this->config);

        parent::__construct($di);
    }
}
```

3. Create an application `config` file in the `app/config/config.php` file:

```php
<?php

return new \Phalcon\Config([
    'application' => [
        'controllersDir' => APP_PATH . '/app/controllers/',
        'modelsDir'      => APP_PATH . '/app/models/',
        'viewsDir'       => APP_PATH . '/app/views/',
        'libraryDir'     => APP_PATH . '/app/library/',
        'logsDir'        => APP_PATH . '/app/logs/',
        'baseUri'        => '/',
        'debug'          => true
    ],
    'database'   => [
        'adapter'  => 'Mysql',
        'host'     => 'localhost',
        'username' => 'root',
        'password' => '',
        'dbname'   => 'my_blog',
        'charset'  => 'utf8'
    ],
    'metaData' => [
        'metaDataDir' => APP_PATH . '/app/cache/metaData/',
    ],
    'modelsCache' => [
        'lifetime' => 86400 * 30,
        'cacheDir' => APP_PATH . '/app/cache/data/',
        'prefix'   => 'myblog-cache-data-'
    ],
    'volt' => [
        'cacheDir'    => APP_PATH . '/app/cache/volt/',
        'compiledExt' => '.php',
        'separator'   => '_',
    ]
]);
```

4. Create an application initialization method, `Bootstrap::run`, in the `app/library/Bootstrap.php` file:

```php
public function run()
{
  $em = new \Phalcon\Events\Manager();
  $this->setEventsManager($eventsManager);
  $di = $this->_dependencyInjector;
```

```php
    foreach ($this->loaders as $service) {
      $serviceName = ucfirst($service);
      $this->{'init' . $serviceName}($di, $this->config, $em);
    }

    $di->setShared('eventsManager', $em);

    return $this->handle()->getContent();
  }
```

5. Next, create all the methods required for the application service initialization. Use the `Bootstrap::loaders` class property, which was created in Step 2, to define the methods. Use the **CamelCase** style, adding the `init` prefix to the name of every method:

```php
protected initEnvironment($di, $config, $em)
{
  if (true == $config->application->debug) {
    ini_set('display_errors', 1);
    ini_set('display_startup_errors', 1);
    error_reporting(E_ALL | E_STRICT);

    if (extension_loaded('xdebug')) {
      ini_set('xdebug.collect_params', 4);
    }
  } else {
    ini_set('display_errors', 0);
    ini_set('display_startup_errors', 0);
    error_reporting(E_ALL ^ E_NOTICE);
  }

  if (is_readable(APP_PATH . '/vendor/autoload.php')) {
    include APP_PATH . '/vendor/autoload.php';
  }
}

protected initLogger($di, $config, $em)
{
  $di->set('logger', function ($file = 'main', $format =
null) use ($config) {
      $path   = $config->application->logsDir . $file .
'.log';
      $format = $format ?: $config->application->logFormat;
      $logger = new \Phalcon\Logger\Adapter\File($path);
```

```
        if ($format) {
          $formatter = new \Phalcon\Logger\Formatter\Line($format);
          $logger->setFormatter($formatter);
        }

        return $logger;
    });
}

protected initLoader($di, $config, $em)
{
    $di->setShared('loader', function () use ($config, $em) {
      $loader = new \Phalcon\Loader();
      $namespaces = [
        'MyBlog\Models' => $config->application->modelsDir,
        'MyBlog\Controllers' => $config->application-
>controllersDir,
        'MyBlog' => $config->application->libraryDir
      ];

      $loader->registerNamespaces($namespaces);
      $loader->setEventsManager($em);
      $loader->register();

      return $loader;
    });
}
```

6. Use the implementation just described to create all the methods, which you need
   for service initialization. It is evident that all the values of the loaders array are
   in actual fact the initializer names, which we call sequentially. The order of these
   values defines the method call order. You can use the following code template as
   an example:

```
protected initMethodName($di, $config, $eventsManager)
{
    // Some initialization

    return ...; // may be omitted to return null
}
```

How it works...

The first thing that should be observed is that we have used a `Bootstrap` class. Phalcon uses a **Dependency Injection** (**DI**) container to handle all the services you may need to use in your application. We have passed it as a parameter to the `Bootstrap` class constructor, in which we will set up our application.

In the class constructor, we create a DI container. If it wasn't passed as a parameter, include the application configuration by placing it into a container for future use and create an instance, `Phalcon\Mvc\Application`. Note that we already use the `APP_PATH` constant, previously defined. Let's remember how it was defined:

```
define('APP_PATH', realpath(dirname(__DIR__)));
```

We have also created a `loader` class property, which we will discuss later.

We have added the application configuration in a separate file. Usually, it is worthwhile due to the fact that according to the application growth, the configuration of the application elements and services will grow. It is much more convenient to have the whole configuration in one place, rather than scattered all over the application. Here we have specified the main application paths and parameters of the database connection, metadata cache, models, and views. We have defined five directories for our application; these are `controllers`, `models`, `views`, `class library`, and `logs`. Besides this, we have specified directories for the metadata cache of models and for the data itself, as well as a view cache directory. If these directories do not exist, it is time to create them. All we need for our application is presented here.

In the `Bootstrap::run` method we have created the event manager, which we can use at any point, subscribed to its events, and passed it to the application. You must not forget the loaders field we have already defined. We will use it right at the present moment. When iterating through the array, we form the method name, `ucfirst($service)`. Then we register a new event in the event manager (of course, we can subscribe to this event now) and call this method by passing the DI container, the application configuration, and the event manager into it.

Next, let's have a look at the most important of initializer methods. The first one is the application environment configuration. There is nothing out of the ordinary here; we define the application error reporting level in an emergency. Note that error output enabling is designed and suitable only for development and must not be used in ready-made production systems. Finally, we include the **Composer** autoloader, if there is one, and configure the **xdebug** extension to make our application debugging more convenient. Note that it is highly recommended to use at least **Xdebug v2.2.3** for better compatibility with Phalcon.

Next, we've just created a quite powerful logger, which we can use in different ways. The code snippet is as follows:

```
$this->di->get('logger', ['some_file'])->debug('Some text ...');
```

This code, which if used, for example, in a controller, will tell the logger to create the following file on the disk if it is missing there:

```
/var/www/myBlog/app/logs/some_file.log
```

The path for the log creation is formed according to the configuration just defined. The logger will write the following to that file:

```
[Tue, 28 Jul 15 22:09:02 -0500][DEBUG] Some text ...
```

And the following code:

```
$this->di->get('logger')->debug('Some text ...');
```

We will use the `main.log` file. Additionally, we are able to define the message format in our log files. In order to get that done, we need to pass the format as the second array element on the `get` method, like this:

```
get('logger', ['some_file', "%date% - %message%"])
```

Also, we can define the format in our configuration file.

The next method we need is the autoloader initialization method. We have created one more method in our `Bootstrap` class and initialized the class `autoloading` component in this method. It means that we have registered the necessary namespaces there. We have defined the namespace as `MyBlog` for all future library classes, located in `app/library/`, in relation to the application root (think back to our configuration file), and have added paths for the namespaces of models and controllers, which are located in `app/models/` and `app/controllers/`, respectively, to the autoloading. Phalcon Loader will register the namespaces we may need, and PHP will search for some classes within the `MyBlog\Models` namespace in `/var/www/myBlog/app/models/`, within the `MyBlog\Controllers` namespace in `/var/www/myBlog/app/controllers/`, and any other classes contained within the `MyBlog` namespace in `/var/www/myBlog/app/library/` (for example, `MyBlog\Acl` or `MyBlog\Utils\Backup`). In future, as the structure of our application grows, we will always be able to enhance or modify this method.

Finally, when looking at the `Bootstrap::run` method, it becomes apparent that after the successful initialization of all the necessary services, the following parent method, `$this->handle()->getContent()`, is called and returns its result back to the caller. That's just the thing.

The line in the entry point (`index.php`) will display the application output:

```
echo $application->run();
```

If the application throws an exception, we'll write a detailed report into our log file in the `catch` block. We may take it a step further by defining the `errorHandler` method in the `loaders` field of the `Bootstrap` class, and implement the `initErrorHandler` method.

Easily loading code on demand

Here you will learn how to load code on demand by using the **PSR-4** compatible autoloading strategy. We notify the autoloader where the classes are located to load them on demand.

Getting ready

If you are familiar with PHP, you've surely heard of **PSR-0** and **PSR-4** standards, which make it possible to load the required classes automatically at the moment of their call without using such instructions as require and include.

The behavior of `Phalcon\Loader` is based on the PHP's capability of autoloading classes; if any class used in code doesn't exist, a special handler will try to find and load it. `Phalcon\Loader` is designed just for that operation. The loading of only the files needed for a particular class to operate has a positive impact on the application's performance. It helps to avoid wasteful computation, and reduces program memory requirements. This technology is called **Lazy Initialization**.

As of October 21, 2014, PSR-0 has been marked as deprecated. PSR-4 is now recommended as an alternative. Starting from version 3.0.0, the support for prefixes strategy in `Phalcon\Loader` is removed from Phalcon. For that very reason, loading with the use of the PSR-0 standard will be omitted here.

How to do it...

Follow these steps to complete this recipe:

1. Create an autoloader instance in the following way:

```
define('APP_PATH', realpath(dirname(dirname(__DIR__))));

$loader = new \Phalcon\Loader();
$loader->registerNamespaces([
    'MyBlog\Models'      => APP_PATH . '/app/models/',
    'MyBlog\Controllers' => APP_PATH . '/app/controllers/',
    'MyBlog\Library'     => APP_PATH . '/engine/',
]);

$loader->register();
```

2. Now, after configuring the loader in the way shown in the earlier code instance, create the class `MyBlog\Models\Users`, located in `app/models/Users.php`:

```php
<?php

namespace MyBlog\Models;

use Phalcon\Mvc\Model;

class User extends Model
{

}
```

3. Edit `MyBlog\Controllers\IndexController` in `app/controllers/IndexController.php`:

```php
<?php

namespace MyBlog\Controllers;

use Phalcon\Mvc\Controller;

class IndexController extends Controller
{

}
```

4. Edit `MyBlog\Library\SomeClass` in the `engine/SomeClass.php`:

```php
<?php

namespace MyBlog\Library;

class SomeClass
{

}
```

How it works...

The `Phalcon\Loader::registerNamespaces` method gets an associative array, identifying which keys are namespace prefixes and their values are directories where the classes are located in. For instance, after configuring the loader as shown earlier, we can use the following class, `MyBlog\Models\Users`, located in `app/models/Users.php`, `MyBlog\Controllers\IndexController` in `app/controllers/IndexController.php`, and `MyBlog\Library\SomeClass` in `engine/SomeClass.php`.

Let's consider in depth how the class search is carried out when using the namespaces strategy. Let's assume that you have registered the `MyBlog\Library` namespace for the `engine` directory, and then called the class `MyBlog\Library\Some\Example`. After registration, the autoloader knows that the `MyBlog\Library` namespace belongs to the `engine` directory. Next, in the remaining part of the class name (`\Some\Example`), the namespace separator (`\`) will be replaced with the directory separator (`/`), and the file extension will be added. Eventually, this will result in forming the path `engine/Some/Example.php`. So, in such a simple and quite fast way, the class loading with the use of the namespace strategy is performed.

It is defined in the PSR-4 standard that the vendor/package pair can refer to any directory or even more. That's why you can easily register the same namespace to be served by several directories:

```
define('ROOT_PATH', realpath(dirname(dirname(__DIR__))));

$loader = new \Phalcon\Loader();

$loader->registerNamespaces([
    'Phalcon' => ROOT_PATH . '/app/library/Phalcon/',
]);

$loader->register();
```

We have used the `Phalcon` namespace here, regardless of the fact that it is already registered by the framework. There is no conflict here. Using the `Phalcon` namespace, PHP will try to find the class among the classes provided by the framework, and after failing to find it, it will try to find it in the directory `app/library/Phalcon/`.

Note that when registering a namespace, which already exists, and an identical class name in this namespace, you will not be able to call this class. For example, if you register the namespace as previously described, and create the `Phalcon\Crypt` class, located in `app/library/Phalcon/Crypt.php`, you will not be able to call it in the following way: `$cryp = new Phalcon\Crypt()`. This is due to the fact that the Phalcon PHP extension is initialized at the earlier stage and PHP knows already about the `Phalcon\Crypt` class.

But let's return to our `Phalcon` namespace, which we have registered before. Now, if we try to create a new class:

```
$myHelper = new Phalcon\MyHelper();
```

Phalcon will search for it in the file `app/library/Phalcon/MyHelper.php`. Just due to the fact that `Phalcon\Loader` uses the fully PSR-4 compatible autoloader, we have no problems with class autoloading when applying such libraries as **Phalcon Incubator** and Phalcon Developer Tools, using the `Phalcon` namespace.

Furthermore, `Phalcon\Loader` provides other class-loading strategies, which are not PSR-4 compatible. We'll consider them briefly later.

`Phalcon\Loader`, as with most autoloaders, provides class loading with the use of directories. This class loading strategy isn't PSR-4 compatible, but it is efficient, and in certain situations, adequate. The loading with the use of directories comes down to the enumeration of all possible directories in an attempt to search for your classes. The `Phalcon\Loader::registerDirs` method receives the array of directories, in which the search will perform:

```
define('ROOT_PATH', realpath(dirname(dirname(__DIR__))));

$loader = new \Phalcon\Loader();
$loader->registerDirs([
  ROOT_PATH . '/components/',
  ROOT_PATH . '/adapters/',
  ROOT_PATH . '/engine/',
]);

$loader->register();
```

We have told the autoloader that our classes are located in three directories: `components`, `adapters`, and `engine`. Note that this strategy is the slowest. Class registering with the use of directories means that, by calling any class, Phalcon will search through these directories to find a class with the same name as the required class. As our project grows, this type of search will have an impact on performance. When using this class loading strategy, it is important to be mindful of the order of your directories, because you could create two classes with the same name in two different directories. If there is one class named `Example` in each of the following directories, components and engine, then, by calling the class:

```
$myComponent = new Example();
```

The first found class will be used which is the one from the `components` directory.

The third option, which can help you register your classes with the use of the `Phalcon\` `Loader` component, is registering classes. This autoloading method is not PSR-4 compatible, but in some cases it is the fastest. This solution may be efficient when using strategies which don't allow for easy retrieval of the file using the namespace and the `class` directory. The following describes how we can register classes in this way:

```
define('ROOT_PATH', realpath(dirname(dirname(__DIR__))));
$loader = new \Phalcon\Loader();
$loader->registerClasses([
   ROOT_PATH . '/components/Awesome/Example.php',
   ROOT_PATH . '/adapters/Base/BaseAdaper.php'
]);
$loader->register();
```

The `Phalcon\Loader:registerClasses` method gets the array of files, among which the search will be performed. Here we have told the autoloader about two classes, `Example` and `BaseAdapter`, and specified the full path to them. For example, now when calling the class `$example = new Example()`, the class located in `components/Awesome/Example.` `php` will be used. Although this method is the fastest, your file list will grow significantly, and with it the time it takes for the search to be carried out, so it will reduce the performance.

The `Phalcon\Loader` component allows you to combine autoloading options. There is no reason why you shouldn't use them all together, if you needed:

```
define('ROOT_PATH', realpath(dirname(dirname(__DIR__))));
$loader = new \Phalcon\Loader();
$loader->registerNamespaces([
   'MyBlog\Models'      => ROOT_PATH . '/app/models/',
   'MyBlog\Controllers' => ROOT_PATH . '/app/controllers/',
   'MyBlog\Library'     => ROOT_PATH . '/engine/',
]);
$loader->registerDirs([
   ROOT_PATH . '/components/',
   ROOT_PATH . '/adapters/',
   ROOT_PATH . '/engine/',
]);
$loader->registerClasses([
   ROOT_PATH . '/vendor/awesome/plugins/Example.php',
   ROOT_PATH . '/adapters/Base/BaseAdaper.php'
]);
$loader->register();
```

In such a manner, we can register the namespaces, the directories, and the classes.

In summary, it should be mentioned that the strategies that are based on the namespaces are faster than those based on the directories. In some cases, the strategy based on the class registering is faster, but only if your project has a small number of classes. In a relatively large project, the fastest strategy is to register the namespaces.

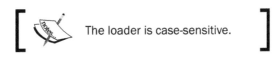 The loader is case-sensitive.

Finally, if the **APC** is enabled, it will be used for the requested file (and this file will be cached).

There's more...

For more information about Lazy Initialization, go to:

`https://en.wikipedia.org/wiki/Lazy_initialization`.

For more detailed information about the PSR-0 standard refer to:

`http://www.php-fig.org/psr/psr-0/, about the PSR-4 standard refer to http://www.php-fig.org/psr/psr-4/`.

Setting up your request entry point

Before you start handling requests, you need to configure your application work environment and prepare all the required components. In this recipe, you will learn what should be done before asking Phalcon to handle an incoming request.

Getting ready

To embark on this recipe, you need to have the web server **Apache** or **Nginx** + **PHP-FPM** installed. Besides this, you should be able to create or change the configuration of the virtual host for your web server and have the proper authority to do so.

How to do it...

Follow these steps to complete this recipe:

1. Create the Nginx virtual host setting as follows:

```
upstream backend {
  server unix:/var/run/php5-fpm.sock;
}

# redirect the request to the non-www domain
```

```nginx
# to choose which domain you prefer
server {
  server_name www.mysite.com;
  return 301 $scheme://mysite.com$request_uri;
}

server {
  listen 80;

  server_name mysite.com;

  error_log  /var/log/nginx/mysite.error.log;
  access_log /var/log/nginx/mysite.access.log;

  index index.php;
  root /var/www/mysite/public;

  try_files $uri $uri/ @rewrite;

  location @rewrite {
    rewrite ^(.*)$ /index.php?_url=/$1 last;
  }

  location ~ \.php$ {
    try_files $uri =404;

    fastcgi_split_path_info ^(.+\.php)(/.+)$;

    fastcgi_pass backend;
    fastcgi_param SCRIPT_FILENAME
$document_root$fastcgi_script_name;
    fastcgi_param PATH_INFO $fastcgi_path_info;
    fastcgi_param PATH_TRANSLATED
$document_root$fastcgi_path_info;
    fastcgi_param   HTTP_REFERER      $http_referer;
    # production | development | staging | testing
    fastcgi_param APP_ENV development;
    fastcgi_buffers 16 16k;
    fastcgi_buffer_size 32k;

    include fastcgi_params;
  }

  location ~* ^/(css|img|js|flv|swf|download)/(.+)$ {
```

```
    root /var/www/mysite/public;
  }

  location ~ /\. {
    return 403;
  }
}
```

2. If you have the Apache web server installed, create the virtual host configuration as follows:

```
<VirtualHost *:80>
  ServerAdmin admin@example.host
  DocumentRoot "/var/www/mysite/public"
  DirectoryIndex index.php
  ServerName mysite.com
  ServerAlias www.mysite.com

  # production | development | staging | testing
  SetEnv APP_ENV development

  <Directory "/var/www/mysite/public">
    Options All
    AllowOverride All
    Allow from all

    RewriteEngine On

    RewriteCond %{REQUEST_FILENAME} !-d
    RewriteCond %{REQUEST_FILENAME} !-f
    RewriteRule ^((?s).*)$ index.php?_url=/$1 [QSA,L]
  </Directory>

  <Files .*>
    Order Deny,Allow
    Deny From All
  </Files>
</VirtualHost>
```

3. Open your bootstrap file and add the URL manager configuration to it:

```
$di->set('url', function () {
    $url = new \Phalcon\Mvc\Url();
    $url->setBaseUri('/');

    return $url;
});
```

4. Then, add the primary routing configuration:

```php
$di->setShared('router', function () {
    $router = new \Phalcon\Mvc\Router();

    if (!isset($_GET['_url'])) {
        $router->setUriSource(Router::URI_SOURCE_SERVER_REQUEST_URI);
    }

    $router->removeExtraSlashes(true);

    $router->add(
        '/',
        [
            'controller' => 'index',
            'action'     => 'index'
        ]
    );

    return $router;
});
```

5. Create a controller, associating it with the routing map defined in the preceding code:

```php
use Phalcon\Mvc\Controller;

class IndexController extends Controller
{
    public function indexAction()
    {
        var_dump($_SERVER);
        return;
    }
}
```

How it works...

We configure the virtual host for our web server. Then, we configure the component `Phalcon\Mvc\Url`. Note that, depending on the installed application root, there may emerge a need to define the base URL. For example, if the document root is `/var/www/mysite`, and your application is installed at `/var/www/mysite/phalcon`, then your base URI (`baseUri`) is `/phalcon/`. When using virtual hosts or if the application is installed in the root directory, the `baseUri` parameter is `/`. By default, Phalcon detects the necessary `baseUri` by itself, but in order to improve performance we recommend to specify it manually.

For creating URIs, the `Phalcon\Mvc\Router` component is used by default. Your application can run with the following default routing pattern:

```
/:controller/:action/:params.
```

Therefore, it's easy to create URIs on this model or by other rules, set in the routing map. When creating an object of the type `Phalcon\Mvc\Router`, you can tell it not to create the default routing. For that purpose, you need to pass `false` to the constructor:

```
$router = new \Phalcon\Mvc\Router(false)
```

Next, we create a router with the default configuration and add a pattern to it, which refers to the site root. By default, the current handling **URI** is taken from the variable `$_GET['_url']`, Phalcon is wired that way, as are the standard **mod-rewrite** rules. Here we use a little trick—we check up whether there is the `_url` (`$_GET['_url']`) key in the superglobal array `$_GET`. In case it is missing, the virtual host configuration doesn't redirect the type `index.php?_url=`. Thus, it's very easy to create a flexible component configuration.

Finally, we create a controller to test our routing with an action, which coincides with the added routing pattern.

There's more...

You can learn about the Apache setup instructions at `http://httpd.apache.org/docs/`, and the complete Nginx documentation at `http://nginx.org/en/docs`. For the **PHP-FPM** configuration directives description, refer to `http://php.net/manual/en/install.fpm.configuration.php`.

For Phalcon installation notes, routing documentation, and generating URLs, refer to `https://docs.phalconphp.com/`.

Understanding the request life cycle

A deeper understanding of the **request life cycle** will lift the veil on the main application mechanisms and offers you the possibility to handle requests more flexibly. This recipe demonstrates how each request usually flows within the framework.

Getting ready

To complete this recipe, you need to have a web server installed and, what is more, you must make the base configuration of your application. Usually, by *base configuration*, we mean that you have your application deployed and have the services configured in all the ways available. You should understand the main class autoloading principles in Phalcon and know how to configure Phalcon Loader. Besides, you need to configure logging in PHP into a readable file.

How to do it...

Follow these steps to complete this recipe:

1. Open the application service configuration and create an event manager, which we will use during further steps:

   ```
   $em = new Phalcon\Events\Manager();
   ```

2. Then, add the following routing setting:

   ```
   $di->setShared('router', function () use ($em) {
     $router = new \Phalcon\Mvc\Router();
     $router->add(
       '/:controller/:action/:params',
       [
         'controller' => 1,
         'action'     => 2,
         'params'     => 3
       ]
     );

     $em->attach('router', new RouterListener);
     $router->setEventsManager($em);

     return $router;
   });
   ```

3. Now we need the router event listener. Create a directory with the name `library` in your project root directory. Add that directory into the Phalcon autoloader and create a class named `RouterListener` in it, inserting the following content:

   ```php
   <?php
   use Phalcon\Mvc\Router;
   use Phalcon\Mvc\Router\Route;
   use Phalcon\Events\Event;
   use Phalcon\Di;

   class RouterListener
   {
     public function beforeCheckRoute(Event $event, Router $router)
     {
       $request = Di::getDefault()->getShared('request');
       error_log('[REQUEST] ' . $request->getMethod() . ": " . $request->getURI());
     }
   ```

```php
    public function matchedRoute(Event $event, Router
$router, Route $route)
    {
        error_log('[ROUTE] matched pattern: ' . $route-
>getPattern());
    }
```

4. Create a `ProductsController` in the `app/controllers` file and place the following code there:

```php
<?php
class ProductsController extends Phalcon\Mvc\Controller
{
    public function viewAction($id)
    {
        $this->tag->setTitle('View Product');
        $this->view->setVars([
            'product_id'    => $id,
            'product_name'  => 'Pizza',
            'product_price' => 12,
        ]);
    }
}
```

5. Then, create a view in `app/views/products/view.volt` and place the following code there:

```
{{ content() }}
<h1>{{ product_name }}</h1>
<p>
    <strong>ID:</strong> {{ product_id }}<br>
    <strong>Price:</strong>
    <span style="text-decoration: line-through">{{
product_price / 0.25 }}</span>
    <strong style="color:darkred">{{ product_price
}}</strong>
</p>
```

6. Add an initial dispatcher setting into the service configuration, as follows:

```php
$di->setShared('dispatcher', function() use ($em) {
    $dispatcher = new Phalcon\Mvc\Dispatcher;

    $em->attach('dispatch', new ActionListener);
    $dispatcher->setEventsManager($em);

    return $dispatcher;
});
```

7. Then, we have to create the **Event Listener**. For this step, create an `ActionListener` class in the `library` directory and put the following content into this class:

```php
<?php
use Phalcon\Events\Event;
use Phalcon\Mvc\Dispatcher;

class ActionListener
{
   public function afterExecuteRoute(Event $event,
Dispatcher $dispatcher)
   {
       $report = [
       $dispatcher->getControllerName() => $dispatcher-
>getControllerClass(),
       $dispatcher->getActionName()      => $dispatcher-
>getActiveMethod(),
       'params'                          => $dispatcher-
>getParams()
     ];

     error_log('[ACTION] ' . json_encode($report));
     }
}
```

8. Open the application services definition and add a view service into the DI container:

```php
$di->setShared('view', function () use ($config, $em) {
   $view = new \Phalcon\Mvc\View();
   $view->setViewsDir($config->get('application')-
>viewsDir);

   $view->registerEngines([
      '.volt' => function ($view, $di) use ($config) {
         $volt = new \Phalcon\Mvc\View\Engine\Volt($view,
$di);
         return $volt;
      }
   ]);

   $em->attach('view', new ViewListener());
   $view->setEventsManager($em);

   return $view;
});
```

9. Finally, create the listener named `ViewListener` in the `library` directory and put the following code into it:

```php
<?php
use Phalcon\Events\Event;
use Phalcon\Mvc\View;

class ViewListener
{
  public function afterRender(Event $event, View $view)
  {
    error_log('[VIEW] ' . $view->getActiveRenderPath());
    return true;
  }
}
```

If you've done it all correctly, after you go to `http://your_site/products/view/1` in your browser, you will see the product card. Note that we use the hostname `your_site` in our example; however, you should use your real project hostname instead.

Additionally, if you look at the content of your `php-log` file, you will see something like this:

```
[30-Sep-2015 02:06:48 Europe/Berlin] [REQUEST] GET:
/products/view/1
[30-Sep-2015 02:06:48 Europe/Berlin] [ROUTE] matched pattern:
/:controller/:action/:params
[30-Sep-2015 02:06:48 Europe/Berlin] [ACTION]
{"products":"ProductsController","view":"viewAction","params":["1"]}
[30-Sep-2015 02:06:48 Europe/Berlin] [VIEW]
/var/www/your_site/app/views/index.volt
```

How it works...

A request life cycle starts with an entry point (for example, `index.php`). All requests are directed to it by the web server (such as Apache, Nginx, and others). The entry point usually doesn't contain much code; it defines only the application object and delegates the control to the last one. The application instance, in turn, uses the **Dependency Injection Container** (**DIC**) and thereby calls different application components one after the other, delegating them the control and if necessary the request context or its current handling result.

The default request life cycle consists of the following stages:

- An **HTTP Request** is handled by the dispatcher and routed to the controller by means of the router pattern.
- The controller performs the action defined in it and passes data to the **View.**
- The View transforms and/or formats the data as appropriate and provides it in a format that is required for the **HTTP Response.**

There are many ways to change the default request handling logic, including:

- Multi module applications
- Halting view rendering
- Non-use of controllers (for example, in a **RESTful** application)
- Working directly with HTTP requests or routers with the immediate return from anonymous functions bound with the defined URIs and even throwing an exception in any of these steps

However, the default request life cycle stages just listed outline the concept of the three main places where we can begin our research.

To demonstrate, we create an event manager, and in it register the **listeners** of the events we are interested in:

- RouterListener
- ActionListener
- ViewListener

In each `listener` method, we log the current request state, that is, which line of the URL request is handled by the `Request` component, which router pattern matches for the address handling, which controller and action are selected by the dispatcher for the request handling, and which view is involved eventually.

Note that we define the routing pattern clearly. We couldn't define the pattern for the handling of the request `/products/view/1` in this recipe, because we've created a routing component with default settings:

```
$router = new \Phalcon\Mvc\Router();
```

Try to comment the adding of your pattern into the routing component and refresh the page. Then, you'll see a matched pattern log entry, like this:

```
[ROUTE] matched pattern: #^/([\w0-9\_\-]+)/([\w0-9\.\_]+)(/.*)*$#u
```

If you take a detailed look at the request **Uniform Resource Identifier** (**URI**) and refer it to this regular expression, it will fall in place that those are a perfect match. But we recommend you to define the pattern clearly and not rely on the default one, since it helps with performance and avoids undesired behaviors.

There's more...

You can see more detailed information about the **Events Manager** at the Phalcon documentation site:

`https://docs.phalconphp.com/en/latest/reference/events.html`

See also

- ▶ The *Easily loading code on demand* recipe, in this chapter
- ▶ The *Setting up your request entry point* recipe, in this chapter

2
Structuring Your Projects

In this chapter, we will cover:

- ▶ Choosing the best place for an implementation
- ▶ Automation of routine tasks
- ▶ Creating the application structure by using code generation tools
- ▶ Getting more power by adding a middleware between Phalcon and your application

Introduction

Often, by creating new projects, developers can face some issues such as what components they should create, where to place them in the application structure, what each component would implement, what naming convention to follow, and so on. Actually, creating custom components isn't a difficult matter; we will sort it out in this chapter. We will create our own component, which will display different menus on your site depending on where we are in the application.

From one project to another, the developer's work is usually repeated. This holds true for tasks such as creating the project structure, configuration, creating data models, controllers, views, and so on. For those tasks, we will discover the power of Phalcon Developer Tools and how to use them. You will learn how to create an application skeleton by using one command, and even how to create a fully functional application prototype in less than 10 minutes without writing a single line of code.

Developers often come up against a situation where they need to create a lot of predefined code templates. Until you are really familiar with the framework it can be useful for you to do everything manually. But anyway, all of us would like to reduce repetitive tasks. Phalcon tries to help you by providing an easy, and at the same time flexible code generation tool named Phalcon Developer Tools. These tools help you simplify the creation of **CRUD** components for a regular application. Therefore, you can create working code in a matter of seconds without creating the code yourself.

Often, when creating an application using a framework, we need to extend or add functionality to the framework components. We don't have to reinvent the wheel by rewriting those components. We can use class inheritance and extensibility, but often this approach does not work. In such cases, it is better to use additional layers between the main application and the framework by creating a **middleware** layer.

The term middleware has a wide range of meanings, but in the context of PHP web applications it means code, which will be called in turns by each request.

We will look into the main principles of creating and using middleware in your application. We will not get into each solution in depth, but instead we will work with tasks that are common for most projects, and implementations extending Phalcon.

Choosing the best place for an implementation

Let's pretend you want to add a custom component. As the case may be, this component allows you to change your site navigation menu. For example, when you have a **Sign In** link on your navigation menu and you are logged in, that link needs to change to **Sign Out**. Then you're asking yourself where the best place in the project to put the code is, where to place the files, how to name the classes, and how to make them autoload by the autoloader.

Getting ready

For successful implementation of this recipe, you must have your application deployed. By this we mean that you need to have a web server installed and configured for handling requests to your application, an application must be able to receive requests, and have implemented the necessary components such as Controllers, Views, and a `bootstrap` file. For this recipe, we assume that our application is located in the `apps` directory. If this is not the case, you should change this part of the path in the examples shown in this chapter.

How to do it...

Follow these steps to complete this recipe:

1. Create the `/library/` directory app, if you haven't got one, where user components will be stored.

2. Next, create the `Elements` (app/library/Elements.php) component. This class extends `Phalcon\Mvc\User\Component`. Generally, it is not necessary, but it helps get access to application services quickly. The contents of `Elements` should be as follows:

    ```php
    <?php

    namespace Library;

    use Phalcon\Mvc\User\Component;
    use Phalcon\Mvc\View\Simple as View;

    class Elements extends Component
    {
      public function __construct()
      {
        // ...
      }

      public function getMenu()
      {
        // ...
      }
    }
    ```

3. Now we register this class in the Dependency Injection Container. We use a shared instance in order to prevent creating new instances by each service resolving resolving as follows:

    ```php
    $di->setShared('elements', function () {
        return new \Library\Elements();
    });
    ```

4. If your `Session` service is not initialized yet, it's time to do it in your `bootstrap` file. We use a shared instance for the following reasons:

    ```php
    $di->setShared('session', function () {
        $session = new \Phalcon\Session\Adapter\Files();
        $session->start();

        return $session;
    });
    ```

5. Create the `templates` directory within the directory with your `views/templates`.

6. Then you need to tell the class autoloader about a new namespace, which we have just entered. Let's do it in the following way:

```
$loader->registerNamespaces([
    // The APP_PATH constant should point
    // to the project's root
    'Library' => APP_PATH . '/apps/library/',
    // ...
]);
```

7. Add the following code right after the tag body in the main layout of your application:

```
<div class="container">
  <div class="navbar navbar-inverse">
    <div class="container-fluid">
      <div class="navbar-header">
        <button type="button" class="navbar-toggle
collapsed" data-toggle="collapse" data-target="#blog-top-
menu" aria-expanded="false">
          <span class="sr-only">Toggle navigation</span>
          <span class="icon-bar"></span>
          <span class="icon-bar"></span>
          <span class="icon-bar"></span>
        </button>
        <a class="navbar-brand" href="#">Blog 24</a>
      </div>
      <?php echo $this->elements->getMenu(); ?>
    </div>
  </div>
</div>
```

8. Next, we need to create a template for displaying your top menu. Let's create it in `views/templates/topMenu.phtml`:

```
<div class="collapse navbar-collapse" id="blog-top-menu">
  <ul class="nav navbar-nav">
    <li class="active">
      <a href="#">Home</a>
    </li>
  </ul>
  <ul class="nav navbar-nav navbar-right">
    <li>
      <?php if ($this->session->get('identity')): ?>
        <a href="#">Sign Out</a>
      <?php else: ?>
        <a href="#">Sign In</a>
```

```
        <?php endif; ?>
      </li>
    </ul>
  </div>
```

9. Now, let's put the component to work. First, create the protected field `$simpleView` and initialize it in the controller:

```
public function __construct()
{
    $this->simpleView =  new View();
    $this->simpleView->setDI($this->getDI());
}
```

10. And finally, implement the getMenu method as follows:

```
public function getMenu()
{
    $this->simpleView->setViewsDir($this->view->getViewsDir());

    return $this->simpleView->render('templates/topMenu');
}
```

11. Open the main page of your site to ensure that your top menu is rendered.

How it works...

The main idea of our component is to generate a top menu, and to display the correct menu option depending on the situation, meaning whether the user is authorized or not.

We create the user component, `Elements`, putting it in a place specially designed for the purpose. Of course, when creating the directory `library` and placing a new class there, we should tell the autoloader about a new namespace. This is exactly what we have done.

However, we should take note of one important peculiarity. We should note that if you want to get access to your components quickly even in HTML templates like `$this->elements`, then you should put the components in the DI container. Therefore, we put our component, `Library\Elements`, in the container named `elements`.

Since our component inherits `Phalcon\Mvc\User\Component`, we are able to access all registered application services just by their names. For example, the following instruction, `$this->view`, can be written in a long form, `$this->getDi()->getShared('view')`, but the first one is obviously more concise.

Although not necessary, for application structure purposes, it is better to use a separate directory for different views not connected straight to specific controllers and actions. In our case, the directory `views/templates` serves for this purpose. We create an HTML template for menu rendering and place it in `views/templates/topMenu.phtml`.

When using the method `getMenu`, our component will render the view `topMenu.phtml` and return HTML. In the method `getMenu`, we get the current path for all our views and set it for the `Phalcon\Mvc\View\Simple` component, created earlier in the constructor. In the view `topMenu` we access the session component, which earlier we placed in the DI container. By generating the menu, we check whether the user is authorized or not. In the former case, we use the **Sign out** menu item; in the latter case, we display the menu item with an invitation to **Sign in**.

Automation of routine tasks

The Phalcon project provides you with a great tool named Developer Tools. It helps automating repeating tasks, by means of code generation of components as well as a project skeleton. Most of the components of your application can be created only with one command. In this recipe, we will consider in depth the Developer Tools installation and configuration.

Getting ready

Before you begin to work on this recipe, you should have a **DBMS** configured, a web server installed and configured for handling requests from your application. You may need to configure a virtual host (this is optional) for your application, which will receive and handle requests. You should be able to open your newly created project in a browser at `http://{your-host-here}/appname` or `http://{your-host-here}/`, where `your-host-here` is the name of your project.

You should have Git installed, too.

In this recipe, we assume that your operating system is Linux. Developer Tools installation instructions for Mac OS X and Windows will be similar. You can find the link to the complete documentation for Mac OS X and Windows at the end of this recipe.

We used the Terminal to create the database tables, and chose MySQL as our RDBMS. Your setup might vary. The choice of a tool for creating a table in your database, as well as a particular DBMS, is yours. Note that syntax for creating a table by using other DBMSs than MySQL may vary.

How to do it...

Follow these steps to complete this recipe:

1. Clone Developer Tools in your home directory:

   ```
   git clone git@github.com:phalcon/phalcon-devtools.git devtools
   ```

2. Go to the newly created directory `devtools`, run the `./phalcon.sh` command, and wait for a message about successful installation completion:

   ```
   $ ./phalcon.sh
   Phalcon Developer Tools Installer
   Make sure phalcon.sh is in the same dir as phalcon.php and that
   you are running this with sudo or as root.
   Installing Devtools...
   Working dir is: /home/user/devtools
   Generating symlink...
   Done. Devtools installed!
   ```

3. Run the `phalcon` command without arguments to see the available command list and your current Phalcon version:

   ```
   $ phalcon

   Phalcon DevTools (3.0.0)

   Available commands:
       commands        (alias of: list, enumerate)
       controller      (alias of: create-controller)
       model           (alias of: create-model)
       module          (alias of: create-module)
       all-models      (alias of: create-all-models)
       project         (alias of: create-project)
       scaffold        (alias of: create-scaffold)
       migration       (alias of: create-migration)
       webtools        (alias of: create-webtools)
   ```

4. Now, let's create our project. Go to the folder where you plan to create the project and run the following command:

   ```
   $ phalcon project myapp simple
   ```

5. Open the website you have just created with the previous command in your browser. You should see a message about the successful installation.

6. Create a database for your project:

   ```
   mysql -e 'CREATE DATABASE myapp' -u root -p
   ```

7. You will need to configure our application to connect to the database. Open the file `app/config/config.php` and correct the database connection configuration. Draw attention to the `baseUri:` parameter if you have not configured your virtual host according to your project. The value of this parameter must be `/` or `/myapp/`. As a result, your configuration file must look like this:

```php
<?php

use Phalcon\Config;

defined('APP_PATH') || define('APP_PATH', realpath('.'));

return new Config([
    'database' => [
        'adapter'      => 'Mysql',
        'host'         => 'localhost',
        'username'     => 'root',
        'password'     => '',
        'dbname'       => 'myapp',
        'charset'      => 'utf8',
    ],
    'application' => [
        'controllersDir' => APP_PATH . '/app/controllers/',
        'modelsDir'      => APP_PATH . '/app/models/',
        'migrationsDir'  => APP_PATH . '/app/migrations/',
        'viewsDir'       => APP_PATH . '/app/views/',
        'pluginsDir'     => APP_PATH . '/app/plugins/',
        'libraryDir'     => APP_PATH . '/app/library/',
        'cacheDir'       => APP_PATH . '/app/cache/',
        'baseUri'        => '/myapp/',
    ]
]);
```

8. Now, after you have configured the database access, let's create a `users` table in your database. Create the `users` table and fill it with the primary data:

```sql
CREATE TABLE `users` (
    `id` INT(11) unsigned NOT NULL AUTO_INCREMENT,
    `email` VARCHAR(128) NOT NULL,
    `first_name` VARCHAR(64) DEFAULT NULL,
    `last_name` VARCHAR(64) DEFAULT NULL,
    `created_at` TIMESTAMP NOT NULL DEFAULT CURRENT_TIMESTAMP
ON UPDATE CURRENT_TIMESTAMP,
    PRIMARY KEY (`id`),
    UNIQUE KEY `users_email` (`email`)
) ENGINE=InnoDB DEFAULT CHARSET=utf8;
```

```
INSERT INTO `users` (`email`, `first_name`, `last_name`)
VALUES
('john@doe.com', 'John', 'Doe'),
('janie@doe.com', 'Janie', 'Doe');
```

9. After that we need to create a new controller, `UsersController`. This controller must provide us with the main CRUD actions on the `Users` model and, if necessary, display data with the appropriate views. Lets do it with just one command:

```
$ phalcon scaffold users
```

10. In your web browser, open the URL associated with your newly created resource, `User`, and try to find one of the users of our database table at `http://{your-host-here}/appname/users` (or `http://{your-host-here}/users`, depending on how you have configured your server for application request handling.

11. Finally, open your project in your file manager to see all the project structure created with Developer Tools:

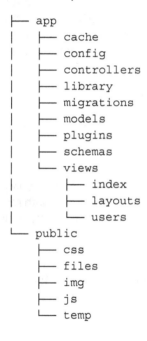

```
├── app
│   ├── cache
│   ├── config
│   ├── controllers
│   ├── library
│   ├── migrations
│   ├── models
│   ├── plugins
│   ├── schemas
│   └── views
│       ├── index
│       ├── layouts
│       └── users
└── public
    ├── css
    ├── files
    ├── img
    ├── js
    └── temp
```

How it works...

We installed Developer Tools with only two commands, `git clone` and `./phalcon`. This is all we need to start using this powerful code generation tool.

Next, using only one command, we created a fully functional application environment. At this stage, the application doesn't represent something outstanding in terms of features, but we have saved time from manually creating the application structure. Developer Tools did that for you! If after this command completion you examine your newly created project, you may notice that the primary application configuration has been generated also, including the `bootstrap` file. Actually, the `phalcon project` command has additional options that we have not demonstrated in this recipe. We are focusing on the main commands. Enter the command `help` to see all available project creating options:

```
$ phalcon project help
```

In the modern world, you can hardly find a web application that works without access to a database. Our application isn't an exception. We created a database for our application, and then we created a `users` table and filled it with primary data. Of course, we need to supply our application with what we have done in the `app/config/config.php` file with the database access parameters as well as the database name.

After the successful database and table creation, we used the `scaffold` command for the pre-defined code template generation, particularly the `Users` controller with all the main CRUD actions, all the necessary views, and the `Users` model. As before, we have used only one command to generate all those files.

Phalcon Developer Tools is equipped with a good amount of different useful tools. To see all the available options, you can use the command `help`. We have taken only a few minutes to create the first version of our application. Instead of spending time with repetitive tasks (such as the creation of the application skeleton), we can now use that time to do more exciting tasks.

Phalcon Developer Tools helps us save time where possible. But wait, there is more! The project is evolving, and it becomes more featureful day by day. If you have any problems, you can always visit the project on GitHub `https://github.com/phalcon/phalcon-devtools` and search for a needed solution.

There's more...

You can find more information on Phalcon Developer Tools installation for Windows and OS X at: `https://docs.phalconphp.com/en/latest/reference/tools.html`. More detailed information on web server configuration can be found at: `https://docs.phalconphp.com/en/latest/reference/install.html`

Creating the application structure by using code generation tools

In the following recipe, we will discuss available code generation tools that can be used for creating a multi-module application. We don't need to create the application structure and main components manually.

Getting ready

Before you begin, you need to have Git installed, as well as any DBMS (for example, **MySQL**, **PostgreSQL**, **SQLite**, and the like), the Phalcon PHP extension (usually it is named **php5-phalcon**) and a PHP extension, which offers database connectivity support using **PDO** (for example, **php5-mysql**, **php5-pgsql** or **php5-sqlite**, and the like). You also need to be able to create tables in your database.

To accomplish the following recipe, you will require Phalcon Developer Tools. If you already have it installed, you may skip the first three steps related to the installation and go to the fourth step.

 In this recipe, we assume that your operating system is Linux. Developer Tools installation instructions for Mac OS X and Windows will be similar. You can find the link to the complete documentation for Mac OS X and Windows at the end of this recipe.

We used the Terminal to create the database tables, and chose MySQL as our RDBMS. Your setup might vary. The choice of a tool for creating a table in your database, as well as particular DBMS, is yours. Note that syntax for creating a table by using other DBMSs than MySQL may vary.

How to do it...

Follow these steps to complete this recipe:

1. First you need to decide where you will install Developer Tools. Put the case in which you are going to place Developer Tools in your home directory. Then, go to your home directory and run the following command:

   ```
   git clone git@github.com:phalcon/phalcon-devtools.git
   ```

2. Now browse to the newly created `phalcon-devtools` directory and run the following command to ensure that there are no problems:

   ```
   ./phalcon.sh
   ```

3. Now, as far as you have Developer Tools installed, browse to the directory where you intend to create your project and run the following command:

```
phalcon project blog modules
```

4. If there were no errors during the previous step, then create a `Help Controller` by running the following command:

```
phalcon controller Help --base-class=ControllerBase —
namespace=Blog\\Frontend\\Controllers
```

5. Open the newly generated `HelpController` in the `apps/frontend/controllers/HelpController.php` file to ensure that you have the required controller, as well as the initial `indexAction`.

6. Open the database configuration in the `Frontend` module, `blog/apps/frontend/config/config.php`, and edit the database configuration according to your current environment. Enter the name of an existing database user and a password that has access to that database, and the application database name. You can also change the database adapter that your application needs. If you do not have a database ready, you can create one now.

7. Now, after you have configured the database access, let's create a `users` table in your database. Create the `users` table and fill it with the primary data:

```
CREATE TABLE `users` (
    `id` INT(11) unsigned NOT NULL AUTO_INCREMENT,
    `email` VARCHAR(128) NOT NULL,
    `first_name` VARCHAR(64) DEFAULT NULL,
    `last_name` VARCHAR(64) DEFAULT NULL,
    `created_at` TIMESTAMP NOT NULL DEFAULT CURRENT_TIMESTAMP ON
UPDATE CURRENT_TIMESTAMP,
    PRIMARY KEY (`id`),
    UNIQUE KEY `users_email` (`email`)
) ENGINE=InnoDB DEFAULT CHARSET=utf8;
INSERT INTO `users` (`email`, `first_name`, `last_name`) VALUES
('john@doe.com', 'John', 'Doe'),
('janie@doe.com', 'Janie', 'Doe');
```

8. Next, let's create `Controller`, `Views`, `Layout`, and `Model` by using the `scaffold` command:

```
phalcon scaffold users --ns-
controllers=Blog\\Frontend\\Controllers —ns-
models=Blog\\Frontend\\Models
```

9. Open the newly generated `UsersController` located in the `apps/frontend/controllers/UsersController.php` file to ensure you have generated all actions needed for user search, editing, creating, displaying, and deleting.

10. To check if all actions work as designed, if you have a web server installed and configured for this recipe, you can go to `http://{your-server}/users/index`. In so doing, you can make sure that the required `Users` model is created in the `apps/frontend/models/Users.php` file, all the required views are created in the `apps/frontend/views/users` folder, and the user layout is created in the `apps/frontend/views/layouts` folder.

11. If you have a web server installed and configured for displaying the newly created site, go to `http://{your-server}/users/search` to ensure that the users from our table are shown.

How it works...

In the world of programming, code generation is designed to lessen the burden of manually creating repeated code by using predefined code templates. The Phalcon framework provides perfect code generation tools, which come with Phalcon Developer Tools.

We start with the installation of Phalcon Developer Tools. Note that if you already have Developer Tools installed, you should skip the steps involving their installation.

Next, we generate a fully functional **MVC** application, which implements the multi-module principle. One command is enough to get a working application at once. We save ourselves the trouble of creating the application directory structure, creating the `bootstrap` file, creating all the required files, and setting up the initial application structure. For that end, we use only one command. It's really great, isn't it?

Our next step is creating a controller. In our example, we use `HelpController`, which displays just such an approach to creating controllers.

Next, we create the table `users` in our database and fill it with data. With that done, we use a powerful tool for generating predefined code templates, which is called `Scaffold`. Using only one command in the Terminal, we generate the controller `UsersController` with all the necessary actions and appropriate views. Besides this, we get the `Users` model and required layout.

If you have a web server configured you can check out the work of Developer Tools at `http://{your-server}/users/index`.

When we use the `Scaffold` command, the generator determines the presence and names of our table fields. Based on these data, the tool generates a model, as well as views with the required fields. The generator provides you with ready-to-use code in the controller, and you can change this code according to your needs. However, even if you don't change anything, you can use your controller safely. You can search for users, edit and delete them, create new users, and view them. And all of this was made possible with one command.

We have discussed only some of the features of code generation. Actually, Phalcon Developer Tools has many more features. For help on the available commands you can use the command `phalcon` (without arguments).

There's more...

For more detailed information on the installation and configuration of PDO in PHP, visit `http://php.net/manual/en/pdo.installation.php`. You can find detailed Phalcon Developer Tools installation instructions at `https://docs.phalconphp.com/en/latest/reference/tools.html`. For more information on Scaffold, refer to `https://en.wikipedia.org/wiki/Scaffold_(programming)`.

Get more power by adding a middleware between Phalcon and your application

This recipe describes how to create your own components that extend Phalcon classes, which are `Dispatcher`, `Router`, `Mvc\Application`, `Mvc\Model`, and so on. So you can easily modify the behavior of any Phalcon component.

Getting ready

In this recipe, we will expand the features of the Phalcon framework by adding some optional layers between your main application and the framework. Our task is to avoid overwriting the main framework classes or extending them by means of inheritance, and to add the previously mentioned features by using a **middleware**. At the beginning we need to have a fully operational application to implement this recipe successfully. It will be enough to have any base application.

After that, we will check out a set of typical tasks and their potential solutions.

How to do it...

Follow these steps to complete this recipe.

Logging critical errors

Let's suppose that you want to log exceptions in your application and to e-mail them to your address. To be aware of all the not so obvious possible errors, you must monitor them constantly. Let's suppose that you decide to filter all the errors and to log only the most critical ones:

1. Create the `BugCatcher`, which will catch the most critical errors:

   ```php
   <?php
   ```

```php
use Phalcon\Events\Event;
use Phalcon\Mvc\User\Plugin;
use Phalcon\Dispatcher;
use Phalcon\Mvc\Dispatcher\Exception as
DispatcherException;
use Phalcon\Mvc\Dispatcher as MvcDispatcher;

class BugsCatcher extends Plugin
{
  /**
   * This action is executed before execute any action
   * in the application
   *
   * @param Event $event
   * @param MvcDispatcher $dispatcher
   * @param \Exception $e
   * @return boolean
   */
  public function beforeException(Event $event,
MvcDispatcher $dispatcher, \Exception $e)
  {
    $code    = $e->getCode();
    $message = $e->getMessage();
    $file    = $e->getFile();
    $line    = $e->getLine();
    $trace   = $e->getTraceAsString();
    $date    = date('Y-m-d H:i:s');

    $body = <<<TEXT
<h1>Error</h1>
<p><em>$date</em></p>
<p>An error was detected in file $file on line $line.</p>

<p>System message: $message</p>
<p>Backtrace:</p>
<pre>$trace</pre>
TEXT;


    mail('alerts@mycompany.com', "Error: {$code}", $body);

    error_log($e->getMessage() . PHP_EOL . $e-
>getTraceAsString());
```

```
        if ($e instanceof DispatcherException) {

            switch ($e->getCode()) {
                case Dispatcher::EXCEPTION_HANDLER_NOT_FOUND:
                case Dispatcher::EXCEPTION_ACTION_NOT_FOUND:
                    $dispatcher->forward(
                        [
                            'controller' => 'errors',
                            'action'     => 'show404'
                        ]
                    );
                    return false;
            }
        }

        $dispatcher->forward(
            [
                'controller' => 'errors',
                'action'     => 'show500'
            ]
        );
        return false;
    }
}
```

2. Subscribe with the newly created plugin for the `dispatch:beforeException` event at the initialization of `Dispatcher` in your `bootstrap` file:

```
$di->setShared('dispatcher', function () use ($di,
$eventsManager) {

    // Handle exceptions and not-found exceptions
    // using BugsCatcher
    $eventsManager->attach('dispatch:beforeException', new
BugsCatcher);

    $dispatcher = new Dispatcher;

    $dispatcher->setEventsManager($eventsManager);

    return $dispatcher;
});
```

Here we told the `Dispatcher` to handle exceptions using `BugsCatcher`. If the exceptions are thrown and can be caught by the `Dispatcher` they will be written to the log with `error_log` as well and an e-mail will be sent out. This is only an example implementation. You could extend and improve it according to your needs; for example, possibly using the mail function wrapper, creating your own error handler, and so on.

Changing the description and keywords meta tags depending on your route

Often we have an SEO optimization task when we need to see our site at least on its accurate search position. In other words, we want to move our site up as high as possible. One of the numerous SEO optimization techniques is changing the `description` and `keywords` meta tags depending on the current request:

1. Create the `Meta` component, which will receive database information needed for filling the `Meta` tags:

```php
<?php

use Phalcon\Mvc\User\Plugin;

class Meta extends Plugin
{
  public function keywords($postId)
  {
    // Method's logic

    echo '<meta name="keywords" content="' . implode(',',
$keywords) . '">';
  }

  public function description($postId)
  {
    // Method's logic ...

    echo '<meta name="description" content="' .
$description . '">';
  }
}
```

2. Register your newly created plugin in the `DI` container. We use a shared instance in order to prevent creating new instances by each service resolving:

```
$di->setShared('meta', function () {
  return new Meta();
});
```

3. Add the call of the two newly created `Meta` plugin methods to the main layout:

```
<!DOCTYPE html>
<html>
  <head>
    <title>My Site</title>
    {{ meta.description(post_id) }}
    {{ meta.keywords(post_id) }}
  </head>
  <body>
    {{ content() }}
  </body>
</html>
```

> Note that the `description` and `keywords` methods receive the current post ID as an argument, therefore, you must pass it in your controllers and also take provisions for when the post ID is not passed.

Receiving site status reports

Imagine that you have a site which, operationally, needs to be checked constantly. You need to receive some site status reports. For that, you have to use a route which enables external requests and transmits all the necessary information. It will be convenient to receive this information in JSON format without handling all the application components in the handler call stack of the designated route. Take a look at the following steps:

1. Create a route in your application, which the status check requests will come to:

```
// Return status if the /ping route is matched
$router->add('/ping', [])->match(function () {

});
```

2. Create the `Status` component, which will collect the data needed for your site status report:

```
<?php

use Phalcon\Mvc\User\Plugin;
```

```php
class Status extends Plugin
{
  protected $statusCode;
  protected $statusReport;

  public function __construct()
  {
    // Some checks and data collection
    // ..

    $this->statusCode = ...
    $this->statusReport = ...
  }

  public function getStatusCode()
  {
    return $this->statusCode;
  }

  public function getStatusReport()
  {
    return $this->statusCode;
  }
}
```

3. Add a component call to the route:

```php
// Return status if the /ping route is matched
$router->add('/ping', [])->match(function () {
  $status = new Status();

  $responseCode = $status->getStatusCode();
  $responseData = $status->getStatusReport();

  $response = $this->getResponse();

  $response->setStatusCode($responseCode);
  $response->setJsonContent($responseData);

  $response->send();
});

// Return status if the /ping route is matched
$router->add('/ping', [])->match(function () {

});
```

Note, routes can have an associated callback that can override the default dispatcher and view behavior only for Phalcon 3.0.0 or higher.

Caching pages to reduce processing

Often we have a task to enhance performance by caching pages. This could be the case of guests or unauthorized users, which can be in fact search engines, bots, off-target audiences, and so on. In brief, those who can overload the site. For these users, you can create a caching the `Middleware` component. We'll check how to use the `CacheMiddleware` component through the example of the `Phalcon\Mvc\Micro` application:

1. Create `CacheMiddleware`, which will check whether the user is authorized or not and take a decision to return the cached content or to let the application generate it again:

```php
<?php

use Phalcon\Mvc\Micro\MiddlewareInterface;

class CacheMiddleware implements MiddlewareInterface
{
  public function call($application)
  {
    $cache   = $application['cache'];
    $session = $application['session'];

    if (!$this->session->has("user-auth")) {
      if ($cache->exists($key)) {
        echo $cache->get($key);

        return false;
      }
    }

    return true;
  }
}
```

2. Next, we pass the object instance to the application:

```php
$app->before(new CacheMiddleware());
```

3. You can call the methods several times to add more events of the same type:

```php
<?php

$app->finish(function () use ($app) {
    // First 'finish' middleware
});

$app->finish(function () use ($app) {
    // Second 'finish' middleware
});
```

> Here we have shown only the principle of creating `CacheMiddleware`.
> Configuring and setting up a `Phalcon\Mvc\Micro` application is
> beyond the scope of this recipe. You can find the link to the complete
> documentation for the `Micro` application at the end of this recipe.

Redirecting the user to the login screen if access to the resource is protected

In many cases, we need to restrict access to resources for unauthorized users. All authorized users will be allowed to access those resources and everyone else will be redirected to the authorization/login page. There are many examples of how to accomplish this. Using Phalcon, you can implement such logic without any additional components. We will implement this using a `Phalcon\Mvc\Micro` application. For other application types, the implementation will be similar:

```php
$app = new Phalcon\Mvc\Micro();

// Executed before every route is executed
// Return false cancels the route execution
$app->before(function () use ($app) {
    if ($app['session']->get('auth') == false) {
        // Redirect the user to the '/login' route
        $app['response']->redirect("/login");

        // Return false stops the normal execution
        return false;
    }

    return true;
});
```

How it works...

We have seen different implementations of the middleware components. The type of middleware and its location can vary depending on the situation. Every application requirement/problem has at least two solutions. By identifying the technical and business requirements, you will be able to implement your components accordingly. In this recipe, we don't implement any particular finished examples. We try to show you the principle of using some additional software layers and different scenarios for their implementation without resting upon one example. Your own solutions can and must be deeper and more specific.

There's more...

For more information about the middleware concept, visit:

`https://en.wikipedia.org/wiki/Middleware`.

For more detailed information about the `Phalcon\Mvc\Micro` application type and the principle of using middleware refer to:

`https://docs.phalconphp.com/en/latest/reference/micro.html`

3

Processing Requests

In this chapter, we will cover:

- ▶ Understanding the default routing strategy for controllers
- ▶ Handling a request along multiple controllers
- ▶ Using flexible key-value action parameter pairs
- ▶ Restricting controllers by managing end user privileges
- ▶ Making unsuccessful requests fail softly
- ▶ Creating a server-sent message server
- ▶ Creating a Websocket server

Introduction

An essential part of any modern framework is processing requests from the web browser and directing them towards the corresponding server side controller logic. This routing strategy can be used for generic common case scenarios as well as complicated custom ones.

A common setup usually involves creating a default routing pattern that will handle the bulk of requests and then defining additional specific routes to handle unique cases. By following this pattern, we can quickly set up an application and then begin to customize it one part at a time. Then sometimes while processing a request it becomes apparent that it is necessary to have the logic flow among a progression of controllers as certain exceptional cases are discovered. This feature allows for a clean and smooth logic flow while eliminating additional code that would cause your code to violate the **DRY** (**Don't Repeat Yourself**) programming principle.

Then we will show you how to use key-value parameters in your URLs to pass data to your controllers. Doing this allows flexibility in your routing while still using the default routing strategy. However, all of this power would be detrimental to your system if you are unable to restrict administrative access to only a certain class of users or to prevent unauthenticated users from viewing private data. So we will create a project to manage end user privileges with classes of users that can access only their prescribed sections of your web application.

At this point, your application is secure and you have a variety of routing strategies to choose from, but even then, sometimes your application logic will hit a critical error or perhaps the user just entered in an incorrect URL. In this case, we will want to show a nice looking error screen to let the user know that something didn't work as expected.

The web is evolving at a tremendous pace and for some types of applications, the traditional request model of browser to server and then back to the browser is just not enough. Sometimes you will need to have the web server to be able to push data to the browser in an efficient manner and the current method of long polling (requesting data every few seconds) will not scale out to large amounts of users. We will show you how to create a persistent connection to the server so that the server can push data to the browser using the server-sent message API. However, while simple and perfect for many use cases, this would not be appropriate, for example, with a chat application or a game and this is where **Websockets** come in. By implementing a Websockets server you will be able to create a long-lived bidirectional communication system between the browser and the server.

Understanding the default routing strategy for controllers

One of the most essential parts of any web framework is having a flexible way of converting browser URLs into a definable logic path on the server, and with Phalcon this is achieved with the `Phalcon\Mvc\Router` class. To start with, it is necessary to have an understanding of the default routing strategy and then later, this can be expanded upon.

The default routing strategy can be described simply in that each web request is assigned to a `Phalcon\Mvc\Controller` class and then to the specific `action` function within that controller. So with each URL, we can begin to think about which PHP controller class the request will be directed to and then which `action` method within that controller will finally handle the request. In this way, groups of common behavior can be grouped together into a single controller for both reducing duplicate code and for organization. The best part is that right from the start, each new `action` function is automatically available by accessing its corresponding URL.

Getting ready

To use this recipe, you will need to have a project skeleton with a configured Phalcon bootstrapper, \Phalcon\Mvc\Router, and at least one \Phalcon\Mvc\Controller. In our example, we will use a project scaffold generated by **Phalcon Developer Tools**.

For testing the recipe results, you need to have a web server installed and configured for handling requests to your application. Your application must be able to take requests, and additionally, there must be such necessary components as controllers, views, and a bootstrap file.

A database is not required for this recipe.

How to do it...

Follow these steps to complete this recipe:

1. First of all, we need to have an application to experiment with. If you already have such an application, you can skip this step. Create a simple application using the following code:

    ```
    phalcon project default_routing simple
    ```

2. Now point the web browser at the root directory of the project. There should be a page with Congratulations! .... if you have PHP and Apache set up properly. (If it doesn't say this then check that the cache directory app/cache is writable by the web server.) Notice that it says This page is located at views/index/index.volt. This is our first hint at the routing path. See if you can guess the controller and action name. If it is not working then check that you have Phalcon added to your PHP modules, that the directory permissions are readable by the web server, and that it is set up to allow .htaccess files.

3. Add /index to the end of the URL in the browser and see if anything changed. Did the browser content change? Well, it shouldn't have, because we didn't actually change the route. What just happened was that the implicit default controller index is now being specifically given as the index. We just overrode the default value with exactly the same value.

4. Next add an additional /index to the URL, so that in total we've added /index/index. Again, this time nothing should have changed. We've now just specified the route action as index and since the default is the same value it will not change the action. Remember that the URL path and the Router route are two different things.

5. Alright, so, while informative, this isn't very exciting so far. So, now we'll add a new action to our `index` controller to see what happens. Add the following method to the controller, `app/controllers/IndexController.php`:

    ```php
    public function testAction()
    {
        return "from controller 'index' and action 'test'.";
    }
    ```

6. Now point the web browser path at `/index/test` to see if our new action is working. So we have created a new action and this new action is automatically reachable by simply entering in the corresponding URL path. This flexibility allows for functionality to be easily added without maintaining a separate list of every URL path to server side logic. This would otherwise become exceedingly tedious after just a short while and default routing to a controller-action is the solution to this problem.

7. So, now we'll draw attention to something that might appear strange at first glance. Notice that the `indexAction` function is completely empty but that somehow when we go to that path it displayed our original `Congradulations!` ... message. So where is that coming from?

8. Navigate to the directory, `app/views`, within the `scaffold` directory to see the views. For now we will only be observing the presence of views and understanding how they fit into the routing strategy, but don't worry, this subject is covered in depth in other recipes. To keep it simple for now, the main `index.volt` is the global template container for all of the views and `index/index.volt` is the template specifically for the route with the `controller` index and `action` index. Whether you choose to use templates or not for an action is purely up to you, and even in a mature application, there are uses for many combinations of this approach.

9. Now we will create a new controller, `app/controllers/HelloController.php`:

    ```php
    <?php

    class HelloController extends \Phalcon\Mvc\Controller
    {
        public function worldAction()
        {
            return 'Hello World';
        }
    }
    ```

10. Now navigate to **hello/world** in your browser to see the message.

Handling a request along multiple controllers

Being able to easily assign URL paths to server side controller logic is a powerful capability. To improve on this, we will be introducing the ability to have requests forwarded from one controller to another controller. This framework design is known as **HMVC** (**Hierarchical Model View Controller**), and this recipe will demonstrate how to work with the Hierarchical part of Phalcon controllers.

Getting ready

To use this recipe, you will need to have a project skeleton with a configured Phalcon bootstrapper, `Phalcon\Mvc\Router`, and three `Phalcon\Mvc\Controller`. In our example, we will use a project scaffold generated by Phalcon Developer Tools.

To test the recipe results, you need to have a web server installed and configured for handling requests to your application. Your application must be able to take requests, and additionally, there must be such necessary components as controllers, views, and a `bootstrap` file.

A database is not required for this recipe.

How to do it...

Follow these steps to complete this recipe:

1. We need to have an application which we will experiment with. If you already have such an application, you can skip this step. Otherwise, create a simple application:

   ```
   phalcon project handling_requests simple
   ```

2. Now point the web browser at the root directory of the project. There should be a page with `Congratulations!  .....` If we see the `Volt directory can't be written` error message then permissions of the directory `app/cache` need to be changed to allow the web server to write to it.

3. Create the controller, `app/controllers/IndexController.php`:

   ```php
   <?php

   class IndexController extends \Phalcon\Mvc\Controller
   {
       public indexAction()
       {
       }
   }
   ```

4. Create the controller, app/controllers/StartController.php:

```php
<?php

class StartController extends \Phalcon\Mvc\Controller
{
    public function indexAction()
    {
        return $this->dispatcher->forward([
            'controller' => 'handle',
            'action'     => 'forward'
        ]);
    }

    public function redirectAction()
    {
        return $this->dispatcher->forward([
            'controller' => 'handle',
            'action'     => 'redirect'
        ]);
    }
}
```

5. Create the controller, app/controllers/HandleController.php:

```php
<?php

class HandleController extends \Phalcon\Mvc\Controller
{
    public function forwardAction()
    {
        return $this->dispatcher->forward([
            'controller' => 'index',
            'action'     => 'index'
        ]);
    }

    public function redirectAction()
    {
        return $this->response->redirect('https://www.packtpub.
com/', true);
    }
}
```

6. Test out a double forward by navigating in the browser to the path start. The `StartController` will forward to the `HandleController`, which will then forward back to the main `IndexController` and so the index view will be displayed (from the `Volt` templates in `app/views`). Next, setting the URL path to `start/redirect` will forward to the `HandleController` but this time we will redirect the browser to the Packt Publishing website.

How it works...

Before we begin to explore the actual use of the controller forwarding technique it is important to have a good understanding of the differences between a redirect and a forward operation.

A `redirect` operation can be described in terms of an externally accessible URL, either on the same website or a different one.

The local relative URL path is:

```
return $response->redirect('controllerName/actionName/?abc=123');
```

The external absolute path is:

```
return $response->redirect('http://our-other-website.com/important_
page', true);
```

A `forward` operation is always purely describing an internal operation to direct the execution to the next path:

```
<?php

return $dispatcher->forward([
    'controller' => 'index',
    'action'     => 'show404'
]);
```

However, this understanding does not yet fully illustrate how very different these two operations are. The redirect operation will send an HTTP header to the user's browser to tell it to change its current path to the new one and to begin a completely new request cycle at the new path, while the forward operation will continue the logic handling operation at the new controller-action location. At this point, the user's browser has not yet been informed of any differences in the internal server operation.

So, with a single request it is possible to forward across multiple controller-actions and then to finally finish with a browser redirect. Notice that redirects are performed with the `\Phalcon\Http\Response` class, while forwards are performed with `\Phalcon\Mvc\Dispatcher`.

Using flexible key-value action parameter pairs

Sometimes in our controller actions we would like to be able to receive named parameters from the route instead of receiving the normal numbered parameters supplied when using the default routing pattern. This is a good strategy for separating the implementation of the routing system from the logical implementation in the controller.

For example, a controller accessing the 0 route parameter instead of string name makes the controller logic brittle because changes to the ordering and structure of the route could cause the parameter ordering to change. Additionally, accessing a parameter by a string name is much more self-documenting than when using an integer.

Getting ready

To use this recipe, you will need to have a project skeleton with a configured Phalcon bootstrapper, `Phalcon\Mvc\Router`, and three `Phalcon\Mvc\Controller`. In our example, we will use a project scaffold generated by Phalcon Developer Tools.

To test the recipe results, you need to have a web server installed and configured for handling requests to your application. Your application must be able to take requests, and additionally, there must be such necessary components as controllers, views, and a `bootstrap` file.

A database is not required for this recipe.

How to do it...

Follow these steps to complete this recipe:

1. First of all, we need to have an application which we will experiment with. If you already have such an application, you can skip this step. Create a simple application:

   ```
   phalcon project key_value_pairs simple
   ```

2. Now point the web browser at the root directory of the project. There should be a page with `Congratulations!` ..... If we see the `Volt directory can't be written` error message then permissions of the directory `app/cache` need to be changed to allow the web server to write to it.

3. Create the controller, `app/controllers/KeyValueControllerBase.php`:

   ```php
   <?php

   class KeyValueControllerBase extends \Phalcon\Mvc\Controller
   {
   ```

```php
    public function beforeExecuteRoute($dispatcher)
    {
        $keyParams = [];
        $params = $dispatcher->getParams();
        foreach ($params as $number => $value) {
            if ($number & 1) {
                $keyParams[$params[$number - 1]] = $value;
            }
        }
        $dispatcher->setParams($keyParams);
    }
}
```

4. Create the controller, `app/controllers/BlogController.php`:

```php
<?php

class BlogController extends KeyValueControllerBase
{
    public function searchAction()
    {
        $params = $this->dispatcher->getParams();

        if (sizeof($params) === 0) {
            return 'Sorry: You must add at least one search
criteria.';
        }

        // One of the key value pairs must be 'publisher/packt'
        if (!isset($params['publisher']) || strtolower($params['pu
blisher']) !== 'packt') {
            return 'Sorry: Packt is the only publisher in this
database.';
        }

        $output = "Searching By: <br><br>\n";
        foreach ($params as $key => $value) {
            $output .= "$key: $value<br>\n";
        }

        return $output;
    }
}
```

5. We will now test that our controllers are working by going to the URL path `blog/search`. There should be a message stating `Sorry: You must add at least one search criteria`. So, now we can try out our key-value pair system by changing the URL path to `blog/search/publisher/packt`. In order to demonstrate parameter checking we have made it so that one of the key-value pairs must be `publisher/packt` in our `searchAction` function, or otherwise a warning message is given. Now that this is working, try adding new key-value pairs to the URL to see the search criteria printed out.

How it works...

The Phalcon dispatch loop controls the execution of the code by triggering a series of events in a specific order. There are two main ways to plug into these events and the first is to attach a listener directly to the `dispatcher` itself and the other is for classes such as `Phalcon\Mvc\Controller` to have a function named after one of the triggered events. In our case, we are using the latter approach in the base controller class, `KeyValueControllerBase`, with the `beforeExecuteRoute` function.

The specific ordering of the events triggered in the dispatch cycle are as follows:

- `beforeDispatchLoop`
- `beforeDispatch`
- `beforeExecuteRoute`
- `initialize`
- `afterExecuteRoute`
- `beforeNotFoundAction`
- `beforeException`
- `afterDispatch`
- `afterDispatchLoop`

You may read about the dispatching loop in detail at: `https://docs.phalconphp.com/en/latest/reference/dispatching.html`

So now let's get back to the two new classes that we added. The `KeyValueControllerBase` is a base class for providing our key-value parameter functionality to any controller that inherits from it. This custom logic is brief and it could easily be expanded upon to provide additional capabilities.

Then, in `BlogController` (or any other derived class of `KeyValueControllerBase`), we can call:

```
$this->dispatcher->getParams();
```

This gets a normal PHP associative array of the key-value pairs. Additionally, it is possible to use the `Dispatcher` method, `getParam`, to check the values of a single key-value.

Restricting controllers by managing end user privileges

Every serious application needs to be able to control access to the logical processes within its framework. Using Phalcon, we can easily create a security system to control access to resources based upon group membership. In this recipe, we will define resources as controller-action pairs, but the primitives of the permission system are general enough that, with a little work, the resources could be broadened to be anything.

In our case, the idea of restricting resources (controller actions) is simple—if a user's group does not have permission to access an action then we will display the message `Unauthorized access`. Later this could be extended to forward the user to a sign-in page or to an alternative page for that resource.

Getting ready

To use this recipe, you will need to have a project skeleton with a configured Phalcon bootstrapper, `Phalcon\Mvc\Router,` and three `Phalcon\Mvc\Controller`. In our example, we will use a project scaffold generated by Phalcon Developer Tools.

To test the recipe results, you need to have a web server installed and configured for handling requests to your application. Your application must be able to take requests, and additionally, there must be such necessary components as controllers, views, and a `bootstrap` file.

A database is not required for this recipe.

How to do it...

Follow these steps to complete this recipe:

1. First of all, we need to have an application which we will experiment with. If you already have such an application, you can skip this step. Create a simple application:

   ```
   phalcon project restrict_controller simple
   ```

2. Now point the web browser at the root directory of the project. There should be a page with `Congratulations!` ..... If we see the `Volt directory can't be written` error message, then permissions of the directory, `app/cache,` need to be changed to allow the web server to write to it.

3. Configure the loader in the file, `app/config/loader.php`:

```php
<?php
$loader = new \Phalcon\Loader();
$loader->registerDirs([
    $config->application->controllersDir,
    $config->application->modelsDir,
    $config->application->pluginsDir
])->register();
```

4. Create a `dispatcher` service in `app/config/services.php` with an attached `DispatcherSecurity` plugin to override the default service:

```php
$di->setShared('dispatcher', function() {
    $securityPlugin = new DispatcherSecurity();
    $securityPlugin->setDI($this);

    $eventsManager = $this->getEventsManager();
    $eventsManager->attach('dispatch', $securityPlugin);

    $dispatcher = new Phalcon\Mvc\Dispatcher();
    $dispatcher->setEventsManager($eventsManager);

    return $dispatcher;
});
```

5. Create an `acl` service in `app/config/services.php`:

```php
$di->setShared('acl', function () {
    // $config is reference inline in the acl.
    $config = $this->getConfig();
    return require_once(__DIR__ . '/acl.php');
});
```

6. Add the plugin, `app/plugins/DispatcherSecurity.php`:

```php
<?php

class DispatcherSecurity extends Phalcon\Mvc\User\Plugin
{
    public function beforeExecuteRoute(Phalcon\Events\Event
$event, Phalcon\Mvc\Dispatcher $dispatcher)
    {
        $roleName = ($this->session->has('role')) ? $this-
>session->get('role') : 'Anonymous';
```

```
        $controllerName = $dispatcher->getControllerName();
        $actionName = $dispatcher->getActionName();

        if (!$this->acl->isAllowed($roleName, $controllerName,
$actionName)) {
            $this->response->setContent('Unauthorized access.');
            $this->response->send();

            return false;
        }
    }
}
```

7. Add `app/controllers/ProfileController.php`:

```php
<?php

class ProfileController extends \Phalcon\Mvc\Controller
{
    public function indexAction()
    {
        return 'Only signed in users should be able to change
their profile';
    }
}
```

8. Add `app/controllers/SecretController.php`:

```php
<?php

class SecretController extends \Phalcon\Mvc\Controller
{
    public function dataAction()
    {
        return 'Only very important users should be able to access
Secret Data.';
    }
}
```

9. Add `app/controllers/SessionController.php`:

```php
<?php

class SessionController extends \Phalcon\Mvc\Controller
{
```

```php
        public function signinAsAdministratorsRoleAction()
        {
            $this->session->set('role', 'Administrators');

            return "You are now signed in with the 'Administrators'
role.";
        }

        public function signinAsMembersRoleAction()
        {
            $this->session->set('role', 'Members');

            return "You are now signed in with the 'Members' role";
        }

        public function signoutAction()
        {
            $this->session->remove('role');

            return "You have successfully signed out.";
        }
    }
```

10. Create app/config/acl.php:

```php
<?php

$resources = [
    'index'   => ['index'],
    'session' => ['index', 'signin', 'signout'],
    'profile' => ['index'],
    'secret'  => ['data'],
];

$publicResources = [
    'index'   => '*',
    'session' => '*'
];

$roles = [
    'Administrators' => [
        'profile' => ['index'],
        'secret'  => ['data'],
    ],
```

```
    'Members' => [
        'profile'  => ['index']
    ],
    'Anonymous' => []
];

$acl = new Phalcon\Acl\Adapter\Memory();
$acl->setDefaultAction(Phalcon\Acl::DENY);

// Add all of the resources to the ACL
foreach ($resources as $controllerName => $actionList) {
    $acl->addResource(new Phalcon\Acl\Resource($controllerName),
    $actionList);
}

// Set the roles and allow specific access for actions
foreach ($roles as $roleName => $role) {
    $acl->addRole($roleName);
    foreach ($role as $controllerName => $actionList) {
        $acl->allow($roleName, $controllerName, $actionList);
    }
}

// Make public resources available to all roles
foreach ($publicResources as $controllerName => $actionList) {
    foreach ($roles as $roleName => $role) {
        $acl->allow($roleName, $controllerName, $actionList);
    }
}

return $acl;
```

How it works...

In our loaders configuration, we add the following line to the `registerDirs` call to allow autoloading of our security plugin:

```
$config->application->pluginsDir
```

Then, in `app/config/services.php`, we define the `dispatcher` and `acl` services. Note that the `dispatcher` and `session` services are automatically provided by the factory default dependency injector and in this instance, we will be using the included default `session` service and overriding the `dispatcher` service.

First we will need to define the ACL service that we will use later in our security plugin. We will pull in the ACL object from the `acl.php config` file:

```
$di->setShared('acl', function () {
    $config = $this->getConfig();
    return require_once(__DIR__ . '/acl.php');
});
```

Then, in `app/config/acl.php`, there are three important declarations: `$resources`, `$publicResources`, and `$roles`. First we must list all controller actions in `$resources`, and every time a new controller or action is added to the system we must add it here as well. Then, if we would like a controller action to always be allowed, we can add it to `$publicResources`. Finally, in `$roles`, we allow specific user roles to be allowed access to individual resources.

Next we create the actual ACL object and then we set its default action to deny first to prevent accidental mistakes in our ACL configuration:

```
$acl = new Phalcon\Acl\Adapter\Memory();
$acl->setDefaultAction(Phalcon\Acl::DENY);
```

Now that we have a functioning ACL system, we will create a new instance of the `DispatcherSecurity` plugin and then set its dependency injector to `$this`, since the service closure is bound to the DI:

```
$di->setShared('dispatcher', function() {
    $securityPlugin = new DispatcherSecurity();
    $securityPlugin→setDI($this);
```

Then we will access the `EventsManager` service to get the object and we will attach the `DispatcherSecurity` object to it so that it will receive notifications of events related to `dispatch`:

```
$eventsManager = $this->getEventsManager();
$eventsManager->attach('dispatch', $exceptionPlugin);
```

Finally, we will create a new `Dispatcher` and then attach the `EventsManager` object to it. This allows the dispatchers events to be available to other components:

```
$dispatcher = new Phalcon\Mvc\Dispatcher();
$dispatcher->setEventsManager($eventsManager);
```

Now that we have set up the `dispatcher`, we will take a look at the `DispatcherSecurity` plugin. We have added a `beforeExecuteRoute` method so that the security plugin can implement logic before allowing the execution to continue to the route destination (controller-action) pair:

```
public function beforeExecuteRoute(Event $event, Dispatcher
$dispatcher)
```

Next we will check to see if the session variable `role` has been set and if not then we will make the default role to be `Anonymous`. Note that by requesting the session service, the PHP session is automatically started. Then we obtain the controller and action name, since in our permission scheme, we are defining these as the resource:

```
$roleName = ($this->session->has('role')) ? $this->session-
>get('role') : 'Anonymous';
$controllerName = $dispatcher->getControllerName();
$actionName = $dispatcher->getActionName();
```

Next we will access the `acl` service and ask it to determine if the role can access the resource, and we will cancel the route if it fails:

```
 if (!$this->acl->isAllowed($roleName, $controllerName, $actionName))
 {
     $this->response->setContent('Unauthorized access.');
     $this->response->send();
     return false;
 }
```

Making unsuccessful requests fail softly

In any web application, there will eventually be errors and it is important to be able to handle them in a graceful manner. The Phalcon dispatch cycle is capable of intercepting PHP exceptions as well as missing routes. On a production system, it is good security practice to disable the output of PHP exceptions on the page and then this typically just produces a white screen for the user. While this is an improvement over displaying possibly sensitive exception information to the user it is not as professional as it could be. In this recipe, we will create a framework that is capable of gently handling these situations and displaying a clean page for the end user.

Getting ready

To use this recipe, you will need to have a project skeleton with a configured Phalcon bootstrapper, `Phalcon\Mvc\Router`, and three `Phalcon\Mvc\Controller`. In our example, we will use a project scaffold generated by Phalcon Developer Tools.

To test the recipe results, you need to have a web server installed and configured for handling requests to your application. Your application must be able to take requests, and additionally, there must be such necessary components as controllers, views, and a `bootstrap` file.

A database is not required for this recipe.

How to do it...

Follow these steps to complete this recipe:

1. First of all, we need to have an application which we will experiment with. If you already have such an application, you can skip this step. Otherwise, create a simple application:

    ```
    phalcon project request_errors simple
    ```

2. Now point the web browser at the root directory of the project. There should be a page with `Congratulations!` ..... If we see the `Volt directory can't be written` error message, then permissions of the directory `app/cache` need to be changed to allow the web server to write to it.

3. Configure the loaders in the file, `app/config/loader.php`:

    ```php
    <?php

    $loader = new \Phalcon\Loader();
    $loader->registerDirs([
        $config->application->controllersDir,
        $config->application->modelsDir,
        $config->application->pluginsDir
    ])->register();
    ```

4. Add `dispatcher` service to `ExceptionPlugin` in `app/config/services.php`:

    ```php
    $di->setShared('dispatcher', function() {
        $exceptionPlugin = new ExceptionPlugin();
        $exceptionPlugin->setDI($this);

        $eventsManager = $this->getEventsManager();
        $eventsManager->attach('dispatch', $exceptionPlugin);

        $dispatcher = new Phalcon\Mvc\Dispatcher();
        $dispatcher->setEventsManager($eventsManager);

        return $dispatcher;
    });
    ```

5. Add the file, `app/plugins/ExceptionPlugin.php`:

    ```php
    <?php

    class ExceptionPlugin extends Phalcon\Mvc\User\Plugin
    ```

```php
{
    public function beforeException(Phalcon\Events\Event $event,
Phalcon\Mvc\Dispatcher $dispatcher, $exception)
    {
        switch ($exception->getCode()) {
            case Phalcon\Mvc\Dispatcher::EXCEPTION_HANDLER_NOT_
FOUND:
            case Phalcon\Mvc\Dispatcher::EXCEPTION_ACTION_NOT_
FOUND:
                $dispatcher->forward([
                    'controller' => 'error',
                    'action'     => 'show404',
                ]);
                return false;
                break;
        }

        $dispatcher->forward([
            'controller' => 'error',
            'action'     => 'unhandledException',
        ]);
        return false;
    }

}
```

6. Add the controller, `app/controllers/ErrorController.php`:

```php
<?php

class ErrorController extends Phalcon\Mvc\Controller
{
    public function show404Action()
    {
    }

    public function unhandledExceptionAction()
    {
    }
}
```

7. Add the controller, `app/controllers/OopsController.php`:

```php
<?php:
```

```
class OopsController extends Phalcon\Mvc\Controller
{
    public function indexAction()
    {
        throw new \Exception('Error');
    }
}
```

8. Create the view, `app/views/error/show404.volt`:

```
<div style="display: inline-block; padding: 30px; background-color: green;">
  There was a 404 Error
</div>
```

9. Create the view, `app/views/error/unhandledException.volt`:

```
<div style="display: inline-block; padding: 30px; background-color: yellow;">
  There was an error
</div>
```

10. In the web browser, go to the following paths:

   ❑ *oops*: You should see a yellow box with *There was an error*

   ❑ *ThisPage/DoesNotExist*: You should a green box with *There was a 404 Error*

How it works...

The Phalcon dispatch loop controls the execution of code by triggering a series of events in a specific order. There are two main ways to plug into these events; the first is to attach a listener directly to the `dispatcher` itself and the other is to attach a plugin to the `dispatcher` so that it is notified of the events. This latter method has the advantage that plugins can be developed independently of each other to handle different aspects of the program.

The loader needs to be able to find the `plugins` directory, so we add the following to the list of directories that are searched when requesting a class that is not already available:

```
$config→application→pluginsDir
```

Then in our services configuration `app/config/services.php`, we define the `dispatcher` service. Note that because this service is core to the system it will be automatically created by the factory default dependency injector. However, in this case we are overriding the default service with a custom one.

First we will create a new instance of the `ExceptionPlugin` and then set its dependency injector to `$this` since the service closure is bound to the DI:

```
$di->setShared('dispatcher', function() {
    $exceptionPlugin = new ExceptionPlugin();
    $exceptionPlugin->setDI($this);
```

Then we will access the `EventsManager` service to get the object and then we will attach the `ExceptionPlugin` object to it so that it will receive notifications of events related to `dispatch`:

```
$eventsManager = $this->getEventsManager();
$eventsManager->attach('dispatch', $exceptionPlugin);
```

Finally, we will create a new `Dispatcher` and then attach the `EventsManager` object to it so that it can notify the following:

```
$dispatcher = new Phalcon\Mvc\Dispatcher();
$dispatcher->setEventsManager($eventsManager);
```

Now that we have set up the `dispatcher`, we will take a look at the `ExceptionPlugin`. We have added a `beforeException` method to intercept the handling rather than letting it bubble all of the way up to terminate the PHP script. We have set up this plugin to handle a variety of different types of exceptions.

Notice that we have named the method after the name of the event:

```
public function beforeException(Event $event, Dispatcher $dispatcher,
$exception)
{
```

First we will try to catch a few different types of exceptions to determine if it is caused by a route that could not be matched to a controller action. The first case, EXCEPTION_HANDLER_NOT_FOUND, checks if the controller could not be found and the next case, EXCEPTION_ACTION_NOT_FOUND, checks if the `action` method could not be found.

Then, if the route has failed, we redirect to `ErrorController` and execute the `show404Action` method. Finally, we return `false` to notify the `dispatcher` that the current action is canceled. This has important implications in security related `dispatcher` plugins:

```
switch ($exception->getCode()) {
    case Phalcon\Mvc\Dispatcher::EXCEPTION_HANDLER_NOT_FOUND:
    case Phalcon\Mvc\Dispatcher::EXCEPTION_ACTION_NOT_FOUND:
        $dispatcher->forward([
            'controller' => 'error',
```

```
                'action'        => 'show404',
        ]);
        return false;
        break;
    }
}
```

Finally, we handle all other exceptions in a generic way by forwarding to the
unhandledException action on the ErrorController:

```
$dispatcher->forward([
    'controller' => 'error',
    'action'     => 'unhandledException',
]);
```

Finally, we are arriving at the actions and, since we created the views for those actions, it will
automatically display them.

Creating a server-sent message server

The server-sent event API is a great new alternative to using AJAX for long polling the server for
updates. This new API has a very simple JavaScript interface as well as an easy to understand
server implementation and it is also more efficient while having a built-in **reconnection**
feature. If your application requires a simple data feed or there is a need for a rapid prototype
then the server-sent API might be the ideal choice.

Getting ready

To use this recipe, you will need to have a project skeleton with a configured Phalcon
bootstrapper, Phalcon\Mvc\Router, and three Phalcon\Mvc\Controller. In our
example, we will use a project scaffold generated by Phalcon Developer Tools.

To test the recipe results, you need to have a web server installed and configured for handling
requests to your application. Your application must be able to take requests, and additionally,
there must be such necessary components as controllers, views, and a bootstrap file.

A database is not required for this recipe.

How to do it...

Follow these steps to complete this recipe:

1. First of all, we need to have an application which we will experiment with. If you already have such an application, you can skip this step. Create a simple application:

   ```
   phalcon project server_sent simple
   ```

2. Now point the web browser at the root directory of the project. There should be a page with `Congratulations!` ..... If we see the `Volt directory can't be written` error message, then permissions of the directory `app/cache` need to be changed to allow the web server to write to it.

3. Create the controller, `app/controllers/MessagesController.php`:

   ```php
   <?php

   class MessagesController extends ControllerBase
   {
       public function indexAction()
       {
       }

       public function retrieveAction()
       {
           $this->response->setHeader("Content-Type", "text/event-stream");
           $this->response->send();
           $this->view->disable();

           // Remove one level of output buffering
           ob_get_clean();

           $count = 0;
           while ($count < 3) {
               $count++;

               // Send the 'update' event
               echo "event: phalcon-message\n";
               echo 'data: {"time": "' . date(DATE_ISO8601) . '"}';
               echo "\n\n";
   ```

```
                    ob_flush();
                    flush();
                    sleep(1);
                }
            }
        }
```

4. Create the view, `app/views/messages/index.volt`:

```
<div id="messages"></div>

<script>
    var messages = document.getElementById('messages')

    var evtSource = new EventSource("messages/retrieve");
    evtSource.addEventListener("phalcon-message", function(e) {
        var data = JSON.parse(e.data);

        var newElement = document.createElement("li");
        newElement.innerHTML = data.time;
        messages.appendChild(newElement);
    }, false);
</script>
```

5. Point the web browser at the path `messages` to load the JavaScript which will create the `EventSource` object to retrieve the server-sent messages at the path, `messages/retrieve`.

How it works...

When the browser is pointed at path messages, it loads the view that we have placed in the directory, `app/views/messages/index.volt`. This view loads the HTML fragment, which is where we will place the time of day from each new data update:

```
<div id="messages"></div>
```

This creates an `EventSource` object, which implements the server-sent message API. This will then connect to our Phalcon framework at the `messages/retrieve` path, which is automatically directed by the default routing to the `retrieveAction` method on the `MessagesController`:

```
var evtSource = new EventSource("messages/retrieve");
```

We then listen to any `phalcon-message` events coming from this connection. Then, delving into this event listener, we are simply converting the JSON string into a plain object and then appending the `time` property into the HTML so that we can visibly track the updates.

Now we are ready to investigate the PHP code in the `MessagesController` that is responsible for sending these messages.

First, in order to allow the browser `EventSource` to recognize the stream we must set the response header content type to `"text/event-stream"`. If this is not set then the browser may not properly handle the `EventSource` stream and before any data is received by the browser, we first need to transmit the header to the browser. We are using the normal Phalcon dependency injected response for this instead of directly calling the PHP function `header` so that we do not circumvent the normal output buffering operations of our Phalcon system. It is possible for other components in the system to set additional headers during the dispatch cycle, and some of these could be important security features that could be dangerous to omit:

```
$this->response->setHeader("Content-Type", "text/event-stream");
$this->response->send();
```

As an additional precaution, we disable the view rendering to ensure that we do not receive warnings in our logs or accidentally output a view if there is an error later:

```
$this->view->disable();
```

Now we are ready to speak about output buffering. In the vast majority of cases in a Phalcon application, we want the normal operation cycle to handle the actual transmitting of data so that it is efficiently sent all at once at the end of the request handling. This common assumption doesn't work well for a server-sent message because the entire point is to deliver timely updates to the browser.

If we don't first address output buffering then all of the text that we send to the browser won't actually be delivered until the very end of the request handling phase and so all of the messages will be delivered all at once. So, in order to gain direct access to the first output buffer, we will need to destroy the second level of buffering:

```
// Remove one level of output buffering
ob_get_clean();
```

Now we are at a level of output buffering, in which we can precisely determine when data is transmitted to the browser. We will iterate on our loop three times, and during each iteration, we will send a message to the browser so that it can be caught by the JavaScript event handler that we added.

The simplicity of the server-sent event API is that a complete message package can be sent with just the three lines of code. We are defining an event called `phalcon-message`, then we are including data with it, and then finally ending it with two newline characters, `"\n\n"`, to indicate that the message is complete.

Now take a look at the following code within our loop:

```
    // Send the 'phalcon-message' event
echo "event: phalcon-message\n";
echo 'data: {"time": "' . date(DATE_ISO8601) . '"}';
echo "\n\n";
```

This is all that is required to create a new event for the browser. However, we are not quite done yet because some data is stuck in the output buffer and has not yet been transmitted to the browser. We can flush this data to the browser with the following code:

```
ob_flush();
flush();
```

Then at the end of the loop we will make the execution stop with the following:

```
sleep(1)
```

In total this will have the effect of sending a total of three messages with a pause of one second after each message.

Now we will take a step back to analyze the behavior of every script cycle. First, JavaScript in the browser connects to our Phalcon server and the result is that a total of three messages are sent to the browser. After this happens, the PHP script dies and we can see a period of several seconds in which no new messages are received and then just as suddenly as they ended the messages start appearing again. This is a result of the automatic reconnection feature of the server-sent message API. So users can connect once and a small error in any part of the application stack won't break the functionality. You can read more about Server-sent events using EventSource at:

```
https://developer.mozilla.org/en-US/docs/Web/API/Server-sent_events/
Using_server-sent_events
```

Creating a Ratchet Websocket server

The Websockets API allows for an entirely new type of web application that until recently was only possible with a normal system application or by using the flash browser plugin. In essence with every communication, the two most important aspects of a Websocket connection between the client and the server are the bidirectional communication and the elimination of the need to transmit HTTP headers on every communication. Previously, when using only web standards (without flash) the only option to retrieve constantly updated content was to *long poll* the server by looping AJAX requests on a timer.

This approach doesn't scale very well at all due to the overhead of the web server request handling, spinning up a PHP process, handling the routing and authentication, and the HTTP headers that need to be sent for each update. Additionally, developers would need to set an arbitrary delay between AJAX polls and then ultimately, this would cause one of the following two problems: if the delay was set too high then the user would need to wait too long for updated data, and if the delay was too short then it would cause an additional burden on the server.

Actually, in any case, repeatedly polling the server is very hard on it and it becomes impractical and expensive with a large user base.

This makes Websockets the only serious option for a chat application, game, or anything else requiring real-time communication. Websockets are the technology that we need and deserve.

However, with this new capability comes an increase in the complexity of our application, due to the need to run an additional Websocket server process. This recipe is a bit different than most others in that we will be creating a multi-module project with both a Web and CLI interface. We will be doing a lot including dabbling in JavaScript, installing third-party components, and creating a command line server program as well as the expected web application.

You may read about the Websockets API at: `https://developer.mozilla.org/en-US/docs/Web/API/WebSockets_API`

Getting ready

To use this recipe you will need to have a project skeleton with a configured Phalcon bootstrapper, `\Phalcon\Mvc\Router`, and at least one `\Phalcon\Mvc\Controller`. In our example, we will use a project scaffold generated by Phalcon Developer Tools.

To test the recipe results, you need to have a web server installed and configured for handling requests to your application. Your application must be able to take requests, and additionally, there must be such necessary components as controllers, views, and a `bootstrap` file.

We need to install **Composer** to be able to install the third-party PHP Websockets library. You may get the open source Composer tool at: `https://getcomposer.org/`

A database is not required for this recipe.

How to do it...

Follow these steps to complete this recipe:

1. We will need to create a Phalcon project with both a `CLI` and `web` environment, so we will use the `modules` project template:

    ```
    phalcon project chat modules
    ```

2. In the Terminal, change the directory into the root directory of the project directory to install the `Ratchet` library:

    ```
    composer require cboden/ratchet:0.4.x-dev
    ```

3. Make sure that the web server can write to the `cache/volt` directory.

4. Add the Websocket port value to the `config` file at `app/config/config.php`:

    ```
            'websocketPort' => 8080,
    return new \Phalcon\Config([
        /// ...
        'application' => [
            // ...
            'websocketPort' => 8080,
        ],
        // ...
    ]);
    ```

5. Configure the scaffold to use our installed Composer packages by opening up the file, `app/config/loader.php`, and adding this line to the end of the file:

    ```
    include BASE_PATH . '/vendor/autoload.php';
    ```

6. Create the file, `app/common/library/Chat.php`:

    ```php
    <?php
    namespace Websocket;

    class Chat implements \Ratchet\MessageComponentInterface
    {
        protected $clients;

        public function __construct()
        {
            $this->clients = new \SplObjectStorage;
        }

        public function onOpen(\Ratchet\ConnectionInterface $conn)
        {
            $this->clients->attach($conn);

            echo "New connection! ({$conn->resourceId})\n";

            foreach ($this->clients as $client) {
                if ($conn !== $client) {
                    // Send connection message to all clients but the
    current one
    ```

```
                        $client->send("Client {$client->resourceId}
connected.");
                }
            }
        }

    public function onMessage(\Ratchet\ConnectionInterface $from,
$msg)
    {
        // Send to all clients but the current one
        foreach ($this->clients as $client) {
            if ($from != $client) {
                $msg = "Client {$client->resourceId} says
\"$msg\"";
                $client->send($msg);
            }
        }
    }

    public function onClose(\Ratchet\ConnectionInterface $conn)
    {
        $this->clients->detach($conn);
    }

    public function onError(\Ratchet\ConnectionInterface $conn, \
Exception $e)
    {
        $conn->close();
    }
}
```

7. Create app/modules/cli/tasks/ChatTask.php:

```php
<?php
namespace Websocket\Modules\Cli\Tasks;

class ChatTask extends \Phalcon\Cli\Task
{
    public function mainAction()
    {
        $websocketPort = $this->getDI()
            ->getConfig()
            ->application->websocketPort;

        $server = \Ratchet\Server\IoServer::factory(
```

```
                    new \Ratchet\Http\HttpServer(
                        new \Ratchet\WebSocket\WsServer(
                            new \Websocket\Chat()
                        )
                    ),
                    $websocketPort
                );

                $server->run();
            }
        }
```

8. Create the controller, `app/modules/frontend/controllers/ChatController.php`:

```php
<?php
namespace Websocket\Modules\Frontend\Controllers;

class ChatController extends \Phalcon\Mvc\Controller
{
    public function indexAction()
    {
        $websocketPort = $this->config->application->websocketPort;
        $httpHost = $this->request->getServer('HTTP_HOST');

        // You may need to change the domain name and host
        // port depending upon the system.
        $this->view->setVars([
            'HTTP_HOST'       => $httpHost,
            'WEBSOCKET_PORT' => $websocketPort,
        ]);
    }
}
```

9. Create the view, `app/modules/frontend/views/chat/index.volt`:

```
<h1>Websocket Chat Server</h1>
<div id="messages"></div>

<script>
var conn = new WebSocket('ws://{{HTTP_HOST}}:{{WEBSOCKET_PORT}}');
```

```
conn.addEventListener('open', function(e) {
  addMessage("Connection established!")
  helloWorldPing()
});

conn.addEventListener('message', function(e) {
  addMessage(e.data)
})

function helloWorldPing() {
  if (conn.readyState === conn.OPEN) {
    conn.send('Hello World!');
    setTimeout(helloWorldPing, 3000);
  }
}

function addMessage(message) {
  var messageTag = document.createElement('div');
  messageTag.innerHTML = message;

  // We will display as well as log the message.
  console.log(message)
  document.getElementById('messages')
    .appendChild(messageTag)
}

</script>
```

10. Now we are ready to run our Websocket chat server. On the command line, change into the root `project` directory and then start the server with the following:

    ```
    ./run chat
    ```

11. Now open up a browser window to point to the path, `/chat`. Open up the web browser developer tools and view the contents of the **Console** pane. There should be a message with the contents **Connection established!**. Now, keep this window open and open a second window to the same `/chat` path and then open the **Console** pane in this window as well. Now view the first window and we should see that the second window sent it a message. Now the two windows will communicate with each other every three seconds.

How it works...

Now we will look at our `Ratchet Chat` class in `app/library/Chat.php`. During a Websocket life cycle, there will be an `open` and `close` event and many `message` events. This class simply adds handlers for these three cases.

In the open event, we will first save the connection in our `SplObjectStorage` object. Note that the echo `New connection...` line does not send anything to the client and instead simply sends the text to standard output which in this case is our command terminal. Next we will send a message to each other client to notify them that a new client connected to the server:

```php
public function onOpen(Ratchet\ConnectionInterface $conn)
{
    $this->clients->attach($conn);
    echo "New connection! ({$conn->resourceId})\n";

    foreach ($this->clients as $client) {
        if ($conn !== $client) {
            // Send connection message to all clients but the current
one
            $client->send("Client {$client->resourceId} connected.");
        }
    }
}
```

Next in our `message` event handler we will simply broadcast a received message to every other client connected to the server:

```php
public function onMessage(Ratchet\ConnectionInterface $from, $msg)
{
    // Send to all clients but the current one
    foreach ($this->clients as $client) {
        if ($from != $client) {
            $msg = "Client {$client->resourceId} says \"$msg\"";
            $client->send($msg);
        }
    }
}
```

Finally, in the `close` event handler, we will simply remove the client connection from the `SplObjectStorage` object:

```php
public function onClose(Ratchet\ConnectionInterface $conn)
{
    $this->clients->detach($conn);
}
```

So far we have covered the most important part of understanding Websockets on the server. However, what would quickly become obvious in a real application is that we need a way to specify specific actions to perform on each message. Eventually, one would begin to do something such as encoding the message in JSON format and to look at a field such as `type` or `action` to see which function should be performed. So, one could find that they are reinventing the wheel, and this is where **WAMP (Web Application Messaging Protocol)** comes in.

Unfortunately, `Ratchet` doesn't currently support the latest versions of the WAMP protocol that modern JavaScript Websocket libraries support and this is where the `Thruway` library comes in. `Thruway` builds upon `Ratchet` and so the lessons learned here will be a good start to building a high-end Phalcon Websocket server.

Now, back to building our Websocket server. We need a way to run our `Chat` event handler and the most direct way to accomplish this is to wrap the chat application in several layers. At the heart of this is an asynchronous event loop. This is important because it means that the CPU will only spend time on the loop when there is something to be done and it will not long poll using a wait timer.

Back in the introduction, we discussed how having the browser long poll the web server for AJAX updates is not very efficient. Well it's just as inefficient from within a server process as well and this is why using a PHP event extension that hooks into the operating system functionality is essential to a performant Websocket app. In the case of Ratchet it is capable of using three different loop extensions depending upon what is installed.

Now lets look at the `mainAction` of our `ChatTask`. Notice the `$websocketPort` argument on the `HttpServer` object. This is the TCP port that the Websocket server will listen on. We defined this setting in the configuration service instead of hardcoding the value into the application since this makes it much easier to reason about the settings that can change in a project:

```
public function mainAction()
{
    $websocketPort = $this->getDI()
        ->getConfig()
        ->application->websocketPort;

    $server = \Ratchet\Server\IoServer::factory(
        new \Ratchet\Http\HttpServer(
            new \Ratchet\WebSocket\WsServer(
                new \Websocket\Chat()
            )
        ),
        $websocketPort
    );

    $server->run();
}
```

Now we are ready to look at the front part of the Websockets. Since this is the part of the solution that is delivered to the client through the web server, we must use the `frontend` scaffold. The JavaScript used to connect it is delivered through the view located at `frontend/app/views/chat/index.volt`.

First we will connect to the server at the domain, `HTTP_HOST` and port `WEBSOCKET_PORT`:

```
var conn = new WebSocket('ws://{{HTTP_HOST}}:{{WEBSOCKET_PORT}}');
```

These `view` variables are set in the `ChatController`:

```
$this->view->setVars([
    'HTTP_HOST'      => $httpHost,
    'WEBSOCKET_PORT' => $websocketPort,
]);
```

The handling of events on the client and server are very similar. For the server and client, we have an `open`, `close`, and `message` event.

We will listen to the `open` event on the connection. This event will trigger when a connection is made. We will then call the `helloWorldPing` function which will then send the message `Hello World!` to the server (which will then broadcast to all other clients) and we will repeat this every three seconds:

```
conn.addEventListener('open', function(e) {
  addMessage("Connection established!")
  helloWorldPing()
});

function helloWorldPing() {
  if (conn.readyState === conn.OPEN) {
    conn.send('Hello World!');
    setTimeout(helloWorldPing, 3000);
  }
}
```

Next we will simply log incoming messages to the JavaScript console:

```
conn.addEventListener('message', function(e) {
  addMessage(e.data)
})
```

Finally, rather than repeat code in multiple events, we place all of the code for logging to the console and displaying the messages in the HTML into a single `addMessage` function:

```
function addMessage(message) {
  var messageTag = document.createElement('div');
  messageTag.innerHTML = message;

  // We will display as well as log the message.
  console.log(message)
  document.getElementById('messages')
    .appendChild(messageTag)
}
```

Important reading:

- ▸ https://developer.mozilla.org/en-US/docs/Web/API/WebSockets_API
- ▸ React PHP: http://reactphp.org/
- ▸ Ratchet: http://socketo.me/
- ▸ Thruway: https://github.com/voryx/Thruway

4

Dealing with Data

In this chapter, we will cover:

- ▸ Applying your own naming conventions to models
- ▸ Defining relationships between models
- ▸ Using the query builder for complex yet fluent model querying
- ▸ Being aware of PHQL capabilities
- ▸ Fetching models from raw SQL queries
- ▸ Getting the most out of your RDBMS of choice
- ▸ Using models and information repositories
- ▸ Storing models across multiple databases

Introduction

Data is the cornerstone of an application and it is important to be able to do the most with it. Sometimes you will have inherited a database from a previous developer and it will have table names that are strange or simply not appropriate for Phalcon models. We will demonstrate how to use Phalcon models independently of the database schema so that you can integrate Phalcon into an existing application while staying true to the Phalcon way.

We will also be defining relations between models to allow a powerful application structure.

The Phalcon model system is built upon a common subset of all of the possible database features. In other words, to ensure a consistent experience across the supported databases, some unique features are not supported in the base Phalcon system. However, the Phalcon database layer is capable of being extended with custom functionality unique to the database of choice. It will be up to the developer to decide if a particular non-standard database feature is a must-have for sacrificing database portability.

The Phalcon ORM system is powered by the very powerful PHQL, which is ultimately converted to SQL before being processed by the database. So PHQL can be thought of as a subset of SQL with powerful Phalcon integration features.

We'll first take a step back from diving straight into PHQL and we'll use the query builder to construct queries using its chainable API. The query builder is particularly useful for developers who are still learning or who are using a supported IDE which can autocomplete the chainable method names.

Then we'll construct queries using fully formed PHQL statements as well as extending the database dialect to support custom functions. Then, if this doesn't provide enough flexibility, we'll work directly with raw SQL statements while using Phalcon models as a central point of knowledge. This will allow us to reap the benefits of our high level model system while being able to go as low level as needed.

Preparation

To test the recipe results, you need to have a web server installed and configured for handling requests to your application. Your application must be able to take requests and there must be necessary components such as controllers, views, and a `bootstrap` file.

This chapter will use a `chapter_04` database so that each recipe doesn't need to provide redundant schema.

Import this table into the database named `chapter_04`:

```
DROP TABLE IF EXISTS 'cars_legacy123';
CREATE TABLE 'cars_legacy123' (
   'id' int(11) NOT NULL AUTO_INCREMENT,
   'name_legacy_abc' varchar(25) COLLATE utf8_unicode_ci NOT NULL,
   PRIMARY KEY ('id')
) ENGINE=InnoDB AUTO_INCREMENT=5 DEFAULT CHARSET=utf8 COLLATE=utf8_
unicode_ci;
INSERT INTO 'cars_legacy123' VALUES (1,'mustang'),(2,'camaro'),(3,'hum
mer'),(4,'porsche');

DROP TABLE IF EXISTS 'colors';
CREATE TABLE 'colors' (
   'id' int(11) NOT NULL AUTO_INCREMENT,
   'name' varchar(25) COLLATE utf8_unicode_ci NOT NULL,
   PRIMARY KEY ('id')
) ENGINE=InnoDB AUTO_INCREMENT=6 DEFAULT CHARSET=utf8 COLLATE=utf8_
unicode_ci;
```

```
INSERT INTO 'colors' VALUES (1,'green'),(2,'blue'),(3,'red'),(4,'black
'),(5,'white');

DROP TABLE IF EXISTS 'hats';
CREATE TABLE 'hats' (
  'id' int(11) NOT NULL AUTO_INCREMENT,
  'name' varchar(25) COLLATE utf8_unicode_ci NOT NULL,
  PRIMARY KEY ('id')
) ENGINE=InnoDB AUTO_INCREMENT=6 DEFAULT CHARSET=utf8 COLLATE=utf8_
unicode_ci;
INSERT INTO 'hats' VALUES (1,'sombrero'),(2,'fedora'),(3,'tophat'),(4,
'baseball'),(5,'panama');

DROP TABLE IF EXISTS 'hats_colors';
CREATE TABLE 'hats_colors' (
  'id' int(11) NOT NULL AUTO_INCREMENT,
  'hats_id' int(11) NOT NULL,
  'colors_id' int(11) NOT NULL,
  PRIMARY KEY ('id')
) ENGINE=InnoDB AUTO_INCREMENT=6 DEFAULT CHARSET=utf8 COLLATE=utf8_
unicode_ci;
INSERT INTO 'hats_colors' VALUES (1,1,3),(2,1,4),(3,2,4),(4,3,5),(5,4
,2);

DROP TABLE IF EXISTS 'posts';
CREATE TABLE 'posts' (
  'id' int(11) NOT NULL AUTO_INCREMENT,
  'title' varchar(50) CHARACTER SET latin1 NOT NULL,
  'text' text CHARACTER SET latin1 NOT NULL,
  PRIMARY KEY ('id'),
  FULLTEXT KEY 'text' ('text')
) ENGINE=MyISAM AUTO_INCREMENT=4 DEFAULT CHARSET=utf8 COLLATE=utf8_
unicode_ci;
INSERT INTO 'posts' VALUES (1,'Technology','Technology is
a very powerful force that seeks to change society for the
better.'),(2,'Life','Where did we come from and where do we
go?'),(3,'Cars','Cars that go fast are generally more popular than
those that go slowly.');
```

Applying your own naming conventions to models

In this recipe, we will introduce workarounds for instances when we are not in control of the column naming used in our database schema. This situation can arise when the system is already under the constraints of other development environments or when working with a legacy system.

Getting ready

This recipe uses the `chapter_04` database that we set up in the chapter introduction and Phalcon Developer Tools, which we will use to set up a project skeleton.

How to do it...

Follow these steps to complete this recipe:

1. We need to have an application skeleton for experimentation. If you already have such an application, you can skip this step. Create a project skeleton using the `simple` template:

   ```
   phalcon project model_conventions simple
   ```

2. Now point the web browser at the root directory of the project. There should be a page with `Congratulations!` ..... If we see the `Volt directory can't be written` error message, then permissions of the directory `app/cache` need to be changed to allow the web server to write to it.

3. Ensure that your `configuration` file is set up with the correct host, database, username, and password. This recipe will use the `chapter_04` database that we established in the introduction to `chapter_04`.

4. Create the model, `app/models/Hats.php`:

   ```php
   <?php

   class Hats extends Phalcon\Mvc\Model
   {
   }
   ```

5. Create the model, `app/models/Cars.php`:

   ```php
   <?php

   class Cars extends Phalcon\Mvc\Model
   {
   ```

```
    public function getSource()
    {
        return "cars_legacy123";
    }

    public function columnMap()
    {
        return [
            'id'              => 'id',
            'name_legacy_abc' => 'name'
        ];
    }
}
```

6. Create the controller, `app/controllers/IndexController.php`:

```php
<?php

class IndexController extends ControllerBase
{
    public function indexAction()
    {
        $sombrero = Hats::findFirstByName('sombrero');
        $porsche = Cars::findFirstByName('porsche');

        return $sombrero->name . ' - ' . $porsche->name;
    }
}
```

7. In the browser, go to the root path of the project. You should see `sombrero - porsche`.

How it works...

Our model in `app/models/Hats.php` is about as simple as it could be:

```
class Hats extends Phalcon\Mvc\Model {}
```

In an ideal case, this is all that is needed for Phalcon to be able to use the database table for querying, inserting, and deleting records. Although we can create `class` variables for each `table` field, it is unnecessary for this recipe because the model's metadata is obtained from the table. It's easy!

Our next `Cars` model is a bit of a tragic case. We have inherited a schema in which the table and column names are just awful and, because it is part of a legacy system we can't just rename them. We are not out of luck, however, because Phalcon allows both the table name and field names to be defined independently from what is stored in the database.

First we will set the table source to allow Phalcon to find the data:

```
public function getSource()
{
    return "cars_legacy123";
}
```

Next we will map the columns from the database to our ideal names that we would like to work with from within Phalcon:

```
public function columnMap()
{
    return [
        'id'              => 'id',
        'name_legacy_abc' => 'name'
    ];
}
```

Now we look at the in `app/controllers/IndexController.php`. The specifics of how this works will be described in a later recipe but, simply, we are able to search the database for the records by their name:

```
$sombrero = Hats::findFirstByName('sombrero');
$porsche = Cars::findFirstByName('porsche');
```

Defining relationships between models

In this recipe, we will learn how to create relationships between two or more `Phalcon\Mvc\Model` classes. This will allow us to use the third normal database form without needing to repeatedly specify primary keys and foreign keys for basic queries.

Getting ready

This recipe uses the `chapter_04` database that we set up in the chapter introduction and Phalcon Developer Tools, which we will use to set up a project skeleton.

How to do it...

Follow these steps to complete this recipe:

1. We need to have an application skeleton for experimentation. If you already have such an application, you can skip this step. Create a project skeleton using the `simple` template:

    ```
    phalcon project model_relations simple
    ```

2. Now point the web browser at the root directory of the project. There should be a page with `Congratulations!` ..... If we see the `Volt directory can't be written` error message then permissions of the directory `app/cache` need to be changed to allow the web server to write to it.

3. Ensure that your `configuration` file is set up with the correct host, database, username, and password. This recipe will use the `chapter_04` database that we established in the introduction.

4. Create the model, `app/models/Hats.php`:

    ```php
    <?php

    class Hats extends Phalcon\Mvc\Model
    {
        public function initialize()
        {
            $this->hasManyToMany(
                "id",
                "HatsColors",
                "hats_id",
                "colors_id",
                "Colors",
                "id",
                [
                    'alias' => 'colors'
                ]
            );
        }
    }
    ```

5. Create the model, `app/models/Colors.php`:

    ```php
    <?php

    class Colors extends Phalcon\Mvc\Model
    {
    ```

```php
        public function initialize()
        {
            $this->hasManyToMany(
                "id",
                "HatsColors",
                "colors_id",
                "hats_id",
                "Hats",
                "id",
                [
                    'alias' => 'hats'
                ]
            );
        }
    }
```

6. Create the model, `app/models/HatsColors.php`:

```php
<?php

class HatsColors extends Phalcon\Mvc\Model
{
}
```

7. Create the controller, `app/controllers/RelationsController`:

```php
<?php

class RelationsController extends Phalcon\Mvc\Controller
{
    public function indexAction()
    {
        $this->response->appendContent('<h3>Hats</h3>');
        foreach(Hats::find() as $hat) {
            $this->printHatColors($hat);
        }

        $this->response->appendContent('<h3>Colors</h3>');
        foreach(Colors::find() as $color) {
            $this->printColorHats($color);
        }

        $this->response->send();
    }
```

```php
        private function printHatColors($hat)
        {
            $colors = $hat->getRelated('colors');

            $this->response->appendContent($hat->name . ':');
            if ($colors->count() > 0) {
                foreach ($colors as $color) {
                    $this->response->appendContent(' ' . $color->name);
                }

            } else {
                $this->response->appendContent(' without color');
            }
            $this->response->appendContent('<br>');
        }

        private function printColorHats($color)
        {
            $hats = $color->getHats();

            $this->response->appendContent($color->name . ':');
            if ($hats->count() > 0) {
                foreach ($hats as $hat) {
                    $this->response->appendContent(' ' . $hat->name);
                }

            } else {
                $this->response->appendContent(' without hats');
            }
            $this->response->appendContent('<br>');
        }
    }
```

8. In the browser, go to the relative path `relations` from the root of the project's webspace. There should be a `Hats` and `Colors` header with their relation data printed out for each record.

How it works...

In our recipe, we have created three models; `Hats`, `Colors`, and `HatsColors`. Two of them are storing actual data (such as their name) and the third model, `HatsColors`, stores primary key combinations that Phalcon will use to link a `Hat` to multiple `Colors` and also a `Colors` to multiple `Hats`. Notice that we are using the plural form when naming models as this reminds us that we are dealing with a set of data.

First we will look at the `Hats` model's `initialize` function. This function is used to configure the model's metadata service with the relationship data. What this code does is link up the `Hats` primary key field `id` to the `HatsColors` field `hats_id` and then links the `HatsColors` field `colors_id` to the `Colors` primary key field `id`. Then it assigns a relationship alias, named `colors`, so that we can easily access the related data by calling it by its name:

```php
public function initialize()
{
    $this->hasManyToMany(
        "id",
        "HatsColors",
        "hats_id",
        "colors_id",
        "Colors",
        "id",
        [
            'alias' => 'colors'
        ]
    );
}
```

However, this only allows us to use relations in a single direction from `Hats` to `Colors`, and so in order to be able to have the same functionality from the other direction we must also define this relationship in the `Colors` model. Notice the strong similarity in the setup:

```php
public function initialize()
{
    $this->hasManyToMany(
        "id",
        "HatsColors",
        "colors_id",
        "hats_id",
        "Hats",
        "id",
        [
            'alias' => 'hats'
        ]
    );
}
```

Finally, in `RelationsController`, we call out to the query functionality that is built into `Phalcon\Mvc\Model`.

Here we call the static `find` method on our `Hats` model to receive a `Phalcon\Mvc\Model\Resultset\Simple` object with our records but for now we don't need to know much about this class, other than that it is an object that can be iterated upon to access individual records:

```
foreach(Hats::find() as $hat) {
    $this->printHatColors($hat);
}
```

Now in the `printHatColors` function, we will retrieve all of the related color records for our `Hats` model. Note that we can also pass in additional query parameters to this function, but we'll cover that in a later recipe. So really, this is where the magic happens because with this simple call, we are able to hide the complexity of a third normal database relationship to obtain all of the related records. Take a look at the following code snippet:

```
private function printHatColors($hat)
{
    $colors = $hat->getRelated('colors');
```

At this point $colors contains all of the `Colors` records that are related to `$hat`. Due to the nature of a many-to-many relationship, `$colors` could be of size 0, 1, or many. So each hat can have any number of colors and each color can have any number of hats. Additionally, each color may have no hats and each hat may have no colors (as strange as a colorless hat would be in real life).

So now we will iterate through the `Phalcon\Mvc\Model\Resultset\Simple $colors` object in the same way as we iterated through `$hats` and print out the results.

Notice that we are using `$this->response->appendContent()` for our output instead of writing directly to the standard output with `echo`. We are allowing the `response` service to handle the output so that HTTP headers and buffers can be automatically used and all of the output correctly inserted into the content area of a Volt layout.

Now we will skip past all of the simple output formatting to the `printColorHats` function. This function is a mirror image of the `printHatsColors` function except that it uses the shorthand magic method to obtain the related records:

```
private function printColorHats($color)
{
    $hats = $color->getHats();
```

Using the query builder for complex yet fluent model querying

Phalcon has a powerful query builder that can generate queries without writing PHQL or SQL. This is accomplished by creating a `Phalcon\Mvc\Model\Query\Builder` object and then chaining a series of methods together to generate a `Phalcon\Mvc\Model\Query`. This technique also has an advantage of having IDE support through the Developer Tools integration.

Getting ready

This recipe uses the `chapter_04` database that we set up in the chapter introduction and the Phalcon Developer Tools which we will use to set up a project skeleton.

How to do it...

Follow these steps to complete this recipe:

1. We need to have an application skeleton for experimentation. If you already have such an application, you can skip this step. Create a project skeleton using the simple template:

   ```
   phalcon project query_builder simple
   ```

2. Now point the web browser at the root directory of the project. There should be a page with `Congratulations! .....` If we see the `Volt directory can't be written` error message, then permissions of the directory `app/cache` need to be changed to allow the web server to write to it.

3. Ensure that your `configuration` file is set up with the correct host, database, username, and password. This recipe will use the `chapter_04` database that we established in the chapter introduction.

4. Create the model, `app/models/Hats.php`:

   ```php
   <?php

   class Hats extends Phalcon\Mvc\Model
   {
       public function initialize()
       {
           $this->hasManyToMany(
               "id",
               "HatsColors",
   ```

```
                "hats_id",
                "colors_id",
                "Colors",
                "id",
                [
                    'alias' => 'colors'
                ]
            );
        }
    }
```

5. Create the model, app/models/Colors.php:

```php
<?php

class Colors extends Phalcon\Mvc\Model
{
    public function initialize()
    {
        $this->hasManyToMany(
            "id",
            "HatsColors",
            "colors_id",
            "hats_id",
            "Hats",
            "id",
            [
                'alias' => 'hats'
            ]
        );
    }
}
```

6. Create the model, app/models/HatsColors.php:

```php
<?php

class HatsColors extends Phalcon\Mvc\Model
{
}
```

7. Create the controller, app/controllers/BuilderController.php:

```php
<?php

class BuilderController extends Phalcon\Mvc\Controller
```

```
{
    public function example1Action()
    {
        $builder = $this->modelsManager
            ->createBuilder();

        $builder = $builder->from('Hats');
        $builder = $builder->where('Hats.name = "panama"');
        $builder = $builder->orWhere('Hats.name = "baseball"');

        $query = $builder->getQuery();
        $generatedSql = $query->getSql()['sql'];
        $hats = $query->execute();

        $this->response->appendContent($generatedSql .
'<br><br>');
        foreach ($hats as $hat) {
            $this->response->appendContent($hat->name . '<br>');
        }
        $this->response->send();
    }

    public function example2Action()
    {
        $hats = $this->modelsManager
            ->createBuilder()
            ->from('Hats')
            ->join('Colors')
            ->distinct(true)
            ->inWhere('Colors.name', ['black', 'red'])
            ->getQuery()
            ->execute();

        foreach ($hats as $hat) {
            $this->response->appendContent($hat->name . '<br>');
        }
        $this->response->send();
    }
}
```

8. Point the browser at `/builder/example1` of the root path of the project. There should be a SQL statement at the top of the page followed by the printout of hats returned from the query.

9. Point the browser at `/builder/example2` to see the print out of the hats returned from the query.

How it works...

Let's take a look at `example1Action` in `BuilderController`.

Here we are calling to the DI service called `modelsManager` and asking it to create a `Phalcon\Mvc\Model\Query\Builder` object for us:

```
public function example1Action()
{
    $builder = $this->modelsManager
        ->createBuilder();
```

Here we are calling a series of methods on the `$builder` object to add additional conditions and requirements to it. Notice after each call saving a new reference to the `$builder` object:

```
$builder = $builder->from('Hats');
$builder = $builder->where('Hats.name = "panama"');
$builder = $builder->orWhere('Hats.name = "baseball"');
```

Although this is perfectly valid, in the next example we will demonstrate a cleaner way to chain the entirety of the query building process into one concise sequence. For now this approach allows us to talk about the class types of the return objects as we build the query.

Now that we have the basic requirements for a SQL statement we can generate a `Phalcon\Mvc\Model\Query` object:

```
$query = $builder->getQuery();
```

We will store the actual SQL generated from our query. This feature is very useful when debugging a troublesome program, but for now we are only doing it for learning purposes:

```
$generatedSql = $query->getSql()['sql'];
```

Finally, we will retrieve our hat models:

```
$hats = $query->execute();
```

Now we have all of the data that we need, so we will print out the generated SQL from our query and also print out all of the hats that were retrieved:

```
$this->response->appendContent($generatedSql . '<br><br>');
foreach ($hats as $hat) {
    $this->response->appendContent($hat->name . '<br>');
}
$this->response->send();
```

Now let's look at our second example in `example2Action`.

We are now chaining the entire query process into one long execution without storing the intermediate objects:

```
$hats = $this->modelsManager
    ->createBuilder()
    ->from('Hats')
    ->join('Colors')
    ->distinct(true)
    ->inWhere('Colors.name', ['black', 'red'])
    ->getQuery()
    ->execute();
```

We are starting with the `Hats` model with `->from('Hats')` and then we are joining it against the `Colors` model with `->join('Colors')`. Due to the defined relationship between our `Hats` and `Colors` model which goes through `HatsColors`, we are able to automatically fill in the join conditions between three tables with just these two lines. Powerful stuff!

We need to declare that we do not want duplicate models returned with `->distinct(true)` as this is the standard SQL behavior.

Now we are ready to add a condition to the `WHERE` clause of the query by adding the call `->inWhere('Colors.name', ['black', 'red'])`. Notice that we are passing in an array of two values with the second argument. This creates placeholders in the SQL and then fills in their bind values during execution. This is more secure and allows us to bind an entire array automatically and this is something that native PDO database access does not support. Additionally as we'll learn later if we bind all values in our query then Phalcon can cache the PHQL to be used later.

At this point, we still have a builder object and, by calling `getQuery`, we retrieve the `Phalcon\Mvc\Model\Query` object which we then execute to receive the `Phalcon\Mvc\Model\Resultset\Simple` that contains all of our models and can be iterated upon.

There are a few other features supported by the query builder and they can be found at: `https://docs.phalconphp.com/en/latest/reference/phql.html#creating-queries-using-the-query-builder`

Being aware of PHQL capabilities

PHQL (Phalcon Query Language) is one of the most innovative and powerful parts of Phalcon and by using it we gain some features and security protections over the standard direct PDO access. Normally, if these features were added to an **ORM (Object Relation Model)** then it would have higher performance penalties but with Phalcon it is essentially unnoticeable because the parser uses highly optimized native libraries written in the C language. We gain a lot of powerful features and if any of these features turn out to be undesirable for us then we can disable each of them on a global or individual query level.

Let's review some of the main benefits over using PDO and standard SQL that we have covered in other recipes. For starters, PHQL understands our model storage details by referencing DI services and by the actual PHP model class implementation where we establish relationships and other settings. This allows us to think in a generality that hides much of the tedium involved in switching between the database and programming mindset. For example, by defining model classes in our PHP code we are able to have PHQL do many things, such as fill in the mundane primary key to foreign key conditions on table joins, understand which database connection to use when retrieving records, how to translate odd table and field names into ideal names for use in our code, and the ability to add custom functions to our query conditions.

In this recipe, we will discuss some other smaller features which, when combined with the power already outlined creates the PHQL experience. We will discuss things, such as how to disable the use of literal values directly in the PHQL statement and to instead force placeholders to be used, how to disable implicit relationship join conditions, how to cast field data to the original types on model data hydration, and how to have PHQL automatically expand array values into placeholders.

Getting ready

This recipe uses the `chapter_04` database that we set up in the chapter introduction and Phalcon Developer Tools, which we will use to set up a project skeleton.

How to do it...

Follow these steps to complete this recipe:

1. We need to have an application skeleton for experimentation. If you already have such an application, you can skip this step. Create a project skeleton using the `simple` template:

   ```
   phalcon project phql_capabilities simple
   ```

2. Now point the web browser at the root directory of the project. There should be a page with `Congratulations!` . . . . . If we see the `Volt directory can't be written` error message, then permissions of the directory `app/cache` need to be changed to allow the web server to write to it.

3. Ensure that your `configuration` file is set up with the correct host, database, username, and password. This recipe will use the `chapter_04` database that we established in the chapter introduction.

4. Create the model, `app/models/Colors.php`:

```php
<?php

class Colors extends Phalcon\Mvc\Model
{
    public function initialize()
    {
        $this->hasManyToMany(
            "id",
            "HatsColors",
            "colors_id",
            "hats_id",
            "Hats",
            "id",
            [
                'alias' => 'hats'
            ]
        );
    }
}
```

5. Create the model, `app/models/Hats.php`:

```php
<?php

class Hats extends Phalcon\Mvc\Model
{
    public function initialize()
    {
        $this->hasManyToMany(
            "id",
            "HatsColors",
            "hats_id",
            "colors_id",
            "Colors",
            "id",
            [
                'alias' => 'colors'
            ]
        );
    }
}
```

6. Create the model, `app/models/HatsColors.php`:

```php
<?php

class HatsColors extends Phalcon\Mvc\Model
```

```
    {
    }
```

7. Create the controller, `app/controllers/PhqlController.php`:

```php
<?php

class PhqlController extends Phalcon\Mvc\Controller
{
    public function basicJoinAction()
    {
        $phql = "SELECT Hats.* FROM Hats JOIN Colors WHERE Colors.
name = 'red'";
        $query = new Phalcon\Mvc\Model\Query($phql, $this-
>getDI());
        $this->response->appendContent('<p>' . $query->getSql()
['sql'] . '</p>');

        $hats = $query->execute();
        $this->response->appendContent('<ul>');
        foreach ($hats as $hat) {
            $this->response->appendContent('<li>' . $hat->name .
'</li>');
        }
        $this->response->appendContent('</ul>');

        $this->response->send();
    }

    public function noImplicitJoinsAction()
    {
        $phql = <<<PHQL
SELECT Hats.* FROM Hats
INNER JOIN HatsColors ON HatsColors.hats_id = Hats.id
INNER JOIN Colors ON Colors.id = HatsColors.colors_id
WHERE Colors.name = 'red'
PHQL;
        $query = new Phalcon\Mvc\Model\Query($phql, $this-
>getDI(), [
            'enable_implicit_joins' => false
        ]);
        $this->response->appendContent('<p>' . $query->getSql()
['sql'] . '</p>');
```

```
        $hats = $query->execute();
        $this->response->appendContent('<ul>');
        foreach ($hats as $hat) {
            $this->response->appendContent('<li>' . $hat->name .
'</li>');
        }
        $this->response->appendContent('</ul>');

        $this->response->send();
    }

    public function bindSimpleAction()
    {
        $phql = "SELECT Hats.* FROM Hats JOIN Colors WHERE Colors.
name = :color:";
        $query = new Phalcon\Mvc\Model\Query($phql, $this-
>getDI(), [
            'phqlLiterals' => false
        ]);
        $this->response->appendContent('<p>' . $query->getSql()
['sql'] . '</p>');

        $query->setBindParams([
            'color' => 'red'
        ]);
        $hats = $query->execute();

$this->response->appendContent('<ul>');
        foreach ($hats as $hat) {
            $this->response->appendContent('<li>' . $hat->name .
'</li>');
        }
        $this->response->appendContent('</ul>');

        $this->response->send();
    }

    public function bindArrayAction()
    {
        $phql = "SELECT Hats.* FROM Hats JOIN Colors WHERE Colors.
name IN ({colors:array})";
        $query = new Phalcon\Mvc\Model\Query($phql, $this-
>getDI());
```

```
                    $query->setBindParams([
                       'colors' => ['red', 'green', 'black']
                    ]);
                    $hats = $query->execute();

                    $this->response->appendContent('<ul>');
                    foreach ($hats as $hat) {
                        $this->response->appendContent('<li>' . $hat->name .
    '</li>');
                    }
                    $this->response->appendContent('</ul>');

                    $this->response->send();
            }
        }
```

8. Point the browser at the following paths:

    ❑   `/phql/basicJoin`

    ❑   `/phql/noImplicitJoins`

    ❑   `/phql/bindSimple`

    ❑   `/phql/bindArray`

How it works...

First let's look at the three models that we created.

The `Colors` model defines a `hasManyToMany` relationship to the `Hats` model that goes through `HatsColors`, and then defines an alias for that relationship, called `hats`. This will allow us to get all related hats by simply calling `getHats()` on any `Colors` object:

```
class Colors extends Phalcon\Mvc\Model
{
    public function initialize()
    {
        $this->hasManyToMany(
            "id",
            "HatsColors",
            "colors_id",
            "hats_id",
            "Hats",
            "id",
            [
                'alias' => 'hats'
```

```
                    ]
                );
        }
    }
```

Next, with the `Hats` model, we define another `hasManyToMany` relationship but in the opposite direction, and this time we create a `colors` relationship alias:

```
class Hats extends Phalcon\Mvc\Model
{
    public function initialize()
    {
        $this->hasManyToMany(
            "id",
            "HatsColors",
            "hats_id",
            "colors_id",
            "Colors",
            "id",
            [
                'alias' => 'colors'
            ]
        );
    }
}
```

To conclude our models setup, the `HatsColors` model is just an empty shell of a class, but it is required for the `hasManyToMany` relationships to work:

```
class HatsColors extends Phalcon\Mvc\Model {}
```

Now we'll look at the actions in our `PhqlController` class.

In `basicJoinAction`, we are taking advantage of our defined relationship from `Hats` to `Colors` by letting the PHQL fill in the `JOIN` condition for us. Notice that there isn't an `ON` condition that would normally be required when working with an SQL join. Take a look at the following code:

```
$phql = "SELECT Hats.* FROM Hats JOIN Colors WHERE Colors.name = 'red'";
$query = new Phalcon\Mvc\Model\Query($phql, $this->getDI());
```

Next we obtain the generated SQL from the query object for debugging purposes. When the query `execute` method is called this SQL will be sent to the underlying PDO object.

```
$query->getSql()['sql']
```

Finally, we execute the query to get our `Phalcon\Mvc\Model\Resultset\Simple` object, and then we iterate on it to get our `Hats` model objects:

```
$hats = $query->execute();
foreach ($hats as $hat) {
    // ...
}
```

Next we will demonstrate how to turn off implicit PHQL joins in the `noImplicitJoinsAction`.

Now that we are not going to allow the PHQL system to fill in the join conditions from the defined relationships we must add them ourselves. This example demonstrates what PHQL normally does for us, as well as giving us a way of deliberately defining the relationship in a situation where PHQL is not capable of generating the SQL that we require.

In the following code, we are using **Heredoc** string format to be able to make it easier to read and write long PHQL statements:

```
        $phql = <<<PHQL
SELECT Hats.* FROM Hats
INNER JOIN HatsColors ON HatsColors.hats_id = Hats.id
INNER JOIN Colors ON Colors.id = HatsColors.colors_id
WHERE Colors.name = 'red'
PHQL;
```

Next we will create the query object, and this time we will be passing in an option to inform the query to disable implicit joins:

```
$query = new Phalcon\Mvc\Model\Query($phql, $this->getDI(), [
    'enable_implicit_joins' => false
]);
```

Next, in the `bindSimpleAction`, we will demonstrate how to bind values to placeholders. In a later recipe, we will learn how this allows the PHQL query cache to save the query to increase performance and memory if it is reused, but in this recipe we will only look into the practical and security implications of it.

This time in our PHQL, we use the `:color:` placeholder instead of specifying red directly in the query:

```
$phql = "SELECT Hats.* FROM Hats JOIN Colors WHERE Colors.name =
:color:";
```

Note that PHQL uses a colon on both sides of the placeholder, while PDO only uses a prefix colon.

We will create the query object this time by passing in an option to disable the use of PHQL literals. Although it is not required to use this option to use placeholders, by using it, you are enforcing their use:

```
$query = new Phalcon\Mvc\Model\Query($phql, $this->getDI(), [
    'phqlLiterals' => false
]);
```

Be sure to look at the output of the `$query->getSql()['sql']` call in this action to see how the PHQL statement is translated into SQL suitable for the underlying PDO object.

For experimentation purposes, try changing the PHQL in this action to use a literal value just as the previous two actions used. It should generate an error.

Note that the use of PHQL literals can be disabled on a project-wide basis by adding the following code in the configuration stage of the project:

```
Phalcon\Mvc\Model::setup([
    'phqlLiterals'       => false
]);
```

Finally, in `bindArrayAction`, we demonstrate a very nice feature of PHQL that will allow us to bind an entire array of values using a placeholder. This feature is far beyond what PDO offers, because the PHQL placeholder will be expanded to the appropriate number of placeholders in the SQL statement. Without this feature, we are required to do some very tedious or complicated custom work to create the correct number of placeholders ourselves:

```
$phql = "SELECT Hats.* FROM Hats JOIN Colors WHERE Colors.name IN
({colors:array})";
```

Then it's as simple as creating the query and passing in the correct values for the array placeholder, `{colors:array}`:

```
$query = new Phalcon\Mvc\Model\Query($phql, $this->getDI());
$hats = $query->execute([
    'colors' => ['red', 'green', 'black']
]);
```

Fetching models from raw SQL queries

In this recipe, we will learn how to retrieve data using raw SQL for when PHQL doesn't meet our needs. Although PHQL does a lot, and can be extended by using custom database specific dialects, it isn't always enough. It would be terrible if we were simply out of luck and unable to fulfill a niche need and fortunately, Phalcon is able to get out of the way and to provide us raw SQL access to our database service. This means that we can use PHQL based technology for almost everything in our system and then, if we hit a wall, we can switch over to writing the query directly with SQL.

Note: One potential downside to consider when using raw SQL is that if we are doing so to implement database implementation specific vendor features then it could make our system no longer able to work with other databases.

Getting ready

This recipe uses the `chapter_04` database that we set up in the chapter introduction and Phalcon Developer Tools, which we will use to set up a project skeleton.

How to do it...

Follow these steps to complete this recipe:

1. We need to have an application skeleton for experimentation. If you already have such an application, you can skip this step. Create a project skeleton using the `simple` template:

    ```
    phalcon project raw_sql simple
    ```

2. Now point the web browser at the root directory of the project. There should be a page with `Congratulations!` ..... If we see the `Volt directory can't be written` error message, then permissions of the directory `app/cache` need to be changed to allow the web server to write to it.

3. Ensure that your configuration file is set up with the correct host, database, username, and password. This recipe will use the `chapter_04` database that we established in the chapter introduction.

4. Create the model, `app/models/Hats.php`:

    ```php
    <?php

    class Hats extends Phalcon\Mvc\Model
    {
        public static function findFirstByRelatedColor($colorName)
    ```

```
        {
            $hat = new Hats();
            $color = new Colors();
            $hatColor = new HatsColors();

            $sql = <<<SQL
SELECT Hats.* FROM '{$hat->getSource()}' Hats
INNER JOIN '{$hatColor->getSource()}' HatsColors ON Hats.id =
HatsColors.hats_id
INNER JOIN '{$color->getSource()}' Colors ON Colors.id =
HatsColors.colors_id
WHERE Colors.name = :colorName
LIMIT 1
SQL;

            $connection = $hat->getReadConnection();
            $row = $connection->fetchOne($sql, Phalcon\Db::FETCH_
ASSOC, [
                'colorName' => $colorName
            ]);
            if (!$row) {
                return false;
            }

            return Phalcon\Mvc\Model::cloneResultMap(new Hats(), $row,
            Phalcon\Mvc\Model::DIRTY_STATE_PERSISTENT);
        }

    public static function findByRelatedColor($colorName)
        {
            $hat = new Hats();
            $color = new Colors();
            $hatColor = new HatsColors();

            $sql = <<<SQL
SELECT Hats.*
FROM '{$hat->getSource()}' Hats
INNER JOIN '{$hatColor->getSource()}' HatsColors ON Hats.id =
HatsColors.hats_id
INNER JOIN '{$color->getSource()}' Colors ON Colors.id =
HatsColors.colors_id
WHERE Colors.name = :colorName
SQL;
```

```
        // We are getting the connection service from the model
instead of from the
        // DI because each model can define its own connection
service.
        $connection = $hat->getReadConnection();
        $results = $connection->query($sql, [
            'colorName' => $colorName
        ]);

        return new Phalcon\Mvc\Model\Resultset\Simple(null, $hat,
$results);
    }

}
```

5. Create the model, `app/models/Colors.php`:

```php
<?php

class Colors extends Phalcon\Mvc\Model
{
}
```

6. Create the model, `app/models/HatsColors.php`:

```php
<?php

class HatsColors extends Phalcon\Mvc\Model
{
}
```

7. Create the controller, `app/controllers/SqlController.php`:

```php
<?php

class SqlController extends Phalcon\Mvc\Controller
{
    public function findFirstByRelatedColorAction()
    {
        $colorName = $this->request->getQuery('color', null,
'black');

        $hat = Hats::findFirstByRelatedColor($colorName);
        $this->response->appendContent($hat->name);
        $this->response->send();
    }
```

```php
    public function findByRelatedColorAction()
    {
        $colorName = $this->request->getQuery('color', null,
'black');

        $resultset = Hats::findByRelatedColor($colorName);
        foreach ($resultset as $record) {
            $this->response->appendContent($record->name);
            $this->response->appendContent('<br>');
        }
        $this->response->send();
    }


    public function lowLevelAction()
    {
        $colorName = $this->request->getQuery('color', null,
'black');

        $hat = new Hats();
        $color = new Colors();
        $hatColor = new HatsColors();

        $sql = <<<SQL
SELECT Hats.name as hats_name, Colors.name colors_name
FROM '{$hat->getSource()}' Hats
INNER JOIN '{$hatColor->getSource()}' HatsColors ON Hats.id =
HatsColors.hats_id
INNER JOIN '{$color->getSource()}' Colors ON Colors.id =
HatsColors.colors_id
WHERE Colors.name = :colorName
SQL;

        $dbh = $hat->getReadConnection()
->getInternalHandler();
        $stmt = $dbh->prepare($sql);
        $stmt->execute([
            'colorName' => $colorName
        ]);
        $results = $stmt->fetchAll(PDO::FETCH_ASSOC);

        foreach ($results as $row) {
            $this->response->appendContent($row['hats_name'] . ':
' . $row['colors_name']);
```

```
        $this->response->appendContent('<br>');
    }

        $this->response->send();
    }
}
```

8. Point the browser at `/sql/findByRelatedColor?color=black`. You should see the hats `sombrero` and `fedora` printed out.

9. Point the browser at `/sql/findFirstByRelatedColor?color=black`. You should see the hat `sombrero` printed out.

10. Point the browser at `/sql/lowLevel`. You should see the hats `sombrero` and `fedora` printed out without their colors.

How it works...

In this recipe, we demonstrate two approaches to dealing with raw SQL; the first method utilizes as much of the built-in Phalcon infrastructure as possible and actually returns Phalcon models wrapped in a standard `Phalcon\Mvc\Model\Resultset\Simple` object, and the second method goes straight to a low-level PDO as soon as possible and returns a PHP array of rows with the fields from two joined tables.

Before we look at the code, let's discuss the general approach taken in the two static methods that we declared in our `Hats` model.

In our `Hats` model, we have created two static methods that are based upon the naming conventions of the static find methods available in Phalcon models. For example, if we wanted to quickly find only the first `Hats` model that matched a name, then we could call `Hats::findFirstByName($color)`. This magic PHP method is provided by the `Phalcon\Mvc\Model` class for each property. So, in this convention, we have named our static model functions `findFirstByRelatedColor` and `findByRelatedColor`. Both of these methods return standard Phalcon framework objects that one would expect after performing a query.

If we wanted, we could implement all of the static `find...` methods, and by doing so we could create our own model querying implementation while still using `Phalcon\Mvc\Model` class as a central repository of business knowledge. In fact, as we will soon see, we are already doing a bit of this in our recipe by retrieving the database table name from the model instead of hardcoding it into our SQL. Additionally, we are also retrieving the database connection directly from the `Hats` model instead of assuming that it is the typical `db` service. This allows us to take advantage of the lesson provided in another recipe, by breaking our models out into more than one database. In short, we can avoid hardcoding service related configurations directly into our raw SQL code.

Now let's look at our `Hats` model code.

In the static method, `findFirstByRelatedColor`, we start out by instantiating three objects for each of the models that we will use in our SQL. Even though we will not be using these objects directly in our queries, we need to instantiate them to be able to retrieve metadata and specific service configuration data from them:

```
$hat = new Hats();
$color = new Colors();
$hatColor = new HatsColors();
```

Now we will look at the actual generated SQL. Notice that we are using the heredoc format with hard line returns after each major SQL section as this provides a clean, readable format:

```
    $sql = <<<SQL
SELECT Hats.* FROM '{$hat->getSource()}' Hats
INNER JOIN '{$hatColor->getSource()}' HatsColors ON Hats.id =
HatsColors.hats_id
INNER JOIN '{$color->getSource()}' Colors ON Colors.id = HatsColors.
colors_id
WHERE Colors.name = :colorName
LIMIT 1
SQL;
```

We are calling `getSource()` on each model object so that we can still take advantage of table aliases. Putting that aside, what is left is a typical third normalized SQL join that is beyond the scope of this recipe to discuss in great detail. We are joining `Hats` to `HatsColor` and then finally to `Color`. Notice that since we are creating the SQL, we will need to specify the join condition ourselves. Next we have a single `WHERE` condition to match the color to the placeholder `:colorName`.

Note: If we wanted, we could also use actual table field names from the models meta data cache.

PHQL uses the placeholder style with a colon before and after the name, while standard PDO only uses a single colon before the placeholder name.

Now we will look at how to access lower level database connections and how to use these connections to execute queries:

```
$connection = $hat->getReadConnection();
```

Here, `$connection` is not a direct PDO object as it is wrapped in a `Phalcon\Db\Adapter\` `Pdo` object. This will be deep enough for us to achieve a lower level approach while still allowing the Phalcon framework to help us out. In a later example, we will demonstrate the most low level approach.

Next we utilize the `fetchOne` method to return normal PHP array results for the model. Here we must use the `Phalcon\Db::FETCH_ASSOC` constant to inform PDO how we would like the results to be returned. We also use the third argument to pass in our bind values for the placeholder `:colorName`:

```
$row = $connection->fetchOne($sql, Phalcon\Db::FETCH_ASSOC, [
    'colorName' => $colorName
]);
```

We will then return `false` if a matching record could not be found to remain consistent with Phalcon conventions:

```
if (!$row) {
    return false;
}
```

At this point, we know that we have a valid record, so we will simply call `cloneResultMap` to create a new model with the appropriate flags set. In this case, we want to inform the model that it came from a persistent location, so even though we used raw SQL here to retrieve the record, we still can use the normal model saving methods to update the database:

```
return Phalcon\Mvc\Model::cloneResultMap(new Hats(), $row,
    Phalcon\Mvc\Model::DIRTY_STATE_PERSISTENT);
```

As we have finished that method, now let's take a look at `Hats::findByRelatedColor`. It uses the same setup as `findFirstByRelatedColor` and so we will just skip ahead to look at only the different part at the end.

We will get a `Phalcon\Db\Adapter\Pdo` `$connection` object the same, but this time, since we want to retrieve many records, we will make a call to the `query` method to retrieve a `Phalcon\Db\Result\Pdo` object:

```
$connection = $hat->getReadConnection();
$results = $connection->query($sql, [
    'colorName' => $colorName
]);
```

Now we will return the normal simple `resultset` object with our results. We will reuse our `$hat` model object for the metadata references since we don't need it for anything else:

```
return new Phalcon\Mvc\Model\Resultset\Simple(null, $hat, $results);
```

Now we are ready to look at `SqlController` to see how we invoked our `Hats` methods. In each of these three controller actions, we add a nice call to the request service query variable `color` so that we can test out the search with different values. For example, we can search for `red` by appending `?color=red` to each corresponding route URL. In our actions, we have set the color `black` as the default:

```
public function findByRelatedColorAction()
{
    $colorName = $this->request->getQuery('color', null, 'black');
```

So, simply, we can retrieve the first `Hat` that has the matching color with:

```
$hat = Hats::findFirstByRelatedColor($colorName);
```

And for all `Hats`, matching that color with:

```
$resultset = Hats::findByRelatedColor($colorName);
```

Finally, we will look at a very low level SQL approach in the `lowLevelAction` method. The initial set up starts the same as the other actions, but once we get to the SQL it diverges a lot.

Skipping straight to the SQL, we see here that the SQL will return two fields from different tables and so we cannot force this into a `Phalcon\Mvc\Model` object:

```
$sql = <<<SQL
SELECT Hats.name hats_name, Colors.name colors_name
FROM '{$hat->getSource()}' Hats
INNER JOIN '{$hatColor->getSource()}' HatsColors ON Hats.id =
HatsColors.hats_id
INNER JOIN '{$color->getSource()}' Colors ON Colors.id = HatsColors.
colors_id
WHERE Colors.name = :colorName
SQL;
```

This time we will go deeper by calling `getInternalHandler()` to return an actual PDO database handler:

```
$dbh = $hat->getReadConnection()
    ->getInternalHandler();
```

The following is all very standard PDO query code. Notice that we are passing in `PDO::FETCH_ASSOC` instead of `Phalcon\Db::FETCH_ASSOC`, since this direct PDO code is not related to Phalcon:

```
$stmt = $dbh->prepare($sql);
$stmt->execute([
```

```
        'colorName' => $colorName
]);
$results = $stmt->fetchAll(PDO::FETCH_ASSOC);
```

In this last example, we went all of the way to raw SQL and PDO access but we were still able to take advantage of Phalcon model definitions to construct the SQL in a way that relies less upon hardcoding directly in the SQL.

Getting the most out of your RDBMS of choice

The Phalcon ORM is quite powerful and it allows the same PHQL search language to be used across multiple databases, including MySQL, PostgreSQL, and SQLite. Underlying all of the built-in database adapters is support for common SQL functions that are in common between all of the supported systems, or at least can be easily mapped to each one.

However, sometimes it may be necessary to use a feature of a particular database system that is not supported by the built-in database adapters. In this recipe, we will be extending the MySQL adapter with a *dialect* that allows it to use the fulltext indexing capability of that system.

Getting ready

This recipe uses the `chapter_04` database that we set up in the chapter introduction and Phalcon Developer Tools, which we will use to set up a project skeleton.

This chapter uses Composer to install the Phalcon Incubator classes.

How to do it...

Follow these steps to complete this recipe:

1. We need to have an application skeleton for experimentation. If you already have such an application, you can skip this step. Create a project skeleton using the `simple` template:

   ```
   phalcon project extend_database simple
   ```

2. Now point the web browser at the root directory of the project. There should be a page with `Congratulations!` ..... If we see the `Volt directory can't be written` error message, then permissions of the directory `app/cache` need to be changed to allow the web server to write to it.

3. Ensure that your configuration file is set up with the correct host, database, username, and password. This recipe will use the `chapter_04` database that we established in the chapter introduction.

4. Install the Phalcon incubator with Composer from within the root directory of the recipe:

```
composer require phalcon/incubator
```

5. Configure the loader to use the library path for the class lookup in the file, `app/config/loader.php`, and to use the Composer autoloader file:

```
$loader->registerDirs(
    [
        // Other paths ...
        $config->application->libraryDir
    ]
) register();

require BASE_PATH . '/vendor/autoload.php';
```

6. Add the following line to your database configuration in `app/config/config.php`:

```
'dialectClass' => 'Phalcon\Db\Dialect\MysqlExtended'
```

7. Add the `dialectClass` setting to the db service:

```
if (isset($config->database->dialectClass)) {
    $params['dialectClass'] = $config->database->dialectClass;
}
```

8. Create the model, `app/models/Posts.php`:

```
<?php

class Posts extends Phalcon\Mvc\Model
{
}
```

9. Create the controller, `app/controllers/QueryController.php`:

```
<?php:

class QueryController extends Phalcon\Mvc\Controller
{
    public function indexAction()
    {
        $sql = "SELECT * FROM Posts WHERE FULLTEXT_MATCH_
BMODE(text, '+technology')";
        $query = new Phalcon\Mvc\Model\Query($sql, $this-
>getDI());
        $posts = $query->execute();
```

```
        foreach ($posts as $post) {
                $this->response->appendContent("{$post->id}: {$post-
>text}<br>");
        }
        $this->response->send();
    }
}
```

10. In the browser, go to the `/query` in the root path of the project. You should see **1: Technology is a very powerful force that seeks to change society for the better**.

How it works...

The built in Phalcon MySQL database adapter only supports a subset of the possible functions available on the database server and our class, `MysqlExtended`, adds some new functions for MySQL specific behavior. This approach allows us to know specifically when we are implementing vendor specific features that will not be available on other supported databases such as PostgreSQL.

The configuration of our database adapter is almost entirely the same as normal except that we are adding a single line to the configuration that specifies that we also use our dialect class to provide extra functionality. This is accomplished with the following line in our database configuration:

```
'dialectClass' => 'Phalcon\Db\Dialect\MysqlExtended'
```

Now let's look in our dialect class. The source for this can be found at:

```
https://github.com/phalcon/incubator/blob/master/Library/Phalcon/Db/
Dialect/MysqlExtended.php
```

Notice that this class only implements a single public method, `getSqlExpression`. The body of this method is made up of a switch statement that we'll get into shortly, but first, notice the very end of the function where, if there were no matches, we simply return the default behavior:

```
return parent::getSqlExpression($expression, $escapeChar);
```

Inside of the switch statement, we are implementing two new functions: `FULLTEXT_MATCH` and `FULLTEXT_MATCH_BMODE`. Notice that for each new defined function, we are constructing and returning a new expression from values in the `$expression` variable. How this works is that Phalcon is parsing the PHQL and is able to identify a function call and extract the arguments, and it is up to us to generate the actual SQL condition fragment that will be returned. So really, we could do anything here as long as we generate a SQL fragment that our chosen database can understand.

So, in the `FULLTEXT_MATCH` definition, we see that we are returning the SQL fragment:

```
return 'MATCH(' . join(', ', $arguments) . ') AGAINST (' .
$this->getSqlExpression($expression["arguments"][$length]) . ')';
```

So again, to review: Phalcon parses the PHQL and we can intercept particular function calls with our database dialect class to return new valid SQL condition fragments; otherwise, Phalcon will attempt to use the default behavior, if it is defined.

Moving on to our `QueryController`, we are executing a query with PHQL that uses our new defined function `FULLTEXT_MATCH_BMODE`.

First we'll look at the PHQL. Here we are calling one of our new functions:

```
$sql = "SELECT * FROM Posts WHERE FULLTEXT_MATCH_BMODE(text,
'+technology')";
```

Next we define the query and execute it. Notice that we pass in the DI as the second argument. This is a good example of the power and ease of using the Phalcon DI system, as all that is needed to fully hook the `Query` class up to all of the services is:

```
$query = new Phalcon\Mvc\Model\Query($sql, $this->getDI());
$posts = $query->execute();
```

Next we iterate on the $posts Phalcon\Mvc\Model\Resultset\Simple object to add each record to the output buffer, and then we send the response to the browser:

```
foreach ($posts as $post) {
    $this->response->appendContent("{$post->id}: {$post->text}<br>");
}
$this->response->send();
```

Using models as information repositories

In this recipe, we will explore how to use model events to tie additional data to our models outside of the normal database service layer. The approach in this recipe can be adapted to handling file uploads, sending e-mails, or any other activity that exceeds the typical *store everything in the database* technique.

Getting ready

This recipe uses its own database schema and the Phalcon Developer Tools, which we will use to set up a CLI project skeleton. This project will require command line usage.

This recipe requires the `gmp` PHP extension.

This recipe will use the `openssl_random_pseudo_bytes` function to create **UUIDs** (**Universally Unique Identifiers**), and so you will need to ensure that this is enabled in the PHP configuration. On Linux and OSX, this should already be enabled but on Windows, with environments like WAMP, it may require manually enabling it in the `php.ini` file and then restarting the web server.

How to do it...

Follow these steps to complete this recipe:

1. We need to have a CLI application skeleton for experimentation. If you already have such an application, you can skip this step. Create a project skeleton using the `cli` template to create a command line application:

```
phalcon project model_repository cli
```

2. Create the database, `model_repository` and import the following into it:

```
DROP TABLE IF EXISTS 'entries';
CREATE TABLE 'entries' (
    'id' int(11) NOT NULL AUTO_INCREMENT,
    'uuid' varchar(255) NOT NULL,
    PRIMARY KEY ('id')
) ENGINE=InnoDB DEFAULT CHARSET=latin1;
```

3. Add the `dataDir` setting to the `application` section of the `config` at app/config/config.php:

```
'application' => [
    // ...
    'dataDir'        => BASE_PATH . '/data'
    // ...
],
```

4. Create the directory, `data`, in the root path of the recipe.

5. Create the model, `app/models/Entries.php`:

```php
<?php

class Entries extends Phalcon\Mvc\Model
{
    public $id;
```

```php
    public $uuid;
    private $value;

    public function getValue()
    {
        return $this->value;
    }

    protected function retrieveValue()
    {
        $deepDirectory = $this->getDeepDirectory();
        if (!file_exists($deepDirectory)) {
            throw new \Exception('The deep directory does not
exist.');
        }

        return file_get_contents($deepDirectory . '/' . $this-
>uuid);
    }

    protected function getDeepDirectory()
    {
        $dataDir = $this->getDI()
            ->getConfig()
            ->application->dataDir;

        $deepDir = $dataDir;
        for ($i = 0; $i < 3; $i++) {
            $deepDir .= '/' . $this->uuid[$i];
        }
        return $deepDir;
    }

    protected function beforeValidationOnCreate()
    {
        $data = openssl_random_pseudo_bytes(16);
        $base16 = bin2hex($data);
        $base62 = gmp_strval(gmp_init($base16, 16), 62);
        $padded = str_pad($base62, 22, '0', STR_PAD_LEFT);
        $this->uuid = vsprintf('%s%s%s-%s%s%s%s%s-%s%s%s', str_
split($padded, 2));
    }
```

```php
    protected function afterCreate()
    {
        $deepDirectory = $this->getDeepDirectory();
        if (!file_exists($deepDirectory)) {
            mkdir($deepDirectory, 0770, true);
        }
        file_put_contents($deepDirectory . '/' . $this->uuid,
rand(1, 1000));
    }

    protected function afterDelete()
    {
        // See if you can do this one on your own.
        // Make sure to please not recursively delete your
        // entire file system, project or data folder!!!
    }

    protected function afterFetch()
    {
        $this->value = $this->retrieveValue();
    }

    protected function initialize()
    {
        $this->skipAttributes(['value']);
    }
}
```

6. Create the task, `app/tasks/EntryTask.php`:

```php
<?php

class EntryTask extends \Phalcon\Cli\Task
{
    public function addAction()
    {
        $entry = new Entries();
        if (!$entry->create()) {
            foreach ($entry->getMessages() as $message) {
                error_log($message);;
            }
            return false;
        }
```

```
            echo "Created entry with id: " . $entry->id;
        }

        public function getAction($argv)
        {
            if (!isset($argv[0]) || !is_numeric($argv[0])) {
                throw new \Exception('This action requires a integer
    argument.');
            }
            $id = $argv[0];

            $entry = Entries::findFirstById($id);
            if (!$entry) {
                fwrite(STDERR, 'An entry with that ID could not be
    found.');
                return false;
            }

            echo 'Retrieving stored value: ' . $entry->getValue();
        }
    }
```

7. Open up the command line terminal, change into the `project` directory, and enter in the following command:

    ./run

    You should see: `Congratulations! You are now flying with Phalcon CLI!`.

8. Now execute the following:

    ./run entry add

    You should see `Created entry with ID: SOME_ID`.

9. Use the value that was returned in the place of `SOME_ID` for the next line:

    Now enter the execute:

    ./run entry get SOME_ID

    You should see `Retrieving stored value: SOME_VALUE`, where `SOME_VALUE` is an integer value that was stored and retrieved.

How it works...

In this recipe, we'll skip past the basic configuration since this recipe is more advanced, and we'll start with our `Entries` model, where most of the interesting things happen.

The model has three properties and we have declared `$value` as private because it is not being stored in the database, and we are using the `getter` function, `getValue`, to retrieve it. This helps us to clarify that this property cannot be changed through the normal mechanism and that it is dependent upon other factors. Take a look at the following code:

```
public $id;
public $uuid;
private $value;
public function getValue()
{
    return $this->value;
}
```

Next we'll look at the model event methods, `beforeValidationOnCreate`, `afterCreate`, and `afterFetch`. These events are triggered during the execution cycle of model actions.

In this method, we are creating a UUID value automatically when a model is created. Since PHP doesn't provide nice UUID creation functions, we need to create one ourselves. It is necessary that this is done in `beforeValidationOnCreate` instead of `beforeCreate` since otherwise, Phalcon will complain that a field has a null value. So, we create the UUID value as soon as possible and then we could even check that the value is valid during the validation phase:

```
protected function beforeValidationOnCreate()
{
    $data = openssl_random_pseudo_bytes(16);
    $base16 = bin2hex($data);
    $base62 = gmp_strval(gmp_init($base16, 16), 62);
    $padded = str_pad($base62, 22, '0', STR_PAD_LEFT);
    $this->uuid = vsprintf('%s%s%s-%s%s%s%s%s-%s%s%s', str_
split($padded, 2));
}
```

Next we will perform an action after the model has been successfully added to the database. Notice the getDeepDirectory method we use to return a file storage directory that is unique to this record instance. We will investigate this method soon. Finally, we create a random integer between 1 and 1,000 that we then store in a directory with the UUID as the filename, as shown in the following code snippet:

```
protected function afterCreate()
{
    $deepDirectory = $this->getDeepDirectory();
    if (!file_exists($deepDirectory)) {
        mkdir($deepDirectory, 0770, true);
    }
    file_put_contents($deepDirectory . '/' . $this->uuid, rand(1,
1000));
}
```

Now we are able to store information outside of the database by using model events (sometimes known as **hooks**). In this recipe, we aren't doing anything particularly meaningful since we are simply storing a random integer, but this data could do more important things such as the md5 hash of the contents of a file, or we could use the hook to send an e-mail or to log a message.

Finally, in the afterFetch method, we retrieve the random value that is stored within the filesystem. This model event is fired automatically after any normal Phalcon model query. What is really nice here is that this can also be used when using raw SQL, as covered in a previous recipe! So with that said, it becomes obvious that using the infrastructure of Phalcon models to organize all of your data is the way to go:

```
protected function afterFetch()
{
    $this->value = $this->retrieveValue();
}
```

Finally, in our initialize method, we inform the model that our value property is not part of the normal persistent storage and so it should be ignored:

```
protected function initialize()
{
    $this->skipAttributes(['value']);
}
```

Now let's look at the interesting getDeepDirectory method where we create a nested directory based off of the first characters of the UUID. This is done to prevent a large performance issue that occurs when thousands of files are stored in a single directory since it takes a while to look through the index of a single directory for all of them. Using this approach, dramatically more files can be stored, while keeping the filesystem performant.

First we start off by accessing the `data` directory from the configuration service. It is recommended that any custom directory paths be added to the `config` service instead of hardcoded into the application:

```
$dataDir = $this->getDI()
    ->getConfig()
    ->application->dataDir;
```

Next we create the nested directory path. So, say that our UUID started with `1zA...`, then this directory fragment would become `1/z/A`. So the number of files stored in a single directory grows logarithmically instead of linearly. Take a look at the code used to create the deep directory relative path:

```
$deepDir = $dataDir;
for ($i = 0; $i < 3; $i++) {
    $deepDir .= '/' . $this->uuid[$i];
}
return $deepDir;
}
```

Now let's look at our `Entry` task in `app/tasks/Entry.php`:

This is actually pretty simple. If we are creating an `Entry` model and then we try to save it, if it fails, we output the error messages, and if it succeeds then we output the primary key of the entry so that we can use it in the `getAction` method. Take a look at the following code:

```
public function addAction()
{
    $entry = new Entries();
    if (!$entry->create()) {
        foreach ($entry->getMessages() as $message) {
            error_log($message);;
        }
        return false;
    }
    echo "Created entry with ID: " . $entry->id;
}
```

Let's look at `getAction`.

First we do a few checks to make sure that we have valid arguments. This is a nice addition to make the program a bit more professional:

```
if (!isset($argv[0]) || !is_numeric($argv[0])) {
    throw new \Exception('This action requires a integer
argument.');
}
$id = $argv[0];
```

Now we look up the entry with that ID and if it doesn't exist we will display a nice error message. Notice that this is not exceptional behavior and so we are simply outputting an standard error instead of throwing an exception:

```
$entry = Entries::findFirstById($id);
if (!$entry) {
    fwrite(STDERR, 'An entry with that ID could not be found.');
    return false;
}
```

Finally, we get the value for that entry that was stored in the deep directory. We now have an information repository that transcends the database:

```
echo 'Retrieving stored value: ' . $entry->getValue();
```

Extra Activities: See if you can create an algorithm to delete directories using the afterDelete model event. As we have left it currently, the files will not be removed when the corresponding Entry model is deleted. Be careful, though, not to recursively delete your entire project, root filesystem, or all of the other files. You may apply this approach to creating your own powerful file uploading strategy upon the Phalcon framework.

Storing models across multiple databases

In this recipe, we will introduce a technique for seamlessly merging multiple databases together for use in our models. This has uses such as creating one database for user credentials and many other databases for application data. It can also be useful when working with legacy systems.

Getting ready

This recipe is a bit different in that it defines and uses three separate databases. We will also use the Phalcon Developer Tools to set up a project skeleton.

How to do it...

Follow these steps to complete this recipe:

1. We need to have an application skeleton for experimentation. If you already have such an application, you can skip this step. Create a project skeleton using the `simple` template:

   ```
   phalcon project multiple_databases simple
   ```

2. Create the database, `multiple_database`:

   ```
   DROP TABLE IF EXISTS 'clients';
   CREATE TABLE 'clients' (
     'id' int(11) NOT NULL AUTO_INCREMENT,
     'name' varchar(50) NOT NULL,
     PRIMARY KEY ('id')
   ) ENGINE=InnoDB AUTO_INCREMENT=3 DEFAULT CHARSET=latin1;
   INSERT INTO 'clients' VALUES (1,'Bob'),(2,'Larry');
   ```

3. Create the database, `multiple_database_clients-1`:

   ```
   DROP TABLE IF EXISTS 'products';
   CREATE TABLE 'products' (
     'id' int(11) NOT NULL AUTO_INCREMENT,
     'name' varchar(50) NOT NULL,
     PRIMARY KEY ('id')
   ) ENGINE=InnoDB AUTO_INCREMENT=4 DEFAULT CHARSET=latin1;
   INSERT INTO 'products' VALUES (1,'soap'),(2,'candles'),(3,'cups');
   ```

4. Create the database, `multiple_database_clients-2`:

   ```
   DROP TABLE IF EXISTS 'products';
   CREATE TABLE 'products' (
     'id' int(11) NOT NULL AUTO_INCREMENT,
     'name' varchar(50) NOT NULL,
     PRIMARY KEY ('id')
   ) ENGINE=InnoDB AUTO_INCREMENT=4 DEFAULT CHARSET=latin1;
   INSERT INTO 'products' VALUES (1,'radio'),(2,'phone'),(3,'television');
   ```

5. Change the configuration for the db service to connect to the `multiple_database` database. Then add a new top level array to the `config` file for the client database service by adding the following:

```
'databaseClient' => [
    'adapter'     => 'Mysql',
    'host'        => 'localhost',
    'username'    => 'root',
    'password'    => 'root',
    'charset'     => 'utf8',
],
```

Note: We did not specify a database entry here as we normally would. We will establish this later, in the service definition for this connection. Add this 'dbClient' service to your services configuration file at `app/config/services.php`:

```
$di->setShared('dbClient', function () {
    $config = $this->getConfig();

    $client = Clients::getSelected();

    $class = 'Phalcon\Db\Adapter\Pdo\\' . $config->databaseClient->adapter;
    $params = [
        'host'      => $config->databaseClient->host,
        'username'  => $config->databaseClient->username,
        'password'  => $config->databaseClient->password,
        'dbname'    => 'multiple_database_clients-' . $client->id,
        'charset'   => $config->databaseClient->charset
    ];

    if ($config->databaseClient->adapter == 'Postgresql') {
        unset($params['charset']);
    }

    $connection = new $class($params);

    return $connection;
});
```

6. Create the model, `app/models/Clients.php`:

```php
<?php

class Clients extends Phalcon\Mvc\Model
{
    private static $selected;

    public static function getSelected()
    {
        if (!isset(self::$selected)) {
            throw new Exception('A client has not yet been
selected.');
        }
        return self::$selected;
    }

    public function select()
    {
        if (isset(self::$selected)) {
            throw new Exception('The client may only be selected
once.');
        }
        self::$selected = $this;
    }

    public function initialize()
    {
        $this->setConnectionService('db');
    }
}
```

7. Create the model, `app/models/Products.php`:

```php
<?php

class Products extends Phalcon\Mvc\Model
{
    public $id;

    public $name;
```

```
        public function initialize()
        {
            $this->setConnectionService('dbClient');
        }
    }
```

8. Create the controller, app/controllers/ClientsController.php:

```php
<?php

class ClientsController extends Phalcon\Mvc\Controller
{
    public function indexAction()
    {
        $clientName = $this->request->getQuery('name', null,
'Bob');

        $client = Clients::findFirstByName($clientName);
        if (!$client) {
            return '<p>The client could not be found.</p>';
        }
        $client->select();

        $products = Products::find();

        $this->response->appendContent('<h3>Products</h3><ul>');
        foreach ($products as $product) {
            $this->response->appendContent('<li>' . $product->name
. '</li>');
        }
        $this->response->appendContent('</ul>');

        $this->response->send();
    }
}
```

9. In the browser, go to the following paths:

- ❏ /clients to see a list of products for the client Bob
- ❏ /clients?name=Larry to see products for the client Larry

How it works...

We created three databases for use in this project. The `multiple_databases` database can be considered the core database for the project and the other two are each tied to a specific client record. Let's look at the `dbClient` database service definition:

```
$di->setShared('dbClient', function () {
```

Here we see that we have named the database service a non-standard name, `dbClient`. Later we will need to let our `Products` model know that it needs to use a different database service than the default `db` service.

Skipping ahead a few lines, we see that we are calling a static method on the `Clients` model to get a *selected* client. This `getSelected` static function is something that we added to our `Clients` model and we'll look at it a bit later. For now, all we need to know is that there is a specific client record that we are using. Take a look at the following code:

```
$client = Clients::getSelected();
```

Next we are using the `multiple-database_clients-` prefix for client databases and then applying the primary key from the client record to the database name so that each client will have their own database for storing records. It's possible that these databases could even reside on different servers and this would not need to be hardcoded into the model:

```
$dbConfig['dbname'] = 'multiple-database_clients-' . $client->id;
```

Now we'll look at the `Clients` model.

First notice that we have defined a `private static` property, `$selected`, as well as a static `getter` to retrieve the property. Take a look at the following code:

```php
<?php
class Clients extends Phalcon\Mvc\Model
{
    private static $selected;

    public static function getSelected()
    {
        if (!isset(self::$selected)) {
            throw new Exception('A client has not yet been
selected.');
        }
        return self::$selected;
    }
```

Next we implement a normal `public` function to be called on a specific record that saves itself to the private static property. We will call this later, in the controller, once we have found a specific client record:

```
public function select()
{
    if (isset(self::$selected)) {
        throw new Exception('The client may only be selected once.');
    }
    self::$selected = $this;
}
```

Finally, in the initialize event, we are specifying that this model should use the default db connection service. In this case, we are doing this only to illustrate how a connection service can be manually set and, since it is the same as the default, it doesn't change anything. Take a look at the following code:

```
public function initialize()
{
    $this->setConnectionService('db');
}
```

Next we will look at `Products` model. The only interesting thing happening here is that we are specifying the connection service to be the non-standard `dbClient`. This is the key part that allows our `Products` models to seamlessly reside in another database and possibly on another server. In fact, this connection could be to an entirely different type of database server such as Postgres, MongoDB, or SQLite. Take a look at the following code:

```
public function initialize()
{
    $this->setConnectionService('dbClient');
}
```

Now we'll look at the `ClientsController` code to demonstrate how to tie all of this functionality together:

```
public function indexAction()
{
    $clientName = $this->request->getQuery('name', null, 'Bob');
```

Here we are taking a client name from the query variables and filling in the default `Bob` if none is provided. This allows us to put `?name=Larry` in the URL to specify a different search.

Next we do a very typical search for a single record using the magic method, `findFirstBy...`, that is provided for us by `Phalcon\Mvc\Model`. We then handle a search with no results in a clean way by returning a string that will be included in the `content()` portion of our view layout. Notice that a query miss here is not exceptional behavior and we handle it normally. Take a look at the following code snippet:

```
$client = Clients::findFirstByName($clientName);
if (!$client) {
    return '<p>The client could not be found.</p>';
}
```

Here is the good part, where we select the client record that is then later used to specify which database we will use in the `dbClient` connection service:

```
$client->select();
```

Finally, we search for all products and then we do the routine output formatting and iterating upon the `Products`. Take a look at the following code snippet:

```
$products = Products::find();

$this->response->appendContent('<h3>Products</h3><ul>');
foreach ($products as $product) {
    $this->response->appendContent('<li>' . $product->name . '</li>');
}
$this->response->appendContent('</ul>');

$this->response->send();
}
```

So, we are now able to deal with `Products` models seamlessly, now that they reside in a different database.

5

Presenting Your Application

In this chapter, we will cover the following topics:

- HTML fragments for AJAX-based applications
- Splitting your layout structure
- Volt and dynamic view implementations
- Presenting models nicely
- Reusing view snippets
- Creating your own Volt keywords and methods

Introduction

In any framework that follows the MVC paradigm, we need to work with the `View` component (`\Phalcon\Mvc\View`). Developing a project with a framework means that the views should enjoy the same consideration as the rest of the application layers. It is therefore important to choose a friendly template engine, which can be integrated with the system as a whole, as well as with external dependencies such as JavaScript and CSS, for your project. This template engine must be:

- Easy to use for both developers and layout designers
- Flexible enough to allow the accomplishment of complex tasks, such as AJAX requests, displaying static or dynamic data, or interaction with external libraries
- Efficient in both speed of execution as well as memory consumption

Phalcon offers this kind of template engine; it is called the **Volt Template Engine**. It is easy to use and currently the fastest template engine in the PHP framework world. Volt is written for PHP with C and inspired by the **Jinja** template engine, which was created by *Armin Ronacher*. The Volt syntax is similar to the syntax of many other template engines. Volt's features are primarily integrated with the Phalcon framework. This template engine integrates seamlessly with the framework's components. However, it follows a loosely coupled design, so it can be used as an independent component for your application.

The Volt Template Engine offers developers all the tools functionality with views that are available in all solid template engines. In particular, these are blocks, layouts (including inheritance), partials, the possibility to include the content of one view into another by means of includes, control structures, the passing of parameters to a view, arithmetic operations, macros, creating custom functions, working with objects and any other data types, caching, and much more. Since Volt is also tightly integrated with the Phalcon framework, services registered in the Dependency Injection Container are immediately available, easing the development time.

In this chapter, we will consider some strong points of Volt, but there are, of course, not the whole number of facilities of this brilliant template engine. After you read this chapter, refer to the detailed documentation, which you can find by following the links at the end of the recipes.

HTML fragments for AJAX-based applications

With the rise in popularity of the Internet, sites are becoming more and more interesting and complex. Simply showing the site content or redirecting users to other, required pages are already antiquated methods. The modern user is an experienced consumer. To keep users on your site, you need to keep them interested by providing friendly interfaces. In particular, one of the best technologies we can use is dynamic, new content loading by certain user actions instead of reloading the whole page. By this, we mean AJAX. In this recipe, we will look into how to use the HTML snippets together with the Volt Template Engine in an application which uses AJAX requests.

We will take a look at a small application that works with customers and orders. We will implement a page where you can select a customer and see the last 10 orders of that customer.

Getting ready

For successful implementation of this recipe you need to have an application with Volt Template Engine service configured. In our example, we will use a template application generated by means of the Phalcon Developer Tools, but you can use any other application that you see fit.

Additionally, we need a database where we will create several tables. In this recipe, we will use MySQL as the **RDBMS** (**Relational Database Management System**), with the user as root and without a password. You can adjust this recipe to fit your needs and use a different DBMS, as well as a different user and/or password.

To demonstrate the feasibility of control structures, we will generate our entire application using the **scaffold** command in Phalcon Developer Tools. We will create models, a controller, and base views. If you already have these components created, you can skip this step and adjust the rest of the recipe to your needs.

How to do it...

Follow these steps to complete this recipe:

1. First of all, we need to have an application to experiment with. If you already have such an application, you can skip this step. Create a simple application:

```
phalcon project store simple
```

2. Create a database if you do not have one:

```
echo 'create database volt_test charset=utf8mb4
collate=utf8mb4_unicode_ci;' | mysql -u root
```

3. We will need several tables in the database. If you already have these tables for your experiments you can skip this step, as well as the code generation steps:

```
CREATE TABLE `customers` (
    `id` INT(11) UNSIGNED NOT NULL AUTO_INCREMENT,
    `name` VARCHAR(64) NULL DEFAULT '',
    `email` VARCHAR(255) NOT NULL,
    `address` VARCHAR(255) NULL DEFAULT '',
    `city` VARCHAR(128) NULL DEFAULT '',
    `country` VARCHAR(128) NULL DEFAULT '',
    `postalcode` MEDIUMINT UNSIGNED DEFAULT 0,
    PRIMARY KEY  (`id`),
    UNIQUE KEY `customers_email` (`email`),
    KEY `customers_phone` (`city`)
) ENGINE=InnoDB  DEFAULT CHARSET=utf8;

INSERT INTO `customers` VALUES
(1, 'Wartian Herkku', 'wartian@herkku.com','Torikatu 38',
'Oulu', 'Finland', 90110),
(2, 'Wellington Importadora', 'i@wellington.com','Rua do
Mercado, 12', 'Resende', 'Brazil', 8737363),
(3, 'White Clover Markets', 'white@clover.com','305 - 14th
Ave. S. Suite 3B', 'Seattle', 'USA', 98128),
(4, 'Wilman Kala', 'kala@wilman.com','Keskuskatu 45',
```

```
'Helsinki', 'Finland', 21240),
(5, 'Wolski', 'wolski@gmail.com','ul. Filtrowa 68',
'Walla', 'Poland', 1012);

CREATE TABLE `orders` (
    `id` INT(11) UNSIGNED NOT NULL AUTO_INCREMENT,
    `customer_id` INT(11) UNSIGNED NOT NULL NULL,
    `status` ENUM('open', 'closed') NOT NULL DEFAULT
'open',
    `created_at` TIMESTAMP NOT NULL DEFAULT
CURRENT_TIMESTAMP,
    `sum` DECIMAL(10,2) NOT NULL DEFAULT '0.0',
    PRIMARY KEY (`id`),
    KEY `orders_customer_id` (`customer_id`),
    KEY `orders_created_at` (`created_at`),
    CONSTRAINT `orders_ibfk_1` FOREIGN KEY (`customer_id`)
REFERENCES `customers` (`id`)
) ENGINE=InnoDB DEFAULT CHARSET=utf8;

INSERT INTO `orders` VALUES
(1, 1, 'open','2016-01-11 00:00:01', 157.3),
(2, 1, 'closed','2016-11-01 00:00:01', 57.3),
(3, 1, 'open','2016-02-12 00:00:01', 100),
(4, 1, 'closed','2016-12-02 00:00:01', 5.3),
(5, 1, 'open','2016-03-03 00:00:01', 70.4),
(6, 2, 'closed','2016-04-04 00:00:01', 11.0),
(7, 2, 'closed','2016-02-04 00:00:01', 12.0),
(8, 2, 'open','2016-03-05 00:00:01', 200.0),
(9, 2, 'closed','2016-04-02 00:00:01', 33.22),
(10, 2, 'open','2016-07-07 00:00:01', 44.42),
(11, 3, 'closed','2016-03-08 00:00:01', 145.90),
(12, 3, 'closed','2016-02-09 00:00:01', 11.93),
(13, 3, 'closed','2016-09-01 00:00:01', 22.0),
(14, 3, 'closed','2016-01-01 00:00:01', 234.0),
(15, 3, 'closed','2016-05-05 00:00:01', 345.0),
(16, 3, 'open','2016-08-03 00:00:01', 193.72),
(17, 5, 'closed','2016-07-06 00:00:01', 66.77),
(18, 5, 'closed','2016-10-10 00:00:01', 77.66),
(19, 5, 'closed','2016-10-01 00:00:01', 222.33),
(20, 5, 'open','2016-10-10 00:00:01', 90.0);
```

4. Then, go to the newly created directory and generate a model, a controller, and a view for the Customers table:

```
phalcon scaffold customers --template-engine=volt
```

5. We will need an `order` model, too. Let us create it:

```
phalcon model orders
```

6. At this step, we ensure that all is functioning as it should be. To do this, go to `http://{your-host-here}/customers`.

7. So, after the initial setup is completed, let us create a `listAction` action in the `CustomersController` controller with the following content:

```
public function listAction()
{
    $customers = Customers::find(['columns' =>'id, name']);

    $this->view->setVars(
        [
            'customers'    => $customers,
            'getOrdersUrl' => $this->url-
>get('customers/orders')
        ]
    );
}
```

8. Now we need a view for this action. Create a view with the following content:

```
<div class="page-header">
    <h1>Customers' Orders</h1>
</div>

{{ content() }}

<div class="container">
    <div class="col-md-3">
        <div class="form-group">
            <label for="customers">Select Customer</label>
            {{ select(
                'customer',
                customers,
                'using': ['id', 'name'],
                'useEmpty': true,
                'emptyText': 'Please select',
                'id': 'customers'
            ) }}
        </div>
    </div>

    <div class="col-md-9">
        <div id="orders">
```

```
                     
                </div>
            </div>
        </div>

        <script
         type="application/javascript"
         src="https://code.jquery.com/jquery-2.1.4.min.js">
        </script>

        <script type="application/javascript">
            $("#customers").change(function() {
                var value = $(this).val();
                if ($.isNumeric( value )) {
                    var getOrdersUrl = "{{ getOrdersUrl }}";

                    $.ajax({
                        type: "POST",
                        url: getOrdersUrl,
                        data: {"id": value},
                        success: function(response){
                            $("#orders").html( response );
                        }
                    });
                }
            });
        </script>
```

9. Additionally, we will need an action to handle AJAX requests:

```
public function ordersAction()
{
  if ($this->request->isPost() &&
    $this->request->isAjax()
  ) {
  $customer_id = $this->request->getPost('id', 'int');
    $customer    = Customers::findFirst(
      [
      'conditions' =>'id = :company_id:',
      'bind'       => [ 'company_id' => $customer_id]
      ]
    );

    $this->view->disable();
    $this->view->setVar('customer', $customer);
```

```
    $this->view->partial('partials/customers/orders');
  }
}
```

10. Now, create a partial, located at `partials/customers/orders.volt`, with the following content:

```
<div class="list-group">
    {% for order in customer.Orders %}
        <a href="#" class="list-group-item active">
            <h4 class="list-group-item-heading">
                Order # {{ order.id }}
            </h4>
        </a>
        <a href="#" class="list-group-item">
            <h4 class="list-group-item-heading">
                Content:
            </h4>
            <p class="list-group-item-text">
                Status: {{ order.status }}  <br>
                Date: {{ order.created_at }}  <br>
                Sum: {{ order.sum }} $  <br>
            </p>
        </a>
    {% else %}
        <a href="#" class="list-group-item active">
            <h4 class="list-group-item-heading">
                No orders
            </h4>
        </a>
    {% endfor %}
</div>
```

11. Go to `http://{your-host-here}/customers/list` to ensure that everything is alright. Select different customers, and those who have no orders among them.

How it works...

We have created an experimental application for using HTML snippets together with the Volt Template Engine in an application which uses AJAX requests, and then we created the required tables, models, a controller, and a view in the database. After that we have seen the output of a simple customer list in a drop-down list.

By selecting any element from the list, **jQuery** sends a simple AJAX request to the server at the address that we defined in advance, in `listAction`.

In the controller, the `ordersAction` receives all requests and checks if the request type is suitable for its handling. If this is an AJAX **POST** request, then the action creates a customer instance with the formed search criteria (in this case by, `id`). In this action, we have disabled the page rendering and rendered only the required partial, passing necessary parameters to it. The `Response` object has returned the result of this rendering. In this partial, using Volt Control Structures, we have created the presentable view for displaying the list of orders and the status of the latter.

Of course, we have omitted some things as validation, the handling of errors on the side of jQuery, and message output. Also, we have not created any more entities as `Product`, `OrderItem` or complicated the `Customers` model with additional logic. This was done on purpose. We have removed the additional logic to ensure that the focus remains on the key point, which is how it works. In a real situation, user communication with the database by means of HTML snippets will be much more complicated.

There's more...

For more detailed information on Volt Template Engine refer to:

`https://docs.phalconphp.com/en/latest/reference/volt.html`

See also

▶ The *Presenting models nicely* recipe, in this chapter

Splitting your layout structure

When creating a complex application, you constantly face questions such as: *how to design the application view structure?*, and *how to create layouts and where to place them?*. More often than not, you end up with large parts of templates that are just copied from file to file with minimal changes. In accordance with **DRY methodology**, we will try to define our views in such a manner that they use the hierarchical template system. Thereby reducing the number of places where the view code can be repeated. In this recipe, we will show you how to create templates that inherit from other templates, and then we will see what you will gain from that.

Getting ready

For successful implementation of this recipe, you need to have an application with a configured Volt Template Engine service. In our example, we will use a template application generated by means of the Phalcon Developer Tools, however, you can use any other application that you have set.

How to do it...

Follow these steps to complete this recipe:

1. So, first we need a certain base template which all other templates will inherit from. Create a template located at `views/templates/base.volt`, which contains the following:

    ```
    <!DOCTYPE html>
    <html>
    <head>
        {% block head %}{% endblock %}
        <title>
            {% block title %}{% endblock %} - My Webpage
        </title>
    </head>
    <body>
        <div id="content">
            {% block content %}{% endblock %}
        </div>
        {% block footer %}{% endblock %}
    </body>
    </html>
    ```

2. Now let us create an authorization page template. We could use this template for user registration or authentication, as well as in cases where a user has forgotten his or her password and wants to recover it. Obviously, this template will have a lot of repeating code as the template in the previous step. We need to change it slightly to use all the functional blocks we defined earlier. Create a template located at `views/session.volt` with the following content:

    ```
    {% extends "templates/base.volt" %}
    {% block title %}Sign In{% endblock %}
    {% block head %}
    <link rel="stylesheet" href="auth.css">
    {% endblock %}
    {% block content %}
    {{ content() }}
    {% endblock %}
    ```

3. In order for our `SessionController` to use this exact template, we need to instruct the controller to use it:

    ```
    use Phalcon\Mvc\Controller;

    class SessionController extends extends Controller
    {
    ```

```
        public function onConstruct()
        {
            $this->view->setMainView('session');
        }
    }
```

4. So far, we have assumed that we will not need a footer block in our authorization page template. However, let's create one more template that needs such a block, along with what we have already implemented. Let us suppose that it will be a template for a typical site page. We will call it `views/main.volt` and fill it with the following content:

    ```
    {% extends "session.volt" %}
    {% block head %}
    <link rel="stylesheet" href="auth.css">
    {% endblock %}
    {% block footer %}
    <div id="footer">
    &copy; Copyright 2015, All rights reserved.
    </div>
    {% endblock %}
    ```

5. Let us tell `IndexController` exactly what template it must use:

    ```
    use Phalcon\Mvc\Controller;

    class IndexController extends extends Controller
    {
        public function onConstruct()
        {
            $this->view->setMainView('main');
        }
    }
    ```

How it works...

We have demonstrated the hierarchical inheritance of templates. The child templates can display contents in blocks or even override parent blocks displaying information needed for the particular action. This powerful feature allows us to create very complex, yet flexible views, while not repeating code. If in the future a site-wide change is required, we only need to change it in the parent template and all pages will reflect the change.

This implementation on the application templates is such that every portion of the views defines only the part it is supposed to, without interfering with or directly interacting with other parts. Therefore, every parent template in the vertical hierarchy is abstract in relation to its children and can only process the conceptual blocks you instruct it to.

Note that not all blocks from the parent templates must be replaced in the child ones. You can define or redefine only those which you really need at any particular point of time.

With this approach, you can create a wide hierarchy of templates, splitting each into smaller, more manageable units, and then connect them dynamically in your controllers.

Volt and dynamic view implementations

Integrating the Volt Template Engine in your application allows you to create a very fluid and dynamic application. This can be achieved by using inheritance in your templates, partials, and blocks. In this recipe, we will look at a typical example of using blocks in order to get better responsiveness for the end user, while at the same time accelerating development. This can be achieved by splitting some parts of the main template into blocks, which can be enabled or disabled at will, without the need to replicate them.

Getting ready...

For successful implementation of this recipe, you need to have any application with the configured Volt Template Engine service. In our example, we will use a template application generated by means of Phalcon Developer Tools, however, you can use any other application that you have set.

How to do it...

Follow these steps to complete this recipe:

1. First, we need a ready-to-use application for our recipe. If you already have such an application, you may skip this step. Create a simple application:

   ```
   phalcon project store simple
   ```

2. Now, open the main view template of your application located at `app/views/index.volt` and write the content block as follows:

   ```
   <div class="container">
       {% block menu %}
       {% endblock %}
       {% block content %}
           {{ content() }}
       {% endblock %}
   </div>
   ```

3. Open `IndexController` and change its content:

```php
<?php

class IndexController extends ControllerBase
{
    public function indexAction()
    {
        $this->view->setVar('user', null);
    }
}
```

4. Next, we need to replace the `IndexContoller` view, generated by default, with the following code:

```
{% block menu %}
    {% include 'partials/menu' with ['user' : user] %}
{% endblock %}

{% block content %}
    {% include 'partials/content' with ['user' : user] %}
{% endblock %}
```

5. After we have defined the two partials above, we need to create the template files. Create the partial `partials/menu.volt` with the following content:

```
{% if user is defined %}
  <nav class="navbar navbar-default">
    <div class="container-fluid">
      <div class="navbar-header">
        <a href="#" class="navbar-brand">
            Project name
        </a>
      </div>
      <ul class="nav navbar-nav">
        <li class="active"><a href="#">Home</a></li>
        <li><a href="#">About</a></li>
        <li><a href="#">Contact</a></li>
      </ul>
      <ul class="nav navbar-nav navbar-right">
        <li><a href="#">Logout</a></li>
      </ul>
    </div>
  </nav>
{% endif %}
```

6. Then, create the partial `partials/content.volt` with the following content:

```
{% if user is not defined %}
  <div class="col-md-4 col-md-offset-4">
    <form class="form-signin">
      <h2 class="form-signin-heading">Please sign in</h2>
      <input type="email" class="form-control"><br>
      <input type="password" class="form-control">
      <div class="checkbox">
        <label>
            <input type="checkbox" value="remember-me">
            Remember me
        </label>
      </div>
        <button type="submit" class="btn btn-lg btn-primary
btn-block">Sign in</button>
    </form>
  </div>
{% else %}
  <div class="page-header">
    <h1>Welcome!</h1>
    <p>Hello {{ user.name }}</p>
    <p>We are happy to see you again</p>
  </div>
{% endif %}
```

7. At this step, we can check if it works as expected. Go to `http://{your-host-here}/`. You will see an empty page with an invitation to log in.

8. Now, change `IndexController indexAction`. Add a user to it:

```php
<?php

class IndexController extends ControllerBase
{
    public function indexAction()
    {
        $user = (object) ['name' =>'John Doe'];
        $this->view->setVar('user', $user);
    }
}
```

9. Then go to `http://{your-host-here}/` again. You will see an entirely different page. There must be a navigation menu and a greeting for a user.

How it works...

The Volt Template Engine offers an opportunity to use functional blocks anywhere you need them. With the use of blocks, you can achieve dynamic displaying of content at any point of time in your application.

We have created a template-based application and passed some of the display logic on our views. We managed to show the navigation menu and some conditional content (in this case, the greeting phrase) only to authorized users, while unauthorized ones see the login screen.

Additionally, `Volt` offers the include function, which allows you to include a template within a template. `Include` templates improve performance when they are included inline, since they are precompiled. `include` templates can also have variables passed into them using the `with` keyword. We have used this approach for demonstration purposes.

In this recipe, we have intentionally not covered certain scenarios, such as authenticating a user, creating a user mode, checking credentials against the database, and so on. The purpose was to demonstrate how easy it is to use blocks and define content dynamically.

Presenting models nicely

The Volt Template Engine allows you to display data with control structures. Views of any complexity can be created to manage the way your models are presented. In this recipe, we will demonstrate how to achieve beautiful presentations of your models using Volt control structures.

Getting ready

For successful implementation of this recipe, you need to have any application with the configured Volt Template Engine service. In our example, we will use a template application generated by means of the Phalcon Developer Tools, however, you can use any other application that you have set.

Additionally, we need a database where we will create several tables. In this recipe, we will use MySQL as the RDBMS with a root user and without a password. However, you can use any other RDBMS or username/password combination you like.

To demonstrate the flexibility of control structures, we will generate our application entirely by using the `scaffold` command in Phalcon Developer Tools. We will create models, a controller, and base views. If you already have these components created, you can skip this step, adjusting the rest of the recipe to your needs.

Note that we will skip the stages of configuring your server, virtual hosting, and other adjustments as they are not directly relevant to the current recipe. If you are going to use Phalcon Developer Tools to test the application, you should do it separately.

How to do it...

Follow these steps to complete this recipe:

1. First, we need a working application for our recipe. If you already have such an application, then skip this step. Create a simple application:

   ```
   phalcon project store simple
   ```

2. Create a database if you do not have one:

   ```
   echo 'create database volt_test charset=utf8mb4
   collate=utf8mb4_unicode_ci;' | mysql -u root
   ```

3. We will need to have several pages in this database. If you have them already you may skip this step, as well as the code generation steps:

   ```
   CREATE TABLE `robots` (
   `id` int(10) unsigned NOT NULL AUTO_INCREMENT,
   `name` varchar(70) COLLATE utf8_unicode_ci NOT NULL,
   `type` varchar(32) COLLATE utf8_unicode_ci NOT NULL default
   'mechanical',
   `year` int(11) NOT NULL default 1900,
   `datetime` datetime NOT NULL,
   `text` text NOT NULL,
   PRIMARY KEY (`id`)
   ) ENGINE=InnoDB DEFAULT CHARSET=utf8
   COLLATE=utf8_unicode_ci;

   INSERT INTO `robots` VALUES
   (1,'Robotina','mechanical',1972,'1972/01/01
   00:00:00','text'),
   (2,'Astro Boy','mechanical',1952,'1952/01/01
   00:00:00','text'),
   (3,'Terminator','cyborg',2029,'2029/01/01
   00:00:00','text');

   CREATE TABLE `parts` (
   `id` int(10) unsigned NOT NULL AUTO_INCREMENT,
   `name` varchar(70) COLLATE utf8_unicode_ci NOT NULL,
   PRIMARY KEY (`id`)
   ) ENGINE=InnoDB DEFAULT CHARSET=utf8
   COLLATE=utf8_unicode_ci;
   ```

```
INSERT INTO `parts` VALUES (1,'Head'),(2,'Body'),(3,'Arms'),(4,'Le
gs'),(5,'CPU');

CREATE TABLE `robots_parts` (
`id` int(10) unsigned NOT NULL AUTO_INCREMENT,
`robots_id` int(10) unsigned NOT NULL,
`parts_id` int(10) unsigned NOT NULL,
PRIMARY KEY (`id`),
KEY `robots_id` (`robots_id`),
KEY `parts_id` (`parts_id`),
CONSTRAINT `robots_parts_ibfk_1` FOREIGN KEY (`robots_id`)
REFERENCES `robots` (`id`),
CONSTRAINT `robots_parts_ibfk_2` FOREIGN KEY (`parts_id`)
REFERENCES `parts` (`id`)
) ENGINE=InnoDB DEFAULT CHARSET=utf8 COLLATE=utf8_unicode_ci;

INSERT INTO `robots_parts` VALUES (1,1,1),(2,1,2),(3,1,3);
```

4. Now, go to your newly-created directory and generate a model, a controller, and a view for the `Robots` table:

   ```
   phalcon scaffold robots --template-engine=volt
   ```

5. We will need some more models, so let us create them:

   ```
   phalcon model robots_parts
   phalcon model parts
   ```

6. At this step, we can go to `http://{your-host-here}/robots` to check that everything works properly.

7. Now, let us see which control structures are provided by Volt and how we can use them. Create a `listAction` action in the `RobotsController` controller with the following content:

   ```php
   public function listAction()
   {
       $robots = Robots::find();

       $this->view->setVars(
           [
               'robots' => $robots
           ]
       );
   }
   ```

8. Next, create a view for this action at `views/robots/list.volt`:

```
<div class="page-header">
<h1>
List robots
</h1>
<p>
{{ link_to("robots/new", "Create robots") }}
</p>
</div>

{{ content() }}
<div class="container">
<div class="col-md-6">
<ul class="list-group">
{% for robot in robots %}
<li class="list-group-item">
{{ robot.name|e }}
</li>
{% endfor %}
</ul>
</div>
</div>
```

9. Go to `http://{your-host-here}/robots/list` to ensure that we are successfully displaying the names of the robots in the list.

10. Now let us make our task more complex to demonstrate embedded loops. We will display robot parts now, so change the container code in your view as follows and refresh the page with the robot list:

```
<div class="container">
<div class="col-md-6">
<ul class="list-group">
{% for robot in robots %}
<li class="list-group-item">
{% for robot_part in robot.RobotsParts %}
<span class="badge">
{{ robot_part.Parts.name|e }}
</span>
{% endfor %}
{{ robot.name|e }}
</li>
{% endfor %}
</ul>
</div>
</div>
```

11. Go to `http://{your-host-here}/robots/list` to ensure that we have successfully displayed the names of the robots together with the parts in the list.

12. Now let's add some logic in our view, so that a message is displayed if there are no robot parts in our shop:

```
<div class="container">
<div class="col-md-6">
<ul class="list-group">
{% for robot in robots %}
<a href="#" class="list-group-item active">
<h4 class="list-group-item-heading">
{{ robot.name|e }}
</h4>
</a>

<a href="#" class="list-group-item">
<h4 class="list-group-item-heading">
Parts
</h4>
{% for robot_part in robot.RobotsParts %}
<p class="list-group-item-text">
{{ robot_part.Parts.name|e }}
</p>
{% else %}
<p class="list-group-item-text">
There are no parts to show
</p>
{% endfor %}
</a>
{% endfor %}
</ul>
</div>
</div>
```

13. Go to `http://{your-host-here}/robots/list` to ensure that we successfully displayed the alternative content for those robots for which we do not have spare parts.

14. Now, let's assume that all `cyborgs` must be highlighted. Additionally, we want to label the models of new robots. Change the `RobotsController listAction` and pass a time variable into the view:

```
public function listAction()
{
    $robots = Robots::find();
```

```
    $this->view->setVars(
        [
            'robots'    => $robots,
            'date_time' => strtotime(date('Y-m-d H:i:s'))
        ]
    );
}
```

15. Change the view slightly to highlight any cyborg parts:

```
<div class="container">
<div class="col-md-6">
<ul class="list-group">
{% for robot in robots %}
<a href="#" class="list-group-item active">
<h4 class="list-group-item-heading">
{{ robot.name|e }}
</h4>
{% if  date('Y', date_time) < robot.year %}
<span class="label label-danger">New</span>
{% else %}
<span class="label label-default">Classic</span>
{% endif %}
</a>

<a href="#" class="list-group-item">
<h4 class="list-group-item-heading">
Parts
</h4>
{% for robot_part in robot.RobotsParts %}
<p class="list-group-item-text">
{{ robot_part.Parts.name|e }}
</p>
{% else %}
<p class="list-group-item-text">
There are no parts to show
</p>
{% endfor %}

{% if robot.type is not 'cyborg' %}
{% continue %}
{% endif %}
<p class="list-group-item-text alert alert-warning">
Warning! This is Cyborg
</p>
```

```
</a>
{% endfor %}
</ul>
</div>
</div>
```

16. Let's improve the presentation by using a table to display the robots:

```
<div class="container">

{% for robot in robots %}
    {% if loop.first %}
        <table class="table table-striped">
        <tr>
            <th>#</th>
            <th>Id</th>
            <th>Name</th>
            <th>Type</th>
            <th>Parts</th>
        </tr>
    {% endif %}

    {% if robot.type is 'cyborg' %}
        <tr class="danger">
    {% else %}
        <tr>
    {% endif %}

    <td>{{ loop.index }}</td>
    <td>{{ robot.id }}</td>
    <td>

    <h5>
        {% if  date('Y', date_time) < robot.year %}
            New
        {% else %}
            Classic
        {% endif %}
        {{ robot.name }}
    </h5>

    </td>
    <td>
        {{ robot.type }}
    </td>
```

```
<td>
    {% for robot_part in robot.RobotsParts %}
        <span class="label label-default">
        {{ robot_part.Parts.name|e }}
    </span> 
    {% else %}
        There are no parts to show
    {% endfor %}
</td>

</tr>
{% if loop.last %}
    </table>
{% endif %}

{% endfor %}

</div>
```

17. Go to `http://{your-host-here}/robots/list` to see the new list of robots.

How it works...

The Volt Template Engine provides you with flexible tools for managing lists. With the help of control structures, you can display your data in any view, even if the data passed in the view is an object, array, or array of objects.

We have created a test application to work with Volt Control Structures and then we created the required tables in the database, models, a controller, and view.

Next, we have created the output of a simple list with the names of the robots, showing you how easy it is to work with the `for` loop. Next, we worked with embedded loops. Volt has no difficulty controlling embedded structures of any complexity. Note that to access other models, you can take advantage of model relationships. To get access to other models through relations, you can use **aliases**. We have used a code generation tool without any additional changes. Because of that, our aliases have such names as `RobotsParts`, `Parts`, and so on, which can be different to the coding style you are using in your application. Naturally, you can rename these aliases, making your code more readable and abiding by the coding standard of your choice.

Volt's loops include `for` as well as `else` (or its synonym `elsefor`), offering flexibility in displaying content for when there might be records, or not.

Operators such as `break` and `continue` can also be used for loop termination or control of iterations. The `if` operator (just like in PHP) along with `else/elseif`, checks for variable comparisons.

For the `for` iterations, Volt offers a special variable `loop`, which can be used to further control the iteration. `loop` provides information about the iteration number/counter, the first element, the last element, and more. We have used this functionality at the last step of our recipe to display the robots in a tabular form.

There's more...

For the detailed Volt Template Engine documentation, visit:

```
https://docs.phalconphp.com/en/latest/reference/volt.html
```

See also

> ▸ Creating the application structure by using code generation tools recipe from *Chapter 2, Structuring Your Projects*

Reusing view snippets

Partials are another approach to splitting the rendering process into better-controlled, smaller parts. By using partials, you will be able to place code for the rendering of certain view parts into separate files. Partials allow you to follow the DRY methodology in your view layer. With Phalcon 3.0.0 and later, partials can be situated outside the main project structure, making their use extremely valuable. For example, you can use the same partials for a number of sites located on one server.

Getting ready

For successful implementation of this recipe, you need to have any application with the configured Volt Template Engine service. In our example, we will use a template application generated by means of the Phalcon Developer Tools, however, you can use any other application that you have set.

How to do it...

Follow these steps to complete this recipe:

1. Open any controller and create the `listAction` method in it if you do not have one. In our example, we will use the `Users` controller, but you can use any other available controller you wish:

```
class UsersController extends \Phalcon\Mvc\Controller
{
    public function listAction()
    {
```

```
        }
    }
```

2. Then, create the `list` view for this action:

    ```
    {{ content() }}

    <table class="table">
        <thead>
            <tr>
                <th>Id</th>
                <th>Email</th>
                <th>First Name</th>
                <th>Last Name</th>
                <th>Registered</th>
            </tr>
        </thead>
        <tbody>
        </tbody>
    </table>
    ```

3. Create the `partials` directory in the main `views` directory, and then create the partial `user_table_row.volt` with the following content in it:

    ```
    <tr>

    <td>{{ user.id }}</td>
    <td>{{ user.email }}</td>
    <td>{{ user.first_name }}</td>
    <td>{{ user.last_name }}</td>
    <td>{{ user.created_at }}</td>

    </tr>
    ```

4. Next, in the main view, add a row generator for the user table:

    ```
    <tbody>
        {% for user in users %}
            {{ partial('partials/user_table_row', user) }}
        {% endfor %}
    </tbody>
    ```

5. Finally, you need to pass the array of objects to your view. To demonstrate the potential of using partials, we have used some user-generated data. You can use any other way of returning an array of objects for this part:

    ```
    public function listAction()
    {
    ```

```php
$users = [
    [
        'id'         => 1,
        'email'      =>'john@doe.com',
        'first_name' =>'John',
        'last_name'  =>'Doe',
        'created_at' => date(
            "Y-m-d H:i:s",
            mt_rand(1262055681, time())
        )
    ],
    [
        'id'         => 2,
        'email'      =>'james@doe.com',
        'first_name' =>'James',
        'last_name'  =>'Doe',
        'created_at' => date(
            "Y-m-d H:i:s",
            mt_rand(1262055681, time())
        )
    ],
    // ...
];

$this->view->setVar(
    'users',
    json_decode(json_encode($users))
);
}
```

6. Now, open the page (in our case, this is `/users/list`) and look at the result.

How it works...

Using partials is similar to using subprograms. Once you define the partial, it can be used by other parts of your application or other applications.

We have created the example of a user list using a view and a partial. Our partial is not very complex and it may seem that you can make shift with simple HTML with insertions in iteration. But as a matter of fact, that is not so. As we already mentioned, you can use this partial in different applications and views of an application. If you need to change the presentation of a certain user in the table, you only need to do it in one place rather than remember where you have used the same presentation code. Furthermore, depending on the situation, a certain template fragment can be quite complex, so when you move that code to a separate partial, you can make the code more flexible and readable.

This is not the only usage of partials. Partials can be used as logical blocks for the view layer, such as header, footer, sidebar, and so on. Implementing partials in such a way allows you to use them in your templates wherever the need arises.

Finally, it should be mentioned that the partial() method gets the array of variables which will be accessible only within the limits of that partial as the second parameter. If you do not need to pass data into partial, you can leave out the second parameter.

Creating your own Volt keywords and methods

The Volt Template Engine is quite flexible and can be extended by adding user functions, as well as keywords to the existing ones. In the first part of this recipe, we will add a user extension which will let you use practically any PHP function in Volt, and then we will register a new function, adding a new feature to Volt Template Engine.

Getting ready

For successful implementation of this recipe, you need to have an application with the configured Volt Template Engine service. In our example, we will use a template application generated by means of the Phalcon Developer Tools, however, you can use any other application that you have set.

How to do it...

Follow these steps to complete this recipe:

1. Create the PhpExtension extension and add the following code in it:

```php
<?php

class PhpExtension
{
    public function compileFunction($name, $args = null)
    {
        if (function_exists($name)) {
            if (func_num_args() > 1) {
                $args = array_slice(func_get_args(), 1);
                return $name . '(' . $args[0] . ')';
            } else {
                return $name . '()';
            }
        }
    }
}
```

2. Then, you need to register your extension in the list of available Volt Template Engine extensions using the *bootstrap* file, like so:

```php
<?php

use Phalcon\Di\FactoryDefault;
use Phalcon\Mvc\View;
use Phalcon\Mvc\View\Engine\Volt as VoltEngine;

$di = new FactoryDefault();

/**
 * Setting up the view component
 */
$di->setShared('view', function () {
    $view = new View();

    $view->setViewsDir('../views/');

    $view->registerEngines([
        '.volt' => function ($view, $di) {
            $volt = new VoltEngine($view, $di);

            $options = [
                'compiledPath' =>'../cache/view/',
                'compiledSeparator' =>'_'
            ];

            $volt->setOptions($options);
            $volt->getCompiler()->addExtension(
                new PhpExtension()
            );

            return $volt;
        }
    ]);

    return $view;
});
```

3. Let us check on how it works. For example, at the time of writing, there is no built-in `str_ireplace` function in Volt. Add the following code in your view and check the result in your browser:

```
{{ str_ireplace("three letter word", "duty of everyone",
"The income tax is a THREE letter Word.") }}
```

4. Now we will try to create the `censor` function, which we will use to censor comments in our example site. Change the previous example by adding the `censor` function to the Volt compiler:

```
$volt->getCompiler()->addFunction('censor', function
($arguments) {
    @list($string, $badWords, ) = eval('return [' .
$arguments . '];');

    if (empty($badWords)) {
        return "'{$string}'";
    }

    foreach ((array) $badWords as $key => $badWord) {
        $badWords[$key] = str_replace(
            '\*', '\S*?',
            preg_quote((string) $badWord)
        );
    }

    $regex = '/(' . join('|', $badWords) . ')/ui';

    $result = preg_replace_callback($regex,
function($matches) {
        return str_repeat('*', mb_strlen($matches[1]));
    }, $string);

    if (is_string($result)) {
        return "'{$result}'";
    }

    return "'{$string}'";
});
```

5. Add the following code in your view and check the result in your browser:

```
{{ censor("What the frick, man!", ['frick']) }}
```

How it works...

In actual fact, Volt Template Engine has advantages over other template engines of the PHP world. Firstly, it is the fastest one, because it is written in C. Secondly, as opposed to other template engines, Volt is not required to execute the compiled templates. After a template is compiled, it is not dependent on Volt. In other words, Volt is used only as a compiler for PHP templates. Some other PHP frameworks are adding support and integration with Volt Template Engine just now.

We have used two examples to demonstrate the extensibility of Volt. In the first example, we have created the `PhpExtension` extension, which utilizes the `compileFunction` method. This method runs before every attempt at a function call compilation in any template. The purpose of this extension is to check if the function to be executed in the template is a PHP one. If yes, then it is called from the template. Events in your extensions must return valid PHP code, which will be used as a compilation result instead of one generated in Volt. If the event does not return the string representing the actual PHP code, then the compilation will need to use default functions in the template engine.

Then, we have created a new function, named `censor`, which censors words. The function gets a string (for example, a user comment from your database) as the first parameter, and expects an array of words, which we would like to *bleep*, as the second. If the array parameters have not been passed or are empty, we return the original string. It is definitely not the most elegant implementation, because it uses @ and `eval`; however, it clearly demonstrates how we can extend Volt. Try the example out, experiment with it; log what gets passed in the anonymous function. This example needs work before it can be used in a live application; however, it does illustrate the power of Volt and its extensibility perfectly.

There's more...

For the detailed Volt Template Engine documentation, visit:

```
https://docs.phalconphp.com/en/latest/reference/volt.html
```

6

Making Use of
Advanced Features

In this chapter, we will cover:

- ▸ Registering dependencies in an effective way
- ▸ Using the DI container on different scopes
- ▸ Unleashing the real power of event driven programming
- ▸ Centralizing validations for rock solid business rules
- ▸ Complex routing with regular expressions
- ▸ Using in-memory session handlers
- ▸ Handy persistence for controllers and components
- ▸ Transactional controller actions ensuring consistent operations
- ▸ Auditing complex user actions with simplicity

Introduction

One of the strong points in every framework is its coupling between its components. A tightly coupled framework does not allow the developer to replace framework components in an easy and clear way without any impacts on the working project. Phalcon offers the `Phalcon\Di` component, which implements patterns such as **Dependency Injection** and **Service Locator**, and is itself a container for dependencies. In this chapter, we will discover how to use the `Phalcon\Di` component, and how to deal with dependencies in various places of your code.

One of the most powerful programming techniques is **event driven programming**. By using such an approach, executing the application or its separate parts is defined by events, for example, users clicking on the link, registration, and expiration of a session. Events allow you to solve many tasks, by dividing the application logic into listeners that serve different events. This development approach provides the developer with the power to manipulate listeners as it seems fit for the particular task, or delete them if necessary, while safely keeping the main application running. In this chapter, we will discuss the main principles of working with Phalcon events.

It is hard to imagine a web application which receives data from the outside world, without having data validation processes in place. The data received could be user input, such as in a registration form, user data entry in relevant screens, or even malicious attacks. After users enter data in the relevant form fields and submit the data, it has to be validated. In the case of the user registration form, this includes the uniqueness of the username, the password complexity or length, validity of the e-mail, and so on. In this chapter, we will check data validation techniques for your Phalcon application.

Phalcon's `Phalcon\Mvc\Router` component offers advanced routing capabilities for your application. Using the MVC architecture in your application, you can define even the most complicated routes and route requests to the relevant controllers. Features of `Phalcon\Mvc\Router` can meet the requirements of any type of routing in your application. In this chapter, we will discuss the main principles of routing using regular expressions.

Performance is always a key concern when building a web application, especially in heavy traffic sites. It is common practice to use cache services for storing session data, logs, or even application data. In this chapter, we will look at Session Adapters, storing data in Redis and/or Memcached.

The value of every framework lies in the fact that it offers solutions to various tasks. No framework can offer solutions for all possible tasks because it is not efficient. Such frameworks will become very complex and slow in terms of performance.

Phalcon offers a wealth of tools that can offer solutions to a wide variety of problems. However, it is advisable to extend the existing tools to incorporate new functionality and logic that better suits your project. In this chapter, we will discuss one of the available options for optimizing performance in your application by extending Phalcon's internal classes. Specifically, we will demonstrate this by creating `Behaviors`.

Registering dependencies in an effective way

One of the strengths of Phalcon is the loose coupling of its components. This is achieved primarily by the `Phalcon\Di` component, from which you can retrieve stored objects in it, in any part of your application. You can even create Phalcon objects and use them in any project. For instance, there have been numerous discussions in WordPress meetups, as well as Laravel conferences, on how to use the Volt Template Engine with WordPress or Laravel.

`Phalcon\Di` works as a central container, storing objects in it and making them available throughout your application. As mentioned earlier, those objects are loosely coupled so that you can use whatever you need at any point of your application. The only dependency in your application is the **DI** container.

In this recipe, we will investigate ways that we can use to get around the tight coupling of objects in your project. We will look at how easy it is to register components (or services) in the DI container and how to retrieve those services from it.

Getting ready

To successfully implement this recipe, you need to have a Phalcon application and the Volt engine configured. In our example, we will use a sample application generated by **Phalcon Developer Tools**. However, you can use any other application that is available to you.

You will also need to have a web server installed and configured for handling requests to your application. Your application must be capable of receiving requests and you should have the necessary controllers and views, as well as a `bootstrap` file with a connection to a database. The database should have at least one table.

How to do it...

Follow these steps to complete this recipe:

1. In our test application, we will create some services and register them in the DI container. We will create a listener for database queries. We will call this new component `DbListener`. Its purpose will be to offer real-time debugging information by logging every database query that our application executes. Create the `DbListener` class:

    ```
    use Phalcon\Logger\AdapterInterface;
    use Phalcon\Logger;
    ```

```
class DbListener
{
  protected $logger;

  public function __construct(AdapterInterface $logger)
  {
    $this->logger = $logger;
  }

  public function afterQuery($event, $connection)
  {
    $this->logger->debug($connection->getSQLStatement());
  }
}
```

2. Next, let us define relevant dependencies. First, we need to tell the Di container about our `DbListener`. In other words, we need to introduce it. Open your `bootstrap` file and add the following code there:

```
$di->set('dbListener', [
    'className' => 'DbListener',
    'arguments' => [
        ['type' => 'service', 'name' => 'logger']
    ]
]);
```

3. We now need to register the logger class in the DI container, which will log anything we need in the relevant `log` file:

```
$di->set('logger', function($file = 'main', $format = null) use
($config) {
  $config = $config->get('logs')->toArray();
  $date   = $config['dateFormat'];
  $format = $format ?: $config['format'];

  $logger = new Phalcon\Logger\Adapter\File($config['logsDir'] .
$file . '.log');
  $formatter = new Phalcon\Logger\Formatter\Line($format, $date);
  $logger->setFormatter($formatter);

  return $logger;
});
```

4. We will need to change the connection parameters for the database so that our class is registered with the database service and can act as a listener:

```
$eventsManager = new Phalcon\Events\Manager();

$di->setShared('db', function () use ($config, $eventsManager,
$di) {
    $dbListener = $di->get('dbListener');
    $eventsManager->attach('db', $dbListener);

    $dbConfig = $config->database->toArray();
    $adapter = $dbConfig['adapter'];
    unset($dbConfig['adapter']);

    $class = 'Phalcon\Db\Adapter\Pdo\\' . $adapter;

    $connection = new $class($dbConfig);
    $connection->setEventsManager($eventsManager);

    return $connection;
});
```

5. We also need to change the configuration file to ensure that the parameters needed for our services exist and are valid. Add the following configuration in your `config` file:

```
'logs' => [
    'dateFormat' => 'D j H:i:s',
    'format' => '%date%: [%type%] %message%',
    'logsDir' => APP_PATH . '/app/logs/',
]
```

6. Create the `app/logs` directory if you do not have one.

7. Now it's time to test what we have just done. Launch your application in your browser and open any page. The `app/logs` directory will be empty; since we had no database interactions there are no logs.

8. Add code into an action of your choosing that will interact with your database. For instance, try to get a record from a model. As an example we will use the `Users` model, as follows:

```
Users::findFirst();
```

9. Refresh your page again and have a look into the `app/logs` directory. You will find debugging information about our SQL queries there.

How it works...

Dependencies can be defined in the DI container in various ways. Each registration method has its advantages and disadvantages, and the choice of which one to use relies only on the developer and his/her particular requirements.

We have demonstrated two ways of registering dependencies. The first one is the registration of `DbListener` as an array. This is a very flexible and easy way of registering a dependency. We have set the dependency name, and specified as its body what class we will use. Note that our `DbListener` expects to get a `logger` instance through its `__constructor`. This registration method is called **Constructor Injection**. With it, we pass dependencies/arguments to the class constructor. We are actually instructing the DI container to pass a `logger` object when creating the `DbListener` class. We will also need to register the `logger` class in the DI container for our `DbListener` to work. Whether we register the `logger` before or after the `DbListener` makes no difference.

We have also registered our `logger` class in the DI container using an anonymous function for lazy loading. This method of registering components in the DI container is a bit more complex. We initialize the `logger` with the necessary parameters (such as the configuration in our preceding example). When this component is created, it will use the default parameters that we have defined in the anonymous function. It is important to understand that when registering a service using the anonymous function method, the actual service is not created immediately. It is only instantiated when we first call it or retrieve it from the DI container.

Next is the Events Manager. We have altered the normal behavior of the database component by connecting the `db` event (generated every time there is a database interaction) to our listener class. We registered the listener class in the DI container with the name `dbLogger` so as not to have collisions with other registered components.

Note that from version 2.1 onward it is not necessary to pass the DI container instance into the anonymous function. In other words, you can register the database connection as follows:

```
$di->setShared('db', function () use ($config, $eventsManager) {
    // Here $this is a link to $di
    $dbListener = $this->get('dbListener');
    // The rest of code...
});
```

Again, both services are not initialized until we retrieve them from the DI container. You can easily check this by looking at the `app/log` folder before and after the database query. In this recipe, we showed two methods of registering services in the DI container and lazy loading.

There are many ways of registering dependencies in Phalcon, as stated before. The choice depends on the application needs and the developer.

There's more...

Detailed DI container documentation can be found at: `https://docs.phalconphp.com/en/latest/reference/di.html`

See also

▶ *Creating the application structure by using code generation tools* recipe from Chapter 2, *Structuring Your Projects*

Using the DI container on different scopes

In this recipe, we will discover how to get services from the DI container in any part of your application. We will also demonstrate also that even if you do not use Phalcon components, you can still use the DI container because it is already loaded in memory.

Getting ready

To successfully implement this recipe, you need to have a Phalcon application and the Volt engine configured. In our example, we will use a sample application generated by Phalcon Developer Tools. However, you can use any other application that is available to you.

You will also need to have a web server installed and configured for handling requests to your application. Your application must be capable of receiving requests and you should have the necessary controllers and views, as well as a `bootstrap` file with a connection to a database. The database should have at least one table.

How to do it...

Follow these steps to complete this recipe:

1. We will first need an application to test this recipe. If you already have an application set up, you can skip this step. You can use Phalcon Developer Tools to create one, as follows:

   ```
   phalcon project store simple
   ```

2. Then create a `library` subdirectory in the `app` directory, and create a test class `Service` in the former. The full path to the file will be: `app/library/Service.php`. Insert the following code into the file:

   ```
   class Service
   {
       public function run($var)
   ```

```
        {
                return debug_backtrace();
        }
}
```

3. You need to register the `library` directory in the autoloader so your application can find the new file. Change the file `app/config/loader.php` and add the `library` directory into the autoloader configuration:

```
$loader = new \Phalcon\Loader();

$loader->registerDirs(
        [
                $config->application->controllersDir,
                $config->application->modelsDir,
                __DIR__ . '/../library/'
        ]
)->register();
```

4. Then add the newly created class in the container:

```
$di->set('myService', function () {
        return new Service();
});
```

5. Now let us try to get our service from the DI container. Open `IndexContoller` and change its contents as follows:

```
class IndexController extends ControllerBase
{
        public function indexAction()
        {
                $this->view->setVar('service_from_controller', $this->myService->run(__CLASS__));
        }
}
```

6. Finally, open the view `app/views/index/index.volt` and add the following code:

```
{{ dump(this.myService.run("some string")) }}
{{ dump(service_from_controller) }}
```

7. Open the application's main page in your browser to see the results.

How it works...

One of the most frequently used Phalcon interfaces is `Phalcon\Di\InjectionAwareInterface`. Any class that implements this interface allows you to set it and get it as a service in the DI container.

One of the first classes that implements the `Phalcon\Di\InjectionAware` interface in order of importance is `Phalcon\Di\Injectable`. The `Injectable` class is abstract in nature and implements the magic method `__get`, which can help you get the needed dependency from the DI container at any time. With this architecture, you can access any service that is registered in the DI container in any part of your application. Here is the list of standard Phalcon classes which extend the `Injectable` class:

- `Phalcon\Mvc\Micro`
- `Phalcon\Mvc\Controller`
- `Phalcon\Mvc\View\Simple`
- `Phalcon\Mvc\View\Engine`
- `Phalcon\Mvc\View`
- `Phalcon\Mvc\Application`
- `Phalcon\Cli\Task`
- `Phalcon\Validation`
- `Phalcon\Forms\Form`

What this really means for you, the developer, is that in any area of your application, if you have access to one of the preceding classes, then you also have the `getDi()`, `setDi()`, as well as the magic `__get()` functions. If you call a field of a service in a class that extends the `Phalcon\Di\Injectable`, you are in fact invoking the `__get()` magic method. Behind the scenes, Phalcon will get the current container instance and then search by name the service you requested. There is no performance overhead by using the magic `__get()` method, since once the service is retrieved, it is cached.

 Note that, by using the `__get` method, you actually use shared services. This means that they always will act as **Singletons**.

There's more...

For detailed Phalcon DI documentation, refer to: `https://docs.phalconphp.com/en/latest/reference/di.html`

See also

▶   *The Using code generation tools* recipe

Unleashing the real power of event driven programming

Phalcon offers you a powerful and flexible tool for working with events, the **Events Manager**. The main purpose of this component is to provide an easy interface by which the developer can catch events generated by the application or even events generated outside the application. The Events Manager can not only catch events, but also generate them, potentially notifying a listener that *something has happened*.

In this recipe, we will try to implement listeners of an event such as *user registration*. When a user registers in our application, we will generate an event and subscribed listeners will respond accordingly.

Getting ready

If you have a test application which meets all the requirements, you may skip the recipe steps related to deploying the application and go ahead with the events implementation.

For successful implementation of this example you need a working application for your tests. It must be a fully configured and working application that has a database, models, controllers, and views. Setting up such an application is outside the scope of this recipe. Instead we will use an existing application, called **Vökuró**. You can get the link to the GitHub repository at the end of this recipe.

In addition, you will need to have access to a MySQL RDBMS instance, as well as be able to create a database for your application. Your testing application could work with other RDBMSes, but that setup is also not in the scope of this recipe. You will also need to have Composer installed so that you can update the necessary dependencies.

Finally, you need to have a web server set up so that it can handle the requests of our application.

How to do it...

Follow these steps to complete this recipe:

1. Clone the `phalcon/vokuro` project into a place suitable for you:

    ```
    git clone git@github.com:phalcon/vokuro.git vokuro-events
    ```

2. Go to the newly created `vokuro-events` folder and install the dependencies needed for your project with `Composer`:

   ```
   composer install
   ```

3. Create a database for your application:

   ```
   echo 'CREATE DATABASE vokuro' | mysql -u root
   ```

4. Populate the database with test data:

   ```
   cat schemas/vokuro.sql | mysql -u root vokuro
   ```

5. You will need to configure your web server to serve the requests for your application. Since this is not in the scope of this recipe, we will skip to the next step.

6. Open your application in a browser to ensure that everything works as expected. From this point forward we will start working with events.

7. First, we need to create a listener of the *user registration* event. Create a `Notification` subfolder in the `app/library` folder, and in it create a `Mail` class containing the following:

   ```php
   namespace Vokuro\Notification;

   use Phalcon\Events\Event;
   use Phalcon\Di\Injectable;

   class Mail
   {
     public function afterSaveOnRegister(Event $event, Injectable
   $source, array $data)
     {
       // Change this email to your real email address
       $adminAddress = "admin@mysite.com";
       $subject      = "A new member joined!";
       $template     = "Name: %s, Email: %s, Date: %s\nMessage
   generated from: %s\nEvent: %s";
       $user         = $data['user'];
       $date         = $data['date'];

       mail(
         $adminAddress,
         $subject,
         sprintf(
           $template,
           $user->name,
           $user->email,
   ```

```
            $date,
            get_class($source),
            $event->getType()
        )
    );

    return true;
    }
}
```

> Please note that if your PHP installations are not configured to send mail using the mail PHP function, then most likely the preceding code will not work. The scope of this recipe is not to set your PHP installation up so that it can send mail. If you are unsure on how to do it, you can replace the `mail` function with some other functionality such as logging with `error_log`:

```
error_log(sprintf(
    $template,
    $user->name,
    $user->email,
    $date,
    get_class($source),
    $event->getType()
));
```

8. Next, change your `bootstrap` file by adding the Events Manager in the DI container:

```
$em = Phalcon\Events\Manager();
$em->enablePriorities(true);
$di->setShared('eventsManager', $em);
```

9. Attach the first listener for all events of type `user` in the Events Manager:

```
$em->attach('user', new Vokuro\Notification\Mail(), 10);
```

10. Attach a second listener using an anonymous function, like so:

```
$em->attach('user', function ($event, $component, $data) use ($di)
{
    if ($event->getType() == 'afterSaveOnRegister') {
        $logger = $di->get('logger', ['new_users.log']);
        $user   = $data['user'];
```

```
        $logger->info("Joined new member: {$user->name} ({$user-
>email})");
    }
}, 20);
```

11. Open the `SessionController`, find `signupAction`, and add the following code after saving the user:

    ```
    $eventManager = $this->getDI()->getShared('eventsManager');
    $eventManager->fire('user:afterSaveOnRegister', $this, ['user' =>
    $user, 'date' => date('Y-m-d H:i:s')]);
    ```

12. Open your application in the browser one more time and register a new user by clicking on the **Create an Account button**.

13. Open your `log` file `app/logs/new_users.log` to ensure the entry of the new account is really there. Additionally, if you have PHP configured to send mail using the `mail` function, check your e-mail and search for the new mail.

How it works...

The first thing to do after deploying the application is to create the `Vokuro\Notification\Mail` listener class and the `afterSaveOnRegister` method in it. There are some important points to be made:

▸ Listeners themselves can be created as separate classes or as anonymous functions. The implementation of which method to choose relies on the developer, as well as the task requirements.

▸ If you have created a listener as a separate class, then its methods will act as events for its subscribers. In other words, if the `someEvent` event runs in the system, then your listener that must respond to this event must have the `someEvent` public method in it.

Following that, we make our application events aware by registering the Events Manager and storing it in the DI container. Internally, Phalcon will work with the Events Manager to check whether events need to be fired before, during, or after a particular action. If the event is present then it will be fired.

Finally, we need to consider event priorities and how they will affect our application. You can specify those priorities when calling each event. To enable this functionality, you will need to pass `true` in the `enablePriorities` method, so that the Events Manager can handle each event in the priority that it is meant to be handled.

The next step is the registration of listeners. We have intentionally registered the listeners with two different methods, to demonstrate the difference between the two methods. In general, you should be aware of the following:

► The first argument of the listener registration must be the event we subscribe to. This event can be specific, for example, `user:afterSaveOnRegister`—in this case, a listener will be aware only about this event. Or general—a user—in this case, a listener – will be aware of all events.

► The second argument must be either a listener instance—an object, or an anonymous function.

► The third argument must be the priority, which defines the order that the Events Manager notifies the subscribed listeners. This is an optional parameter.

After registering the listeners, we need to modify the `SessionController`—`signupAction` code, to notify the Events Manager that the `user:afterSaveOnRegister` event is executed. The first argument of the notification is the event itself. The second required argument must be the source of the event or the place where the event is executed. The third parameter will be the data that the listener needs to perform the relevant event action. You can also optionally pass, as the last parameter, a Boolean value, a flag, that can stop the execution of the event if needs be.

You can subscribe several listeners to one event. When the event fires, all subscribed listeners will be notified. The listeners are notified in the order in which they have been registered in the Events Manager, or in priority order in case you have specified it.

Note that your listeners can subscribe to any new events your application has, but also to existing Phalcon ones. At the time of writing, Phalcon has 66 different events. The number of available events that Phalcon offers could have increased by the time this book is published, but the following list will remain the same:

```
acl:afterCheckAccess
acl:beforeCheckAccess
application:afterHandleRequest
application:afterStartModule
application:beforeHandleRequest
application:beforeSendResponse
application:beforeStartModule
application:boot
application:viewRender
collectionManager:afterInitialize
console:afterHandleTask
console:afterStartModule
console:beforeHandleTask
```

```
console:beforeStartModule
console:boot
db:afterQuery
db:afterQuery
db:beforeQuery
db:beforeQuery
db:beginTransaction
db:commitTransaction
db:createSavepoint
db:releaseSavepoint
db:rollbackSavepoint
db:rollbackTransaction
di:beforeServiceResolve
dispatch:afterDispatchLoop
dispatch:afterDispatch
dispatch:afterExecuteRoute
dispatch:afterInitialize
dispatch:beforeDispatchLoop
dispatch:beforeDispatch
dispatch:beforeException
dispatch:beforeException
dispatch:beforeExecuteRoute
dispatch:beforeNotFoundAction
loader:afterCheckClass
loader:beforeCheckClass
loader:beforeCheckPath
loader:beforeCheckPath
loader:beforeCheckPath
loader:pathFound
loader:pathFound
loader:pathFound
loader:pathFound
micro:afterExecuteRoute
micro:afterHandleRoute
micro:beforeException
micro:beforeExecuteRoute
micro:beforeHandleRoute
micro:beforeNotFound
modelsManager:afterInitialize
router:afterCheckRoutes
router:beforeCheckRoute
router:beforeCheckRoutes
router:matchedRoute
```

```
router:notMatchedRoute
view:afterRender
view:afterRender
view:afterRenderView
view:afterRenderView
view:beforeRender
view:beforeRender
view:beforeRenderView
view:beforeRenderView
view:notFoundView
```

There's more...

For more detailed information about event driven programming, check `https://en.wikipedia.org/wiki/Event-driven_programming`.

You can find the Events Manager documentation at `https://docs.phalconphp.com/en/latest/reference/events.html`.

The Vökuró repository is located at `https://github.com/phalcon/vokuro`.

Centralizing validations for rock solid business rules

Phalcon offers flexible tools to validate data such as user input. The `Phalcon\Validation` component is strategically located in its own namespace, so that it can be used at any point and in any part of your application, such as validating posted data from the UI, data before it is saved to the database, data sent to the UI, and so on.

In this recipe, we will create some validators and discuss the common approaches on how to use them in your application.

Getting ready

To successfully implement this recipe, you need to have a Phalcon application and the **Volt** engine configured. In our example, we will use a sample application generated by Phalcon Developer Tools. However, you can use any other application that is available to you.

You will also need to have a web server installed and configured for handling requests to your application. Your application must be capable of receiving requests and you should have the necessary controllers and views, as well as a `bootstrap` file with a connection to a database. The database should have at least one table.

How to do it...

Follow these steps to complete this recipe:

1. Assuming that you do not have an application ready, you will need to create it. We are using Phalcon Developer Tools to do so. Execute the following command to generate your application skeleton:

   ```
   phalcon project validation simple
   ```

2. Next, create a database if you do not have one:

   ```
   echo 'CREATE DATABASE validators' | mysql -u root
   ```

3. We will need to create a table to store data. Log into your MySQL console and execute the following query:

   ```
   CREATE TABLE IF NOT EXISTS 'users' (
       'id' int(10) unsigned NOT NULL AUTO_INCREMENT,
       'name' varchar(255) NOT NULL,
       'email' varchar(255) NOT NULL,
       'password' char(60) NOT NULL,
       'active' char(1) DEFAULT NULL,
       PRIMARY KEY ('id'),
       KEY ('email')
   ) ENGINE=InnoDB  DEFAULT CHARSET=utf8;
   ```

4. Change the database configuration, specifying the correct credentials:

   ```
   'database' => [
           'adapter'      => 'Mysql',
           'host'         => 'localhost',
           'username'     => 'root',
           'password'     => '',
           'dbname'       => 'validators',
           'charset'      => 'utf8',
   ],
   ```

5. Next we will need a controller, a model, and some views to work with the User entity. Phalcon Developer Tools can generate the code for us with the following command:

   ```
   phalcon scaffold users
   ```

6. Create a folder for storing our validators: `app/library/Validators`.

7. Register the new namespace in the `Phalcon\Loader`, which points to our newly created folder:

```
$loader->registerNamespaces([
    'MyApp\Validators' => $config->application->libraryDir .
'Validators/'
]);
```

8. Create a `MyApp\Validators\User` class extending `Phalcon\Validation`:

```
namespace MyApp\Validators;

use Phalcon\Validation;
use Phalcon\Validation\Validator\Email;
use Phalcon\Validation\Validator\PresenceOf;

class User extends Validation
{
  public function initialize()
  {
    $this->add('name', new PresenceOf(['message' => 'The name is
required']));
    $this->add('email', new PresenceOf(['message' => 'The e-mail
is required']));
    $this->add('email', new Email(['message' => 'The e-mail is not
valid']));
  }
}
```

9. In order to test this, we need to add a bit of code in our action. Open the `UsersController` and add the `createAction` method:

```
public function createAction()
{
  if (!$this->request->isPost()) {
    $this->dispatcher->forward([
      'controller' => 'users',
      'action' => 'index'
    ]);
```

```
    return;
}

$validation = new \MyApp\Validators\User();
$data = [
  'name'  => $this->request->getPost(
      'name',
      'striptags'
  ),
  'email' => $this->request->getPost('email', 'email'),
  'password' => $this->request->getPost('password'),
  'active' => $this->request->getPost(
      'active',
      'absint'
  ),
];

$messages = $validation->validate($data);
$errors   = [];

if (count($messages)) {
  foreach ($messages as $message) {
    $errors[] = $message->getMessage();
  }

  $this->flash->error(join('<br>', $errors));

  $this->response->redirect([
    'controller' => 'users',
    'action' => 'create'
  ]);

  return;
}

$user = new Users();
$user->name = $data['name'];
$user->email = $data['email'];
$user->password = $data['password'];
$user->active = $data['active'];

if (!$user->save()) {
```

```
    foreach ($user->getMessages() as $message) {
      $this->flash->error($message);
    }

    $this->dispatcher->forward([
      'controller' => "users",
      'action' => 'new'
    ]);

    return;
  }

  $this->flash->success("user was created successfully");

  $this->response->redirect([
    'controller' => 'users',
    'action' => 'index'
  ]);
}
```

10. Now, open `http://{your-host-here}/users/create`, where `your-host-here` is the hostname of your project. Try to fill the form in different ways, for example, with no username, with no e-mail, or with an e-mail in an incorrect format, and try to save the entered data. You will see an error message.

11. Assume that you have a business requirement, where all registered usernames must be in Latin characters, consisting of the first and last name of the user that wants to register. Additionally, each username must be a minimum of three characters and there must be a space between the first and last name. Let's create a validator to encompass this logic:

```
namespace MyApp\Validators;

use Phalcon\Validation;
use Phalcon\Validation\Message;
use Phalcon\Validation\Validator;

class CorrectName extends Validator
{
  public function validate(Validation $validator, $attribute)
  {
    $value = $validator->getValue($attribute);
    $pattern = '#^[A-Z][a-z]{2,} [A-Z][a-z]{2,}$#';
```

```
        if (!preg_match($pattern, $value)) {
            $message = $this->getOption('message') ?: 'The name is not
    valid';

            $validator->appendMessage(new Message($message, $attribute,
    'CorrectName'));

            return false;
        }

        return true;
    }
}
```

12. To enable this validator, we need to add it to the `MyApp\Validation\Users` object by adding the following line:

```
$this->add('name', new CorrectName(['message' => 'The user name
you entered does not match the required format']));
```

13. Now, open `http://{your-host-here}/users/create` and try to fill it. Enter a user name incorrectly. You should thoroughly test and experiment with different character combinations. Each incorrect entry should produce an error message.

14. Let's assume that data can enter your application in various ways. For instance, if you need to validate data when a user is created, you would also need to validate it when the user is edited. Additionally, if you need to create a console application, which will manipulate data, you will most likely need to apply those validations there, too. To keep your application *DRY*, we can change the `Users` model as shown in the following code. Change the `validation` method in the model so that it uses our validator:

```
use Phalcon\Validation;
use Phalcon\Validation\Validator\Email as EmailValidator;
use MyApp\Validators\CorrectName as NameValidator;

class Users extends \Phalcon\Mvc\Model
{
    public $id;
    public $name;
    public $email;
    public $password;
    public $active;
```

```
      public function getSource()
      {
        return 'users';
      }

      public function validation()
      {
        $validator = new Validation();

        $validator->add(
          'email',
          new EmailValidator()
        );

        $validator->add(
          'name',
          new NameValidator(['message' => 'The user name you entered
  does not match the required format'])
        );

        return $this->validate($validator);
      }
    }
```

15. Now, open `UsersController` and remove the following code from the `createAction` method:

```
$validation = new \MyApp\Validators\User();

$messages = $validation->validate($data);
$errors   = [];

if (count($messages)) {
  foreach ($messages as $message) {
    $errors[] = $message->getMessage();
  }

  $this->flash->error(join('<br>', $errors));

  $this->dispatcher->forward([
    'controller' => 'users',
    'action' => 'new'
  ]);

  return;
}
```

16. Additionally, open `MyApp\Validators\User` and remove the code related to validator from there:

    ```
    $this->add('name', new CorrectName(['message' => 'The user name
    you entered does not match the required format']));
    ```

17. Now, open `http://{your-host-here}/users/create` and try to enter a user name with incorrect data. You will see an error message.

> Note that `Phalcon\Mvc\Model\Validation` is deprecated in Phalcon 3.0.0 in favor of `Phalcon\Validation`. The functionality of both components is merged into one, allowing us to reduce the code base while offering the same functionality as before. The syntax for creating validators in Phalcon 2.0 is different from that in Phalcon 3.0.0. We suggest that you start using Phalcon 3.0.0, since it is a stable version with long term support and many bug fixes. Phalcon 2.0 is no longer supported, but you can still use the same functionality by just changing the validator syntax to match the Phalcon version. For more detailed information on validation changes, check the following post in the Phalcon blog: `http://blog.phalconphp.com/post/phalcon-3-0-0-released`

How it works...

We first create an application, a database with a user table in it, as well as the application structure with a controller and a view for our recipe. We extend the `Phalcon\Validation` component by creating one of our own and enabling validation on specific conditions/data. So far, we use just the stock validators that come with Phalcon. Several validators can be initialized, though, by adding them to the `Phalcon\Validation` object. We have enabled validators when the components are initialized. We have enabled validation in our `UsersController` by instantiating our validator and passing it in the array with the data to be validated.

Then, we created a custom validator. We created it for the purposes of our recipe, but we could have easily used the powerful `Phalcon\Validation\Validator\Regex` to achieve the same result.

The Phalcon framework has a lot of validators out of box which use the `Phalcon\Validation` component, but you can easily create your own custom validators that meet the requirements of your application business logic. The loosely coupled design of this component allows you to create your own validators alongside those provided by the framework. We have then removed the direct validation call from our controller and moved the validation logic in the model. This allowed us to remove duplicate code and achieve the same result—centralizing validator logic.

There's more...

For detailed validation documentation, refer to: `https://docs.phalconphp.com/en/latest/reference/validation.html`

Complex routing with regular expressions

In this recipe, we will specify routes using regular expressions. Specifically, we will check how to allow language specific characters in URLs and ensure that the routing is correctly executed irrespective of language. For instance, if a user needs to visit the Contact Us page in our application, they need to use `http://{your-host-here}/en/contacts` for English, `http://{your-host-here}/ja/`連絡先 for Japanese, or `http://{your-host-here}/it/contatti` for Italian. We may also want to suffix our URLs with `.htm` or `.html` for SEO. With the preceding, the user will be able to see their URL in their native tongue. Finally, to make this recipe a bit more complex, we will differentiate on the results based on the language selection.

Getting ready

To successfully implement this recipe you need to have a Phalcon application and the **Volt** engine configured. In our example, we will use a sample application generated by **Phalcon Developer Tools**. However, you can use any other application that is available to you.

You will also need to have a web server installed and configured for handling requests to your application. Your application must be capable of receiving requests and you should have the necessary controllers and views, as well as a `bootstrap` file with a connection to a database. The database should have at least one table.

How to do it...

Follow these steps to complete this recipe:

1. Assuming that you do not have an application ready, you will need to create it. We are using Phalcon Developer Tools to do so. Execute the following command to generate your application skeleton:

   ```
   phalcon project routing simple
   ```

2. We will need to configure the router in such a way that it redirects requests to the correct controller:

   ```
   $di->setShared('router', function () {
       $router = new Router(false);
   ```

```
$router->removeExtraSlashes(true);

$router->add(
    '/{lang:[a-z]+}/{article:([\w_-]+)(\.html?)?}',
    [
        'controller' => 1,
        'action'     => 'index',
    ]
);


return $router;
});
```

3. We will need to create a base controller that our specific controllers will extend. This controller will contain the common functionality, keeping our application DRY:

```
abstract class LanguageController extends ControllerBase
{
  public function onConstruct()
  {
    $params  = $this->dispatcher->getParams();
    $action = 'index';

    // Translate article here
    $translate = [
      '連絡先'     => 'contacts',
      'contacts' => 'contacts',
      'contatti' => 'contacts',

    ];

    if (isset($translate[$params['article']])) {
      $action = $translate[$params['article']];
    }

    $this->dispatcher->forward([
      'controller' => $params['lang'],
      'action'     => $action
    ]);

    return;
  }
}
```

The scope of this recipe is not to expand on the Phalcon translation adapters. Therefore, we will use stubs here.

4. Now, create a controller for each of the languages. The Japanese controller is demonstrated in the following code. You can replicate the same functionality for other language controllers:

```
class JaController extends LanguageController
{
    public function indexAction()
    {
    }

    public function contactsAction()
    {
        var_dump(
                __CLASS__,
                __METHOD__,
                $_SERVER,
                func_get_args()
        );
        die;
    }
}
```

Go to the address `http://{your-host-here}/ja/連絡先` in your browser to ensure that everything works properly. Try to use a URI with the ending `.html` or `.htm`, or without it at all.

How it works...

We have created the router service and configured it to handle a multi-language URI. The `add()` method has a regular expression as the first parameter, which does all the matching for our route. Regular expressions must match the **PCRE** format.

The first thing that we need to draw our attention to is the named parameters in the route template. In our route, the parameters are named `lang` and `article`. For the action, the parameter is replaced by the defined index value. It is important to understand that the router does not execute any code. It simply collects information from the request and routes the relevant parameters to the `Phalcon\Mvc\Dispatcher` component.

The second parameter in the `add()` method determines which parts of the URI are mapped to the controller, action, or parameters. For our example, the parameters can be empty or not specified. The relevant parts of the URI are retrieved from the wildcards or masks of the regular expression, which are contained in the square brackets. If we use a mask in specifying a route, then we must use its sequence number. Since the router allows for named parameters, we can use those. For instance:

```
// Get "day" parameter
$name = $this->dispatcher->getParam("lang");
// Get "day" parameter
$type = $this->dispatcher->getParam("article");
```

> One thing to note is that we must avoid using special characters in regular expressions for controllers and namespaces. The parameters form class and file names, which exist in the filesystem. You have to be very careful since this could be potentially a security risk. The regular expression `/([a-zA-Z0-9\_\-]+)` is safe.

We built the route in such a way that it points to the relevant language controller. Each individual controller extends the abstract controller, which does all the work. The `onConstruct` method is called first (as always), and in there the selected language is determined. After that we emulate the translation of the article. The rest is paperwork. Using forward, we have just told the dispatcher where it will redirect the request.

There's more...

To find the documentation on the PCRE regular expression format, see: `http://www.php.net/manual/en/book.pcre.php`

You can see the full routing documentation at: `https://docs.phalconphp.com/en/latest/reference/routing.html`

Using in-memory session handlers

Some applications make heavy use of sessions to store user related data or other necessary information for correct operation, while others don't. Since Phalcon offers the DI container, where we can store various services, we can take advantage of it and store our session service there, ensuring that the session starts only when the application requires it to do so. Phalcon offers a simple yet powerful object oriented interface to work with sessions. In this recipe, we will discuss how to configure and use the session component with adapters such as **Memcached** and **Redis**.

Getting ready

To implement this recipe, we don't need a fully deployed or working application. We can demonstrate the functionality in a simple script. However, you will need to have the appropriate PHP extensions enabled, as well as access to a `Memcached` and/or `Redis` server. We will use **telnet** and **redis-cli** for testing, so these utilities need to be installed in your system. Any other alternative utilities that perform the same tasks can also be used.

How to do it...

Follow these steps to complete this recipe:

1. We will concentrate on the `Phalcon\Session\Adapter\Redis` adapter. We will configure it and check how it works to understand the main principles of the session component. Create a file and name it `session-redis.php`. Place the following code in it (substituting the `host` and `port` parameters for your installation):

    ```php
    use Phalcon\Di;
    use Phalcon\Session\Adapter\Redis as RedisSession;

    $di = new Di();

    // Start the session the first time when some
    // components request the session service
    $di->setShared('session', function () {
        $session = new RedisSession([
            'uniqueId'   => 'my-private-app',
            'host'       => 'localhost',
            'port'       => 6379,
            'persistent' => false,
            'lifetime'   => 3600,
            'prefix'     => 'my_'
        ]);

        $session->start();
        return $session;
    });
    ```

2. Since the service is configured, we will now try to save some data in the session. Add the following code after the service registration configuration:

    ```php
    $data = [
        "abc" => "123",
        "def" => "678",
    ```

```
        "xyz" => "zyx"
    ];

    $session = $di->get('session');
    $session->write($sessionID, serialize($data));
```

3. Save the file and execute the script in the command line using the following command:

   php session-redis.php.

4. If everything went well, we will not see any output or errors on the screen. To check what has been written in the session, we need to use the Terminal. Open it and run the following command:

   redis-cli

5. You will get to the Redis console. Run the `get` command to see if the data was actually saved:

   get my_abcdef123456

 Check the key. It consists of two parts: the prefix (`my_`), and the session ID (`abcdef123456`), which was defined in the script.

6. We can now check if the data was actually saved in the session. Put the following code in our script right after the session writing section:

   ```
   var_dump($session->read($sessionID));
   ```

7. You will see something like this:

   ```
   string(66) "a:3:{s:3:"abc";s:3:"123";s:3:"def";s:3:"678";s:3:"xyz"
   ;s:3:"zyx";}"
   ```

8. We will now check what happens if we delete the data and check the results. Add the following code in the `session-redis.php` and run the script again:

   ```
   $session->destroy($sessionID);
   ```

9. Open the Redis console and run the `get` command to see the data:

   get my_abcdef123456

10. The output should be something like this:

    127.0.0.1:6379> get my_abcdef123456

    (nil)

11. Let's look at the `Phalcon\Session\Adapter\Libmemcached` in more detail. Create a file named `session-memcached.php` and paste the following code in it (substituting the parameters for `host` and `port`):

```php
use Phalcon\Di;
use Phalcon\Session\Adapter\Libmemcached as MemcachedSession;

$di = new Di();

// Start the session the first time when a
// component requests the session service
$di->setShared('session', function () {
    $session = new MemcachedSession([
        'servers' => [
            [
                "host" => "127.0.0.1",
                "port" => 11211
            ]
        ],
        'client' => [
            \Memcached::OPT_HASH => \Memcached::HASH_MD5,
            \Memcached::OPT_PREFIX_KEY => 'prefix.',
        ],
        'lifetime' => 3600,
        'prefix'   => 'my_'
    ]);

    $session->start();
    return $session;
});
```

12. The service is now configured. We will now try to save some data in the session. Add the following code after the service-registration configuration:

```php
$data = [
    "abc" => "123",
    "def" => "678",
    "xyz" => "zyx"
];

$session = $di->get('session');
$session->write($sessionID, serialize($data));
```

13. Save the file and run the script in the command line using the following command:

`php session-memcached .php`

14. If everything went well, we will not see any output or errors on the screen. To check what has been written in the session, we need to use the Terminal. Open it and run the following command:

```
telnet 127.0.0.1 11211
```

15. Log in to Telnet and run the `get` command to see that the data was actually saved:

```
get my_abcdef123456
```

16. You will see something like this:

```
telnet 127.0.0.1 11211
Trying 127.0.0.1...
Connected to 127.0.0.1.
Escape character is '^]'.
get my_abcdef123456
VALUE my_abcdef123456 0 74
s:66:"a:3:{s:3:"abc";s:3:"123";s:3:"def";s:3:"678";s:3:"xyz";s:3:"
zyx";}";
END
```

17. We can now check if the data was actually saved in the session. Put the following code in our script right after the session writing section:

```
var_dump($session->read($sessionID));
```

18. You will see something like this:

```
string(66) "a:3:{s:3:"abc";s:3:"123";s:3:"def";s:3:"678";s:3:"xyz"
;s:3:"zyx";}"
```

19. This output verifies that the data was actually saved. As mentioned before, the key consists of two parts: the prefix (`my_`), and the session ID (`abcdef123456`), which was defined in the script. We will now check what happens if we delete the data and check the results. Add the following code in the `session-memcached.php` and run the script again:

```
$session->destroy($sessionID);
```

20. Open Telnet one more time and run the command `get` to see the status of our data:

```
get my_abcdef123456
```

21. You will see something like this:

```
telnet 127.0.0.1 11211
Trying 127.0.0.1...
```

```
Connected to 127.0.0.1.
Escape character is '^]'.
get my_abcdef123456
END
```

How it works...

Session adapters in Phalcon follow a simple interface to allow easy interaction with the component. We have seen how we can use adapters like `Phalcon\Session\Adapter\Libmemcached` and `Phalcon\Session\Adapter\Redis`. You can create your own adapters for session handling, extending the relevant interface. For example, implementing a file adapter or an adapter with Aerospike or any other session storage would use exactly the same interface. The only difference will be the configuration of the backend when the service is registered in the DI container.

There's more...

More detailed information about session adapter configuration can be found at:
`https://docs.phalconphp.com/en/latest/reference/session.html`

Handy persistence for controllers and components

In this recipe, we will discuss how to improve application performance by caching application content. Our application can use the cached content instead of requesting the same data from the database. There are many implementations for every task. We will look at one of the available scenarios for using cache, but note that it is not the only solution available.

Getting ready

To successfully implement this recipe you need to have a Phalcon application and the Volt engine configured. In our example, we will use a sample application generated by Phalcon Developer Tools. However, you can use any other application that is available to you.

You will also need to have a web server installed and configured for handling requests to your application. Your application must be capable of receiving requests and you should have the necessary controllers and views, as well as a `bootstrap` file with a connection to a database. The database should have at least one table.

In addition, you will need to have access to a MySQL RDBMS instance, as well as be able to create a database for your application. Your testing application could work with other RDBMSes, but that setup is not in the scope of this recipe. You will also need to have composer installed so that you can update the necessary dependencies.

We will use the root user without a password for the database connection. You should adjust the recipe with your own database credentials.

How to do it...

Follow these steps to complete this recipe:

1. Assuming that you do not have an application ready, you will need to create it. We are using Phalcon Developer Tools to do so. Execute the following command to generate your application skeleton:

```
phalcon project blameable
```

2. Next, we will need a database. Create it, if you do not have one, and run the following command in the Terminal:

```
echo 'CREATE DATABASE cachemvc' | mysql -u root
```

3. The next step is to configure our application. Open the configuration file and adjust the database parameters:

```
'database' => [
    'adapter'  => 'Mysql',
    'host'     => 'localhost',
    'username' => 'root',
    'password' => '',
    'dbname'   => 'cachemvc',
    'charset'  => 'utf8',
],
```

4. We will now need to create a table to store posts in our database. Open the Terminal and connect to it your database. Run the following script to create the posts table:

```
CREATE TABLE 'posts' (
'id' BIGINT UNSIGNED NOT NULL AUTO_INCREMENT,
'title' TEXT NOT NULL,
'body' LONGTEXT NOT NULL,
'teaser' TEXT,
PRIMARY KEY (id)
) ENGINE=InnoDB DEFAULT CHARSET=utf8;
```

5. We will also need to insert some test data to be used in our recipe:

```
INSERT INTO 'posts' ('id', 'title', 'body', 'teaser') VALUES
(1, 'The first post', 'some content here ...', 'some teaser here
...'),
(2, 'The second post', 'some content here ...', 'some teaser here
...'),
(3, 'The third post', 'some content here ...', 'some teaser here
...');
```

6. The database is ready for our recipe; we now need to create a controller, a model for the Posts model, and the views. We will use Phalcon Developer Tools to generate the necessary code:

```
phalcon scaffold posts
```

7. We will now need to configure and register the view cache service in the DI container. The service will save the cached data in files and not in memory. We will use this implementation for the purposes of this recipe. In your application, you can use any backend adapter that suits you. Open the bootstrap file and put the following code in it:

```
use Phalcon\Cache\Backend\File as FileCache;
use Phalcon\Cache\Frontend\Output as FrontendOutput;

$di->setShared('viewCache', function () use ($config) {
    $frontCache = new FrontendOutput([
        "lifetime" => 86400 * 30
    ]);

    return new FileCache($frontCache, [
        "cacheDir" => $config->application->cacheDir . 'views/'
    ]);
    }
);
```

8. Then, we need a folder for the cached data. Create the folder app/cache/views.

9. Next, open the Posts model and add the following methods there:

```
public function afterSave()
{
    $this->clearCache();
}
```

```
public function afterDelete()
{
    $this->clearCache();
}

public function clearCache()
{
    if ($this->id) {
        $viewCache = $this->getDI()->getShared('viewCache');
        $viewCache->delete('post-' . $this->id);
    }
}
```

10. Register an event in the Events Manager so that all database queries are logged. We will need this for debugging purposes:

```
$em = new Phalcon\Events\Manager();

$di->setShared('db', function () use ($config, $em) {
  $connection = new Phalcon\Db\Adapter\Pdo\Mysql(
    $config->database->toArray()
  );

  $em->attach('db', function ($event, $connection) {
    if ($event->getType() == 'afterQuery') {
      error_log($connection->getSQLStatement());
    }
  });

  $connection->setEventsManager($em);

  return $connection;
});
```

11. Open the `PostsController` and create the `viewAction` method as follows:

```
public function viewAction($id)
{
  // Enable cache
  $this->view->cache(['key' => 'post-' . $id]);

  // Check for cache
  if ($this->viewCache->exists('post-' . $id)) {
    return;
```

```
        }

    $post = Posts::findFirstByid($id);
    if (!$post) {
      $this->flash->error("post was not found");

      $this->dispatcher->forward([
        'controller' => "posts",
        'action' => 'index'
      )];

      return;
    }

    $this->view->setVar('post', $post);
  }
```

12. Create a view for displaying the post (`app/views/posts/view.phtml`) with the following contents:

```php
<?php echo $this->getContent(); ?>

<h1><?php echo $post->title ?></h1>

<div class="container">
    <?php echo $post->body ?>
</div>
```

13. Your database table has some sample data (we entered them earlier in the recipe). Open its page in your browser at `http://{your-host-here}/posts/view/{post-id-here}` by using the `id` of an existing `post`.

14. We have used an anonymous function as the listener of all `db` events. Since launching the page to read the article, the listener was invoked and the relevant query will be written in the `log` file. Open the `log` file and check that this is the case.

15. Open the `view cache` directory `app/cache/views` to ensure it is empty.

16. Reload the page.

17. Open the `view cache` directory again to ensure that there is a new `cache` file in it.

18. Open the `log` file one more time to ensure that the second query has not been executed.

How it works...

Phalcon offers the `Phalcon\Cache` class, which allows you to easily access cached data. `Phalcon\Cache` is written in C, thus achieving high performance.

First we created our test application with the required models, controllers, and views.

Next we registered the view cache service in our DI container and set it up with a cached data lifetime of one month. Lifetime is the time in seconds that the data will be stored in the cache until it expires. Of course, since this is a configuration variable, you can change it to whatever your application needs. All stored data get the same lifetime by default. You can override the default lifetime when saving data in the cache.

There can be situations when you need to invalidate data in the cache. To do so, you will only need to know the key that the data was stored with. We updated the `Posts` model, adding functionality to remove cached data automatically when a record was saved or deleted, The model will automatically call the `clearCache` method when the events `afterSave` and `afterDelete` are fired. All this happens transparently when you call `$post->save()` or `$post->delete()`. In the `clearCache` method of the model, we retrieve the cache service from the DI container and perform the necessary actions.

Our next step was to create the `viewAction` and an appropriate view. In this action, we enabled the output also cache and checked that the new `cache` file is in the `view cache` directory.

In this recipe, we used one of the caching strategies that Phalcon offers. Other than caching output, you can cache also arbitrary data, using the relevant backend adapter.

Despite the fact that `Phalcon\Cache` is a high performance component, we recommend choosing your caching strategy carefully. It is often the case that the wrong caching strategy will deteriorate performance rather than boost it. Some of the most common areas that caching is applicable, if not necessary, are:

- ▶ You make complex calculations when the same result is returned (or the result changes rarely)
- ▶ You use a lot of helpers and the result is the same
- ▶ You get data from the database and the result does not change (or changes rarely)

There's more...

Detailed online cache documentation can be found at: `https://docs.phalconphp.com/en/latest/reference/cache.html`

Transactional controller actions ensuring consistent operations

In our applications, it is common to perform a number of database operations in one action. The question in every developer's mind is, what if something goes wrong? In that case, we are left in a state where some of the data has been updated while the rest has not. To circumvent this issue, we use database transactions to ensure that either we do a full update of all the related data, or rollback the changes if something goes wrong.

Phalcon offers the `\Phalcon\Mvc\Model\Transaction\*` classes to allow for an easy and convenient way to perform transactional writes to our database. Imagine a business rule in our application, where a `User` entity has at least one `Address` entity. Also assume that our UI has relevant functionality to allow for input of many addresses per user. Once that payload is posted to our controller, we need to first save the user related data and then save any addresses that have been submitted, binding the `User` entity with the `Address` entity with the relevant foreign key. However, if an error happens during that operation, we need to be able to discard all of our changes as a whole. We do that by using transactions.

In this recipe, we will look at the available transaction mechanisms, and demonstrate the basic principles of working with them inside your controllers.

Getting ready

In this recipe, we will need two database tables: a user table and an address table. In this recipe, we will use MySQL, but you can easily use something else, for example, PostgreSQL. If you choose the latter, you might need to modify the syntax of the SQL dump to suit your needs. For the tables mentioned in the previous sections, we will create two models, as well as a test controller.

For this recipe, we are using the Phalcon Developer Tools to generate our test application. You can always use an application you already have.

Setting up your web server and virtual hosts is not in the scope of this recipe. We will assume that they are already set up.

We will use the root user without a password for the database connection. You should adjust the recipe with your own database credentials.

It should also be noted that database normalization also falls outside the scope of this recipe.

How to do it...

Follow these steps to complete this recipe:

1. First, you need an application for the tests. Create it if you do not have one. Run the following command to generate a template application:

   ```
   phalcon project transaction simple
   ```

2. You need a database for your application. Create it if you do not have one using, for instance, the following command in the Terminal:

   ```
   mysql -e 'create database transaction_test charset=utf8mb4
   collate=utf8mb4_unicode_ci;' -u root
   ```

3. Open the application configuration and change the database connection settings according to your credentials:

   ```
   'database' => [
         'adapter'       => 'Mysql',
         'host'          => 'localhost',
         'username'      => 'root',
         'password'      => '',
         'dbname'        => 'transaction_test',
         'charset'       => 'utf8',
   ],
   ```

4. Now we need two tables, one for users and one for addresses. Create them using the following code:

   ```
   CREATE TABLE 'users' (
     'id' INT UNSIGNED NOT NULL AUTO_INCREMENT,
     'name' VARCHAR(255) NOT NULL,
     'email' VARCHAR(255) NOT NULL,
     'password' CHAR(60) NOT NULL,
     'active' CHAR(1) DEFAULT NULL,
     PRIMARY KEY ('id'),
     KEY ('email')
   ) ENGINE=InnoDB  DEFAULT CHARSET=utf8;

   CREATE TABLE 'address' (
     'id' INT UNSIGNED NOT NULL AUTO_INCREMENT,
   ```

```
'users_id' INT UNSIGNED NOT NULL,

'country' VARCHAR(200) NOT NULL,

'state' VARCHAR(200) NOT NULL,

'city' VARCHAR(200) NOT NULL,

'location' VARCHAR(200) NOT NULL,

PRIMARY KEY ('id'),

FOREIGN KEY ('users_id') REFERENCES 'users' ('id') ON UPDATE
CASCADE ON DELETE CASCADE

) ENGINE=InnoDB  DEFAULT CHARSET=utf8;
```

5. Next we need a controller, a form for creating the user, views, and, of course, models. Creating the controllers, models, and views is not in the scope of this recipe. We will simply use Phalcon Developer Tools to create the scaffold for us. However, if all these components exist in your application, you can skip this step. Run the following command in the Terminal:

    ```
    phalcon scaffold users
    ```

6. After the code has been generated, go to `http://{your-host-here}/users/new` to ensure everything works properly. You will see the form for creating the user.

7. Open the view containing this form and add the required address fields there. The code has been simplified on purpose, containing only the relevant parts:

    ```
    <?php echo $this->tag->textField(["address[country]", "size" =>
    30, "class" => "form-control", "id" => "country"]) ?>
    <?php echo $this->tag->textField(["address[state]", "size" => 30,
    "class" => "form-control", "id" => "state"]) ?>
    <?php echo $this->tag->textField(["address[city]", "size" => 30,
    "class" => "form-control", "id" => "city"]) ?>
    <?php echo $this->tag->textField(["address[location]", "size" =>
    30, "class" => "form-control", "id" => "location"]) ?>
    ```

8. Now we can create users with their addresses. Try to open the page in your browser again, fill the fields, and submit the form. You will see that the user has been created successfully, but without an attached address for now.

9. Change the `createAction` method in `UsersController` as demonstrated in the following code by adding an initial validation:

    ```
    public function createAction()
    {
      if (!$this->request->isPost()) {
        $this->response->redirect[
          'controller' => 'users',
    ```

```php
        'action' => 'index'
    ]);

    return;
}

$messages = [];
try {
  $transactionManager =
      new \Phalcon\Mvc\Model\Transaction\Manager();
  $transaction = $transactionManager->get();

  $user = new Users();
  $user->setTransaction($transaction);

  $user->name = $this->request->getPost(
      'name',
      'striptags'
  );
  $user->email = $this->request->getPost(
      'email',
      'email'
  );
  $user->password = $this->request->getPost('password');
  $user->active = $this->request->getPost(
      'active',
      'absint'
  );

  if (!$user->save()) {
    foreach ($user->getMessages() as $message) {
      $messages[] = $message->getMessage();
    }

    $transaction->rollback(
        "Can't save user: <br> * " .
        join('<br> * ', $messages)
    );
  }
```

```
        $this->flash->success(
            'The user was created successfully'
        );
        $transaction->commit();

        $this->response->redirect([
          'controller' => 'users',
          'action' => 'index'
        ]);
      } catch (\Exception $e) {
        $this->flash->error($e->getMessage());

        $this->response->redirect([
          'controller' => 'users',
          'action' => 'new'
        ]);

        return;
      }
    }
```

10. Now, open `http://{your-host-here}/users/new` and enter only the user name, leaving all form fields empty. Try to save this user by submitting the form. You will see an error message.

11. Check the `user` table in your database. You will see that the user you tried to save is not present yet.

12. Let us try to save the user address. Create a model for user addresses (we will use code generation):

    phalcon model address

13. Change the `createAction` method by adding the following code below the block with the `if (!$user->save())` condition:

    ```
    $address = new Address();
    $post = $this->request->getPost("address");
    $address->users_id = $user->id;
    $address->country = $post['country'];
    $address->state = $post['state'];
    $address->city = $post['city'];
    $address->location = $post['location'];
    ```

```
if (!$address->save()) {
    foreach ($address->getMessages() as $message) {
        $messages[] = $message->getMessage();
    }

    $transaction->rollback(
        "Can't save user: <br> * " .
        join('<br> * ', $messages)
    );
}
```

14. Open `http://{your-host-here}/users/new` again, fill the fields related to the `address` model, and try to save the data. You will see an error message.

15. Check the `user` table in your database. You will notice that the user you tried to save is not present. Additionally, the `address` table will be empty.

16. Fill the required fields and try to save it all again. This time the data will be saved correctly.

How it works...

We generated the required skeleton of our test application with controllers, views, models, as well as the database with the necessary tables in it.

We modified the `createAction` method in `UsersController` so that our transaction fails and rolls back. Transactions ensure that all database operations succeed before data is stored in the database. We use isolated transactions. They run in a new connection and ensure that all generated SQL, virtual foreign key checks, and business rules are isolated from the main connection. This transaction type requires a transactional manager that controls every transaction, globally ensuring the correct `roll back/commit` of the operations before the end of the request.

In actual practice, there is not much use in doing it, because Phalcon does not allow you to save the model in case its mandatory fields are not filled. In other words, Phalcon will not store anything in the database until it is sure that there is all the required information. For this reason, there is nothing to roll back. But we have created a skeleton, in which we use the manager a bit later.

Our next step is adding the user address saving logic. We use the previous approach and check whether the model has been saved successfully. If this is not so, then we collect all error messages and display them. At the same time, we roll back the transaction.

Finally, when we ensure that everything goes smoothly we commit the transaction, adding the new user and his or her address.

This example is a bit artificial, of course, but we demonstrate the main aspects of working with transactions.

There's more...

More detailed information about transactions can be found at: `https://docs.` `phalconphp.com/ru/latest/reference/model-transactions.html`

Auditing complex user actions with simplicity

In this recipe, we will demonstrate how you can implement better flexibility and performance in your application by extending internal Phalcon classes instead of using them directly.

Our recipe will demonstrate how we can have a site that stores code snippets from users, and how we can track those changes so as to offer the different revisions of those changes per snippet.

Getting ready

To successfully implement this recipe you need to have a Phalcon application and the Volt engine configured. In our example we will use a sample application generated by Phalcon Developer Tools. However, you can use any other application that is available to you.

You will also need to have a web server installed and configured for handling requests to your application. Your application must be capable of receiving requests and you should have the necessary controllers and views, as well as a `bootstrap` file with a connection to a database. The database should have at least one table.

In addition, you will need to have access to a MySQL RDBMS instance, as well as be able to create a database for your application. Your testing application could work with other RDBMSes, but that setup is also not in the scope of this recipe. You will also need to have a composer installed so that you can update the necessary dependencies.

We will use the root user without a password for the database connection. You should adjust the recipe with your own database credentials.

How to do it...

Follow these steps to complete this recipe:

1. Assuming that you do not have an application ready, you will need to create it. We are using Phalcon Developer Tools to do so. Execute the following command to generate your application skeleton:

   ```
   phalcon project blameable
   ```

2. Then, you need a database. Create it if you do not have one. Run the following command in the Terminal:

   ```
   echo 'CREATE DATABASE blameable' | mysql -u root
   ```

3. We now need to configure our application. Open the configuration file and set the necessary database connection parameters of your environment:

   ```
   'database' => [
       'adapter'  => 'Mysql',
       'host'     => 'localhost',
       'username' => 'root',
       'password' => '',
       'dbname'   => 'blameable',
       'charset'  => 'utf8',
   ],
   ```

4. We will also need several tables in our database, as well as sample data in them. Run the following SQL queries in your database:

   ```
   CREATE TABLE 'users' (
     'id' BIGINT UNSIGNED NOT NULL AUTO_INCREMENT,
     'name' VARCHAR(72) NOT NULL,
     'email' VARCHAR(128) NOT NULL,
     PRIMARY KEY ('id')
   ) ENGINE=InnoDB DEFAULT CHARSET=utf8;


   INSERT INTO 'users' ('id', 'name', 'email') VALUES
   (1, 'John Doe', 'john@doe.com');


   CREATE TABLE 'snippets' (
   ```

```
  'id' BIGINT UNSIGNED NOT NULL AUTO_INCREMENT,

  'user_id' BIGINT UNSIGNED NOT NULL,

  'title' VARCHAR(72) NOT NULL,

  'body' LONGTEXT NOT NULL,

  'created_at' TIMESTAMP NOT NULL DEFAULT CURRENT_TIMESTAMP,

  PRIMARY KEY ('id'),

  FOREIGN KEY ('user_id') REFERENCES 'users' ('id') ON DELETE
CASCADE ON UPDATE CASCADE
) ENGINE=InnoDB DEFAULT CHARSET=utf8;


INSERT INTO 'snippets' ('id', 'user_id', 'title', 'body') VALUES
  (1, 1, 'Example', '<?php phpinfo();');


CREATE TABLE 'audits' (
  'id' BIGINT UNSIGNED NOT NULL AUTO_INCREMENT,

  'user_id' BIGINT UNSIGNED NOT NULL,

  'model_name' VARCHAR(32) NOT NULL,

  'ip_address' INT UNSIGNED NOT NULL,

  'type' CHAR(1) NOT NULL,

  'created_at' TIMESTAMP NOT NULL DEFAULT CURRENT_TIMESTAMP,

  PRIMARY KEY ('id')
) ENGINE=InnoDB DEFAULT CHARSET=utf8;


CREATE TABLE 'audit_details' (
  'id' BIGINT UNSIGNED NOT NULL AUTO_INCREMENT,

  'audit_id' BIGINT UNSIGNED NOT NULL,

  'field_name' VARCHAR(32) NOT NULL,

  'old_value' VARCHAR(32) DEFAULT NULL,

  'new_value' VARCHAR(32) NOT NULL,

  PRIMARY KEY ('id'),

  FOREIGN KEY ('audit_id') REFERENCES 'audits' ('id') ON DELETE
CASCADE ON UPDATE CASCADE
) ENGINE=InnoDB DEFAULT CHARSET=utf8;
```

5. The tables are ready. Now you need a controller, views, and a model for the `Snippet` entity. As stated, we will use Phalcon Developer Tools. To generate the required template code, run the following command:

   `phalcon scaffold snippets`

6. Open your browser and go to `http://{your-host-here}/snippets/edit/1` to ensure that everything is configured properly and you are able to see the existing snippets.

7. Additionally, we need a model for users. Create it by running the following command in the Terminal:

   `phalcon model users`

8. Now create two models required for the audit by running the following commands in the Terminal:

   `phalcon model audits`

   `phalcon model audit_details`

9. Open the `Audits` model and add the following two constants into it:

   `const TYPE_CREATE = 'C';`

   `const TYPE_UPDATE = 'U';`

10. After you have created the required models it is time to try the audit. Create the folder `app/library` and add it into the class autoloader, like so:

```
use Phalcon\Loader;

$loader = new Loader();
$loader->registerDirs(
    [
        $config->application->controllersDir,
        $config->application->modelsDir,
        $config->application->libraryDir,
    ]
);
$loader->register();
```

11. Create a new `Behavior` class named `Blameable` in the newly created `library` directory and place the following code there:

```
use Phalcon\Mvc\ModelInterface;
use Phalcon\Mvc\Model\Behavior;
use Phalcon\Mvc\Model\BehaviorInterface;
```

```php
class Blameable extends Behavior implements BehaviorInterface
{
  public function notify($eventType, ModelInterface $model)
  {
    if ($eventType == 'afterUpdate') {
      return $this->auditAfterUpdate($model);
    }

    return null;
  }

  public function auditAfterUpdate(ModelInterface $model)
  {
    $changedFields = $model->getChangedFields();
    $session = $model->getDI()->getSession();

    if (!$session->has('userId')) {
      return null;
    }

    if (count($changedFields)) {
      $audit = new Audits();

      $request = $model->getDI()->getRequest();

      $audit->user_id = $session->get('userId');
      $audit->model_name = get_class($model);
      $audit->ip_address = ip2long(
            $request->getClientAddress()
      );
      $audit->type = Audits::TYPE_UPDATE;

      $audit->save();

      $originalData = $model->getSnapshotData();
      foreach ($changedFields as $field) {
        $auditDetail = new AuditDetails();

        $auditDetail->audit_id = $audit->id;
        $auditDetail->field_name = $field;
        $auditDetail->old_value = $originalData[$field];
        $auditDetail->new_value = $model->$field;
        $auditDetail->save();
      }
```

```
        return true;
    }

    return null;
    }
}
```

12. We now need to change the `Snippets` model slightly, adding the ability to store snapshots of data, as well as to use the newly created `Behavior`. Change the `Snippets` model as follows:

```php
use Phalcon\Mvc\Model;

class Snippets extends Model
{
    public $id;
    public $user_id;
    public $title;
    public $body;
    public $created_at;

    public function initialize()
    {
        $this->belongsTo(
            'user_id',
            'Users',
            'id',
            ['alias' => 'user']
        );
        $this->keepSnapshots(true);
        $this->addBehavior(new Blameable());
    }

    public function getSource()
    {
        return 'snippets';
    }
}
```

13. It is important to note that in your application, you might not always need to check if the user session exists or if the user is authorized. The creation of an authentication mechanism, as well as the logic for checking whether users are authorized to access a particular method or not, is outside the scope of this recipe. We have skipped this step intentionally, adding only such a check as `if (!$session->has('userId'))` in the `Behavior` class. You will need to adjust the code accordingly to fit the needs of your application. To demonstrate a good starting point, we will emulate this functionality by registering the session service in our DI container. Open the `bootstrap` file and add the following code:

```
$di->setShared('session', function () {
    $session = new \Phalcon\Session\Adapter\Files();
    $session->start();

    return $session;
});
```

14. Next, open the `SnippetsController`, find the `saveAction` method, and add the following code before the model saving block, to emulate the user authentication:

```
$this->session->set('userId', 1);
```

15. Now it is time to check how it works. Go to `http://{your-host-here}/snippets/edit/1` again. You will see a form filled with data from the database. Change the existing data and submit the form. Check the `audits` and `audit_details` tables (we use the Terminal and the MySQL command line tools):

```
SELECT * FROM 'audit_details'\G
SELECT * FROM 'audits'\G
```

How it works...

In this recipe, we have learned how to achieve better performance of Phalcon internal classes by extending them with additional features.

First, we created a test application, database tables, and generated the required skeleton code.

Then, we created a `Behavior` to be used with the Phalcon ORM. Each model fires the `afterUpdate` event after saving the data. We subscribed to this event and implemented the audit mechanism. We collect all necessary data using the `Blameable::auditAfterUpdate`, and then we save this data in the database. This recipe cannot be used in a production environment without thoroughly investigating the actual business requirements and optimizing the code. We just used it for demonstrating our recipe. It is also important to note that we use the snapshot mechanism in Phalcon models.

The snapshot mechanism stores the previous value in our database after the update. We need to enable this mechanism in our model's initialize method:

```
$this->keepSnapshots(true)
```

We could also subscribe to other model generated events, in exactly the same manner as explained previously, and implement the relevant `Behavior` for them.

We could potentially create a base `Model` class extending the `Phalcon\Mvc\Model` class, and have all of our models extend that. Should we put our `audit` code in our base model class, we will end up with all of our models implementing the behavior logic for all models, which might not be what we want. Phalcon provides a flexible tool and interface named `Behaviors`, which allows for the delegation of the necessary logic to any number of classes.

Of course, we could create traits and place that logic there. This solution appears more reasonable as compared to inheritance. But it is not perfect, either. In this case, we must take care to ensure that all traits which we include in a certain model will have conflict-free method names. In any case, it is not always convenient.

There's more...

For a more detailed example of **Blameable Behavior**, refer to the component in the Phalcon `Incubator` repository: `https://github.com/phalcon/incubator/tree/master/Library/Phalcon/Mvc/Model/Behavior`

7
Debugging and Profiling

In this chapter, we will cover:

- ▶ Improved exception reporting
- ▶ Logging messages to the browser console
- ▶ Testing routing
- ▶ Handling abnormal terminations in requests
- ▶ Detecting slow queries

Introduction

Phalcon has powerful debugging and profiling tools to help ensure that your application performs correctly and efficiently. The easiest place to start with an improved debugging experience is to set up the Phalcon **Debug** component. This will provide additional information within a pleasantly themed interface detailing the location and circumstances of the error, which makes it an excellent tool for beginners to intermediate Phalcon developers. It is also possible to log messages directly to the Firefox JavaScript console by using the FirePHP logger. This can save a lot of time by not needing to switch between a system shell window and the browser and it will present a nicer interface for inspecting the log messages. Next we set up a test suite for routing to ensure that each route can reach its final destination. We will then create a plugin for handling abnormal termination in our application dispatch cycle and then another plugin for detecting slow queries in our application.

Improved exception reporting

Phalcon includes a powerful debugging component that can make the process a more casual experience. By instantiating this component early in our application bootstrap, we can receive a visual layout of the **backtrace** and other important states. The backtrace is formatted to include the colored source code of every file that was loaded and it will even highlight the specific line that the error occurred on. Additionally, each core Phalcon class that was loaded during execution will be presented with a link to the official Phalcon documentation.

Getting ready

This recipe uses Phalcon Developer Tools, which we will use to set up a project skeleton, and database access is not required.

How to do it...

Follow these steps to complete this recipe:

1. We need to have an application skeleton for experimentation. If you already have such an application, you can skip this step. Create a project skeleton using the `simple` template:

    ```
    phalcon project improved_exception simple
    ```

2. Now point the web browser at the root directory of the project. There should be a page with `Congratulations!` ..... If we see the `Volt directory can't be written` error message, then permissions of the `cache` directory need to be changed to allow the web server to write to it.

3. First we will need to load the debug component and ensure that all exceptions are left uncaught by a `try...catch` block. If **Developer Tools** were used to create the project then open up the `public/index.php` file and simply comment out the `try... catch` code while leaving the remainder as it is. Now just before the `Application` object is instantiated add the following code to enable the debug component:

    ```
    (new \Phalcon\Debug())->listen();
    ```

4. Add a controller, `app/controllers/FailController.php`:

    ```php
    <?php

    class FailController extends \Phalcon\Mvc\Controller
    {
        public function indexAction()
        {
    ```

```
$itemBuilder = $this->modelsManager
    ->createBuilder(1, 2, 3);
    }
}
```

5. In the browser, go to the path `/fail` from the root path of the project. You should see `BadMethodCallException: Wrong number of parameters`.

How it works...

The `Phalcon\Debug` component registers itself to handle all uncaught exceptions in execution. For this reason, we need to make sure that the exceptions are not handled in the program and so fall out at the end of the script. The component is able to step through the execution backtrace to construct the HTML representation of this data. If we look at the source code of the page, we will see that the CSS and JavaScript used to present this output is coming from `static.phalconphp.com`.

If we look at the tabs in the following screenshot, the exception message we will should see; **Backtrace**, **Request**, **Server**, **Included Files** and **Memory**:

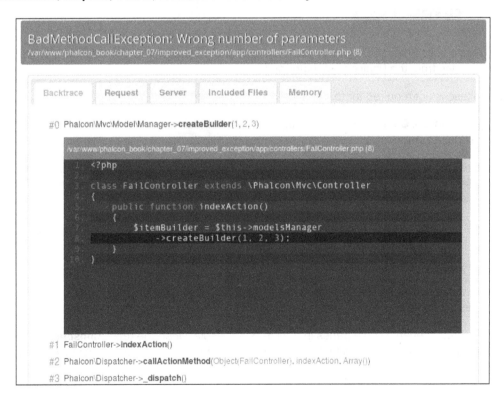

First we'll look at the **Backtrace**. In our example, we should see the stack trace go from **#0** through **#5**. If we look at **#0**, we will see that the component was able to identify that the error took place within an object of type `Phalcon\Mvc\Model\Manager` and so it is able to create a link to the Phalcon documentation there. Then from **#1** through **#4**, we can see the stack trace of each function that was called leading up to this point and finally with step **#5** we are shown the colored source on the `index.php` file. The debug component will show the source of every PHP file along the stack trace.

Next, if we look at **Request** and **Server** we can see the contents of the super globals, `$_REQUEST` and `$_SERVER`. The **Included Files** tab simply lists out all files that were required or included during the program execution. Finally, the **Memory** tab displays the memory used.

Logging server messages to the browser console

In this recipe, we will set up the **Firelogger** extension to send messages from the server to the Firebug JavaScript console.

Getting ready

This recipe uses Phalcon Developer Tools to set up a project skeleton and Composer to install PHP libraries from the Phalcon Incubator project.

A database is not required for this recipe.

We need to install **Composer** for installing the Phalcon Incubator libraries. Get the open source Composer tool at: `https://getcomposer.org/`

In this recipe, we need Firefox with the **Firebug** and Firelogger extensions installed. While using Firefox, open up the following links and click **Add to Firefox** and install, and then restart the browser as needed:

> - **Firebug**: `https://addons.mozilla.org/en-US/firefox/addon/firebug/`
> - **Firelogger**: `https://addons.mozilla.org/en-US/firefox/addon/firelogger/`

Now, with the two Firefox extensions installed, go to any web page and follow the directions given next.

We will need to enable some panes in the Firebug console. Open the tabs—**Console**, **Net** and, **Logger**, and click the **enable** button in each pane to set up the requirements for using Firelogger.

How to do it...

Follow these steps to complete this recipe:

1. We need to have an application skeleton for experimentation. If you already have such an application, you can skip this step. Create a project skeleton using the `simple` template:

   ```
   phalcon project browser_logging simple
   ```

2. Now point the web browser at the root directory of the project. There should be a page with `Congratulations!` ..... If we see the `Volt directory can't be written` error message, then permissions of the `cache` directory need to be changed to allow the web server to write to it.

3. We will need to go to the command line to install the Phalcon **Incubator** libraries. In the Terminal go to the root directory for this recipe and enter the following:

   ```
   composer require phalcon/incubator
   ```

   This will build the `composer.json` file and install the dependencies into the `vendor` directory.

4. We need to add the Composer autoloader our normal *loader* service. Open up `app/config/loader.php` and add the following to the end of the file:

   ```
   include BASE_PATH . '/vendor/autoload.php';
   ```

5. Create the `'logger'` service in your `services.php` file. Note: the class `Phalcon\Logger\Adapter\Firelogger` is being brought in from the `phalcon/incubator` package via the autoloader that we set up:

   ```
   $di->setShared('logger', function () {
       return new Phalcon\Logger\Adapter\Firelogger('debug');
   });
   ```

6. Create `app/controllers/LogController.php` to use the logger:

   ```php
   <?php

   class LogController extends ControllerBase
   {
       public function indexAction()
       {
           $logger = $this->getDI()
               ->getLogger();
   ```

```
$logger->debug('Debug Log');
$logger->log('Normal Log, Same as Debug Log');
$logger->info('Info Log');
$logger->warning('Warning Log');
$logger->error('Error Log');
$logger->critical('Critical Log');

$this->response->appendContent('Check your Firebug Logger
Console for messages.');
$this->response->send();
    }
}
```

7. In the browser, go to path `log`. If the instructions in the **Getting Started** section were followed then we should be able to see the `log` messages in the **Logger** pane of Firebug. If the messages don't appear then try refreshing the browser page while Firebug is open.

How it works...

Now lets look at the ouput of the log messages as they appear in the Firebug console:

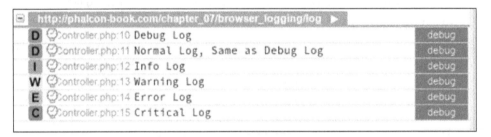

There are two parts to the Firelogger solution—the backend that sends the log messages and the frontend that interprets them. There are several solutions for sending these specially formatted messages to the browser but in our case, the `Phalcon\Logger\Adapter\Firelogger` class from the `phalcon/incubator` package will be doing this for us by sending data encoded in the HTTP response headers. Once they arrive in the browser, the Firelogger extension can be used to display these normally invisible header entries. Firelogger simply leverages the Firebug debugging framework rather than reinventing the wheel. On the far right in purple we see the message `debug`. We defined this fixed message in the `logger` service itself. So it is possible to create multiple logging services with different fixed messages to easily catch our eye.

Next we will notice that there are a total of six different log messages each with their own color coded type on the left.

Creating a route test suite

In this recipe, we will learn how to create a test suite for all of the routes of our application. This is important because it's difficult to check that our controller logic is in fact reachable through the browser URLs. Using this approach, we should be able adapt this routing test suite to any application structure.

Getting ready

This recipe uses Phalcon Developer Tools, which we will use to set up a project skeleton and database access is not required.

How to do it...

Follow these steps to complete this recipe:

1. We need to have an application skeleton for experimentation. If you already have such an application, you can skip this step. Create a project skeleton using the `simple` template:

   ```
   phalcon project route_testing simple
   ```

2. Now point the web browser at the root directory of the project. There should be a page with `Congratulations!` ..... If we see the `Volt directory can't be written` error message, then permissions of the `cache` directory need to be changed to allow the web server to write to it.

3. Create our custom routes setup at `app/config/routes.php`:

   ```php
   <?php

   $router->add('/index([0-9]+)', [
       'controller' => 'index',
       'action'     => 'index'
   ]);

   $router->add('/signin', [
       'controller' => 'session',
       'action'     => 'signin'
   ]);
   ```

4. Add a `router` service to override the default router service that is automatically set up with the factory default dependency injector:

```php
$di->setShared('router', function() {
    $router = new Phalcon\Mvc\Router();

    // Fetch custom routes
    include(APP_PATH . '/config/routes.php');

    return $router;
});
```

5. Add the controller, `app/controllers/SessionController.php`:

```php
<?php

class SessionController extends Phalcon\Mvc\Controller
{
    public function indexAction()
    {
    }

    public function signinAction()
    {
    }

    public function signoutAction()
    {
    }
}
```

6. Add the controller `app/controllers/TestController.php`:

```php
<?php

class TestController extends ControllerBase
{
    public function indexAction()
    {
        $routes = [
            '/index'            => ['index', 'index'],
            '/index12123'       => ['index', 'index'],
            '/index/index'      => ['index', 'index'],
            '/about'            => ['about', 'index'],
```

```
            '/signin'              => ['session', 'signin'],
            '/session/signin'      => ['session', 'signin'],
            '/session/signin/abc'  => ['session', 'signin'],
            '/session/nonsense'    => ['session', 'nonsense'],
            '/session'             => ['session', 'index'],
    ];

    // We will create another router to not interfere with the
normal one.
    $router = new Phalcon\Mvc\Router();

    // Then we will load the application routes onto our new
router so that we can test.
    include(APP_PATH . '/config/routes.php');

    // Testing each route
    foreach ($routes as $route => $destination) {
        list($intendedControllerName, $intendedActionName) =
$destination;

        // Handle the route
        $router->handle($route);

        $this->response->appendContent('Testing ' . $route .
'<br>');

        // Check if some route was matched
        if (!$router->wasMatched()) {
            $this->response->appendContent('The route wasn\'t
matched by any route<br><br>');
            continue;
        }

        $controllerName = $router->getControllerName();
        $actionName = (empty($router->getActionName())) ?
'index' : $router->getActionName();
        if ($controllerName != $intendedControllerName) {
            $this->response->appendContent("Controller
'$controllerName' does not match intended
'$intendedControllerName'" . '<br<br>');
            continue;
        }
```

```
            if ($actionName != $intendedActionName) {
                $this->response->appendContent("Action
'$actionName' does not match intended '$intendedActionName'" .
'<br><br>');
                continue;
            }

            $controllerClass = ucfirst($controllerName) .
'Controller';
            $actionMethod = $actionName . 'Action';
            if (!class_exists($controllerClass, true)) {
                $this->response->appendContent("Controller
'$controllerClass' could not be found.<br><br>");
                continue;
            }
            if (!is_callable([$controllerClass, $actionMethod])) {
                $this->response->appendContent("Method
'$actionMethod' is not callable from '$controllerClass'<br><br>");
                continue;
            }

            $this->response->appendContent("$controllerClass::$act
ionMethod<br><br>");
        }

        $this->response->send();
    }
}
```

7. In the browser, go to the path /test off the base path of the project. You should see a printout of all of the routes and their status if they could be properly reached.

How it works...

In app/config/routes.php, we defined some custom routes for our router. The first route, /index([0-9]+), is a bit silly and this simply allows the route to start with index and to then any number of digits after that. The second route, /signin, is a shortcut for session/signin. This allows us to create a clean sign in URL.

In our services definition file, we added a custom router service that attaches the routes setup in our custom routes.php file. Due to our usage of Phalcon\Di\FactoryDefault as our dependency injector, we don't need to set up a router for the most basic default routing, but for this project, we want to add custom routes, and so we override the default service with our new service.

In our `SessionController`, we have merely created three skeleton methods for the actions that we want to test. It is not necessary to test actual sign in code because that is really a completely different test and the test suite that we created in `TestController` is able to simply test that the final route destination exists.

Now we will look at the real meat of the recipe in our `TestController`. If we look at the `$routes` variable, we will see a listing of various routes and their final controller and action destination. By using this structure, we can virtually test all of our routes from start to finish. There might very well be extra conditions in place that are untestable with this approach, such as URL rewriting performed by the web server. If we assume that part of our setup is working correctly then we can get far with our approach.

With the following two lines, we will create a new `Router` and attach the normal routes to it. We are doing it this way so that we don't pollute our essential router service:

```
$router = new Phalcon\Mvc\Router();
include(APP_PATH . '/config/routes.php');
```

Now we are ready to run the loop on our routes structure. First we save the intended destination controller and action name, and then we run the `route` through the router to see how it interprets it:

```
foreach ($routes as $route => $destination) {
    list($intendedControllerName, $intendedActionName) = $destination;

    $router->handle($route);
```

We check to see if the `router` was unable to make any sense out of the `route`:

```
if (!$router->wasMatched()) {
    $this->response->appendContent('The route wasn\'t matched by any
route<br><br>');
    continue;
}
```

Now that we know the router was able to match the route to a controller and action name we check that the intended and real destinations match:

```
$controllerName = $router->getControllerName();
$actionName = (empty($router->getActionName())) ? 'index' : $router-
>getActionName();

if ($controllerName != $intendedControllerName) {
    $this->response->appendContent("Controller '$controllerName' does
not match intended '$intendedControllerName'" . '<br<br>');
```

```
        continue;
    }
    if ($actionName != $intendedActionName) {
        $this->response->appendContent("Action '$actionName' does not
    match intended '$intendedActionName'" . '<br><br>');
        continue;
    }
```

We build the actual `Controller` class name and `Action` method name that will be called during a normal `Phalcon\Mvc\Dispatcher` cycle:

```
    $controllerClass = ucfirst($controllerName) . 'Controller';
    $actionMethod = $actionName . 'Action';
```

We will check to see that the class exists. We pass in a true value for the second argument on `class_exists` to have it try to load the class using the autoloader:

```
    if (!class_exists($controllerClass, true)) {
        $this->response->appendContent("Controller '$controllerClass'
    could not be found.<br><br>");
        continue;
    }
```

Finally, we test that the `action` method is callable on the actual controller class. This allows us to finally determine if the route can reach its intended destination:

```
    if (!is_callable([$controllerClass, $actionMethod])) {
        $this->response->appendContent("Method '$actionMethod' is not
    callable from '$controllerClass'<br><br>");
        continue;
    }
```

Handling abnormal terminations

It is essential that applications have a means of handling abnormal conditions without hard crashing. In this recipe, we will create a dispatcher plugin that will handle two specific types of exceptional behavior. The first one will allow us to handle HTTP 404 conditions, and the second will allow us to catch any exception that occurs in the dispatcher cycle and display a specific page notifying that an error has occurred. So, by adding this functionality, we will prevent our users from seeing a white screen of death.

Getting ready

This recipe uses Phalcon Developer Tools which we will use to set up a project skeleton and database access is not required.

How to do it...

Follow these steps to complete this recipe:

1. We need to have an application skeleton for experimentation. If you already have such an application, you can skip this step. Create a project skeleton using the `simple` template:

   ```
   phalcon project abnormal_termination simple
   ```

2. Now point the web browser at the root directory of the project. There should be a page with `Congratulations!` ..... If we see the `Volt directory can't be written` error message, then permissions of the `cache` directory need to be changed to allow the web server to write to it.

3. Open up the `app/config/loader.php` file and register the plugins directory by adding `$config->application->pluginsDir` to the `registerDir` call.

4. Add a custom override `dispatcher` service in `app/config/services.php`:

   ```php
   $di->setShared('dispatcher', function() {
       $eventsManager = $this->getEventsManager();

       $exceptionPlugin = new DispatcherExceptionPlugin();
       $exceptionPlugin->setDI($this);
       $eventsManager->attach('dispatch', $exceptionPlugin);

       $dispatcher = new Phalcon\Mvc\Dispatcher();
       $dispatcher->setEventsManager($eventsManager);

       return $dispatcher;
   });
   ```

5. Add the dispatcher plugin to handle exceptions at `app/plugins/DispatcherExceptionPlugin.php`:

   ```php
   <?php

   class DispatcherExceptionPlugin extends Phalcon\Mvc\User\Plugin
   {
       public function beforeException(Phalcon\Events\Event $event,
   Phalcon\Mvc\Dispatcher $dispatcher, $exception)
       {
           //Handle 404 exceptions
           if ($exception instanceof Phalcon\Mvc\Dispatcher\
   Exception) {
   ```

```
            switch ($exception->getCode()) {
                case Phalcon\Mvc\Dispatcher::EXCEPTION_HANDLER_
NOT_FOUND:

                case Phalcon\Mvc\Dispatcher::EXCEPTION_ACTION_NOT_
FOUND:

                    $dispatcher->forward([
                        'controller' => 'errors',
                        'action' => 'show404'
                    ]);
                    break;
            }
        } else {
            $dispatcher->forward([
                'controller' => 'errors',
                'action' => 'exception'
            ]);
        }

        return false;
    }
}
```

6. Add the controller, `app/controllers/ErrorsController.php`:

```php
<?php

class ErrorsController extends ControllerBase
{
    public function show404Action()
    {
        return '404 Message';
    }

    public function exceptionAction()
    {
        $this->response
            ->appendContent('There was an error processing the
request.')
            ->send();
    }
}
```

7. Add the controller, `app/controllers/OopsController.php`:

```php
<?php

class OopsController extends ControllerBase
{

    public function indexAction()
    {
        throw new Exception('Ooops');
    }
}
```

8. In the browser, go to the path, `/nonsense`, off of the base path of the project. You should see `404 Message`.

9. In the browser, go to the path `/oops`. You should see *There was an error processing the request*.

How it works...

The dispatcher service triggers many events during its normal execution cycle. We can attach plugins to catch the events to change the default behavior to meet the needs of our program. In this recipe, we are handling exceptions by attaching to the `beforeException` event. We are able to handle the exceptions in this very convenient way because the dispatcher is able to internally catch exceptions using a normal `try/catch` block, and then generate a `beforeException` event, which passes along that exception as one of the parameters of the event.

Let's first jump right into the `DispatcherExceptionPlugin`, since it is easy to understand on its own. Then we will go through the controllers that we have designed to interact and trigger this plugin behavior and then finally how we created our custom dispatcher service.

We create the `DispatcherExceptionPlugin` by inheriting from the `Phalcon\Mvc\User\Plugin` class. It really doesn't matter what we call our plugin:

```php
class DispatcherExceptionPlugin extends Phalcon\Mvc\User\Plugin
{
```

Next we create a `beforeException` function since the name of the event is `beforeException`:

```php
public function beforeException(Phalcon\Events\Event $event, Phalcon\
Mvc\Dispatcher $dispatcher, $exception)
{
```

The first thing that we will check for is whether the exception was specifically created from within the dispatcher itself due to it not being able to either find the controller class or the `action` method on the controller. If this is the case, we will forward to `ErrorsController` and the `show404Action` method. Note that since an unhandled exception has occurred in all cases, we are putting a single `return false;` at the end of the method rather than for each case.

```php
if ($exception instanceof Phalcon\Mvc\Dispatcher\Exception) {
    switch ($exception->getCode()) {
        case Phalcon\Mvc\Dispatcher::EXCEPTION_HANDLER_NOT_FOUND:
        case Phalcon\Mvc\Dispatcher::EXCEPTION_ACTION_NOT_FOUND:
            $dispatcher->forward([
                'controller' => 'errors',
                'action' => 'show404'
            ]);
            break;
    }
```

If the exception was not of a routing nature then we will redirect to the more generic `exceptionAction` to display an error message about the program execution:

```php
} else {
    $dispatcher->forward([
        'controller' => 'errors',
        'action' => 'exception'
    ]);
}

return false;
```

We will now look at the `ErrorsController`. This controller is critical to our exceptions plugin since on exceptional behavior, we are forwarding to actions on this controller. It's really very simple and each action just outputs some text.

Now we will create a controller whose sole purpose is to trigger an exception that will be caught in the `else` block of our exceptions plugin. The `OopsController` simply throws an exception:

```php
<?php
class OopsController extends Phalcon\Mvc\Controller
{
    public function indexAction()
    {
```

```
        throw new Exception('Ooops');
    }
}
```

By going to the path /oops, we trigger this behavior and we can test out our
ErrorsController::exceptionAction method.

When we go to /nonsense it is a route that does not correspond to an existing controller
action and so the first part of our exceptions plugin is executed.

Finally, we set up all of this behavior in our dispatcher service by overriding the default
Phalcon\Di\FactoryDefault defined service with our own custom service.

We access the existing eventsManager service since we don't need to create a new one:

```
$di->setShared('dispatcher', function() {
    $eventsManager = $this->getEventsManager();
```

Next we create the dispatcher plugin and set its DI to $this, since each service function
is bound to the DI object itself and then we attach the dispatcher to the eventsManager
object:

```
$exceptionPlugin = new DispatcherExceptionPlugin();
$exceptionPlugin->setDI($this);
$eventsManager->attach('dispatch', $exceptionPlugin);
```

Finally, we complete the circle by creating a dispatcher and attach the events manager to the
dispatcher and then, like all services, we return the intended object:

```
    $dispatcher = new Phalcon\Mvc\Dispatcher();
    $dispatcher->setEventsManager($eventsManager);
    return $dispatcher;
});
```

With this approach, we can create any number of dispatcher plugins for any event. Also, keep
in mind that we can attach plugins to dispatcher events anywhere, and not just in the service
definition. For example, if a base controller is used for all controllers then this can be added
to the initialize method of the base controller and it will always execute. It can also be
added to a module definition in a multi-module application as well. Really, it is open ended
and you will need to decide what is the best bit. There is more than one way to accomplish
a goal and so it is up to you to decide the approach.

Detecting slow queries

As an application grows, its SQL queries can become quite complex and so slow that the entire application suffers. Without a clear path toward discovering the slowdown we would be in a difficult spot. This recipe will give us the tools to detect these exceptionally slow queries so that we can begin to develop optimizations or redesigns. Additionally, this will have a pleasant side effect of illustrating some nice details about how the Phalcon **ORM (Object Relational Model)** works by showing us all of the queries that are performed to set up this powerful functionality. Lastly, being able to see the metrics of these queries will give us ideas and entice us to think about how it can be further optimized with query caching.

Getting ready

This recipe uses Phalcon Developer Tools for setting up a project skeleton and a configured database connection for demonstrating the fast queries that are performed when setting up the ORM, as well as the synthetic slow queries that we need to demonstrate a slow query.

How to do it...

Follow these steps to complete this recipe:

1. We need to have an application skeleton for experimentation. If you already have such an application, you can skip this step. Create a project skeleton using the `simple` template:

   ```
   phalcon project slow_queries simple
   ```

2. Now point the web browser at the root directory of the project. There should be a page with `Congratulations! .....` If we see the `Volt directory can't be written` error message then permissions of the `cache` directory need to be changed to allow the web server to write to it.

3. Create a database `slow_queries`:

   ```
   DROP TABLE IF EXISTS 'items';
   CREATE TABLE 'items' (
     'id' int(11) NOT NULL AUTO_INCREMENT,
     'name' varchar(20) NOT NULL,
     PRIMARY KEY ('id')
   ) ENGINE=InnoDB AUTO_INCREMENT=5 DEFAULT CHARSET=utf8;
   INSERT INTO 'items' VALUES (1,'apple'),(2,'car'),(3,'notebook'),(4
   ,'stereo');
   ```

4. Add the model, `app/models/Items.php`:

```php
<?php

class Items extends Phalcon\Mvc\Model
{
}
```

5. Add the following option to the database section of the configuration located at `app/config/config.php`:

```php
'slow_query_time' => 0.1,
```

6. We will be creating a plugin, so set the loader service to load classes from the `app/plugins` directory by adding `$config->application->pluginsDir` to the `registerDirs` call. In the developer tools simple template, this is located in the `app/config/loader.php` directory.

7. Update our db service in the file `app/config/services.php` to use the `SlowQueryPlugin`:

```php
$di->setShared('db', function () {
    // ….

    $connection = new $class([
        // ...
    ]);

    $slowQueryPlugin = new SlowQueryPlugin();
    $slowQueryPlugin->setDI($this);

    $eventsManager = $this->getEventsManager();
    $eventsManager->attach('db', $slowQueryPlugin);
    $connection->setEventsManager($eventsManager);

    return $connection;
});
```

8. Add our slow query detection plugin at `app/plugins/SlowQueryPlugin.php`:

```php
<?php

class SlowQueryPlugin extends Phalcon\Mvc\User\Plugin
{
    public function __construct()
    {
```

```php
        $this->profiler = new Phalcon\Db\Profiler();
    }

    public function beforeQuery($event, $connection)
    {
        $this->profiler->startProfile(
            $connection->getRealSQLStatement(),
            $connection->getSQLVariables(),
            $connection->getSQLBindTypes()
        );
    }

    public function afterQuery($event, $connection)
    {
        $config = $this->getDI()
            ->getConfig();

        $this->profiler->stopProfile();
        $profile = $this->profiler->getLastProfile();

        $sql = $profile->getSQLStatement();
        $totalElapsedSeconds = $profile->getTotalElapsedSeconds();

        if ($totalElapsedSeconds > $config->database->slow_query_
time) {
            error_log("Slow query: '$sql' at $totalElapsedSeconds
seconds.");
        } else {
            error_log("Normal query: '$sql' at
$totalElapsedSeconds seconds.");
        }
    }
}
```

9. Add the controller, `app/controllers/QueriesController.php`:

```php
<?php

class QueriesController extends Phalcon\Mvc\Controller
{
    public function indexAction()
    {
        $db = $this->getDI()
```

```
        ->getDb();

        // This query is very fast
        $db->query('SELECT 1+2+3');

        // This query is slow
        $db->query('SELECT SLEEP(1)');

        // This query is slow
        $db->query('SELECT SLEEP(2)');

        // This query will perform several small queries to access
the models meta data.
        $items = Items::find();

        $this->response->appendContent('Check web server error log
for messages.');
        $this->response->send();
    }
}
```

10. In the browser, go to the path, /queries, off of the root path of the project. After about three seconds we should see the message **Check web server error log for messages**. Now find out where the web server error logs are located and open them up. If we are on a Unix type of system, such as OSX or Linux then we can use the command `tail -f YOUR_LOG_PATH_HERE` in the Terminal to receive a scrolling view of any new entries rather than needing to reopen the file after any changes. Note—replace `YOUR_LOG_PATH_HERE` with the actual path of the log file, as this will vary from system to system. In a typical system, the Apache error log file should be located at the path, `/var/log/apache/error.log`, on a Linux system, and on WAMP for Windows it should be at `C:\wamp\logs\error.log`.

How it works...

By using a Phalcon connection service we gain many benefits over the vanilla PDO database access. In this recipe, we have taken advantage of the `beforeQuery` and `afterQuery` events to easily splice additional functionality into our database service by adding a `Phalcon\Mvc\User\Plugin` object to intercept these two events. We will record some initial state in the `beforeQuery` event and then we close this out in the `afterQuery` event. Then, in our `QueriesController`, we run three explicit queries, one of which is considered *fast* and two that are considered *slow*. Then we run a sort of `meta` query with the static `Phalcon\Mvc\Model::find` method (using the `Items` model) that first obtains the model's metadata for the `Items` model and then finally retrieves the item's records from the database.

Note that all of these models' metadata queries are extremely fast. In fact, to simulate some *slow* queries we had to actually tell the database to go to sleep for a few seconds. So unless your application grows very large or there is an improperly formed SQL statement, then all of the queries should be lightning fast to the range of very small fractions of a second.

Now let's look at the source code.

Let's look at our `db` service setup. We'll skip ahead through the first several lines of the typical setup to talk about how we enable our `SlowQueryPlugin`.

First we create the plugin and then attach the active dependency injector, `$this`, to the plugin. This is a standard way to add a DI to a `Phalcon\Mvc\User\Plugin` object or any object that extends from `Phalcon\Di\Injectable`:

```
$slowQueryPlugin = new SlowQueryPlugin();
$slowQueryPlugin->setDI($this);
```

Next we do the usual sequence of adding the plugin to the events manager and then the events manager to the plugin:

```
$eventsManager = $this->getEventsManager();
$eventsManager->attach('db', $slowQueryPlugin);
$db->setEventsManager($eventsManager);
```

At this point, we have a configured `SlowQueryPlugin` so now let's investigate what it does.

Here we are creating and saving a `Phalcon\Db\Profiler` object that we will later use in the events to record information about each database query:

```php
<?php

class SlowQueryPlugin extends Phalcon\Mvc\User\Plugin
{
    public function __construct()
    {
        $this->profiler = new Phalcon\Db\Profiler();
    }
```

The `beforeQuery` event is fired at the point when we know all of the information that will go into the final query, such as the variables and the bind types. If we want, we can get at this information but we'll be saving that for another recipe:

```php
public function beforeQuery($event, $connection)
{
    $this->profiler->startProfile(
        $connection->getRealSQLStatement(),
```

```
        $connection->getSQLVariables(),
        $connection->getSQLBindTypes()
    );
}
```

Now we will look at the interesting part of the plugin in the `afterQuery` event.

First we get the `config` service at the very beginning of the function. This is merely a nice stylistic approach that, if done for all services in the function, will allow us to quickly review which service dependencies are required:

```
public function afterQuery($event, $connection)
{
    $config = $this->getDI()
        ->getConfig();
```

Next we stop the current profile and then save access to it. The `profiler` stores all of the recorded profiles and it can be iterated upon, but for our use, we only need access to the current one:

```
$this->profiler->stopProfile();
$profile = $this->profiler->getLastProfile();
```

Next we access a few of the recorded values from the profile that we will use in the error log:

```
$sql = $profile->getSQLStatement();
$totalElapsedSeconds = $profile->getTotalElapsedSeconds();
```

Finally, we compare the total time of the query against our cutoff time that we used in our main configuration. It is highly recommended to store settings such as this in the configuration service instead of hardcoding the value into the plugin. Next we log the query SQL and the elapsed time on both cases of both a *slow* and *fast* query:

```
if ($totalElapsedSeconds > $config->database->slow_query_time) {
    error_log("Slow query: '$sql' at $totalElapsedSeconds seconds.");
} else {
    error_log("Normal query: '$sql' at $totalElapsedSeconds
seconds.");
}
```

Now let's look at our `QueriesController` where we perform queries to trigger our `SlowQueryPlugin`.

Our first query is a very simple one, which the database can perform almost instantly. On my development platform, I get a time of 0.00033092498779297 seconds. Fast!

```
$db->query('SELECT 1+2+3');
```

The following two queries are painfully slow. They don't really do anything except for sleeping but our profiler doesn't know that. On my platform, I recorded times of 1.0016000270844 and 2.0019800662994 seconds. There is a small time overhead there due to PHP and Phalcon but that is to be expected. Slow!!!

```
$db->query('SELECT SLEEP(1)');
$db->query('SELECT SLEEP(2)');
```

Finally, for the last operation, we will be doing something that is much more realistic for a normal use case. Here, we simply use some core `Phalcon\Mvc\Model` functionality to retrieve a `Phalcon\Mvc\Model\Resultset\Simple` that contains all of the Items records:

```
$items = Items::find();
```

While looking at the log, we can see that in order to perform this single query we will first need to perform two other queries to obtain the necessary metadata for the `Items` model. This is typical of an ORM, and it's well worth the small overhead to obtain all of the great features that it provides. Well, without using an existing ORM, developers eventually find that they are recreating the wheel, and they end up creating their own in-house one that is inferior and is a waste of time.

As covered in another recipe, we could use a metadata cache service to greatly reduce the cost of doing these queries on each execution of the script. Two easy metadata adapters to use are `Phalcon\Mvc\Model\MetaData\Files` and `Phalcon\Mvc\Model\MetaData\Apc`.

Now let's look at the logs for evaluations of the queries performed:

- `SELECT IF(COUNT(*) > 0, 1, 0) FROM 'INFORMATION_ SCHEMA'.'TABLES' WHERE 'TABLE_NAME' = 'items' AND 'TABLE_ SCHEMA' = DATABASE()`

- `DESCRIBE 'items'`

- `SELECT 'items'.'id', 'items'.'name' FROM 'items'`

- `Adding up to 0.0026521682739 = 0.00079512596130371 + 0.0016450881958008 + 0.00021195411682129`

It's really fast!

Remember—If a model metadata cache is used such as `Phalcon\Mvc\Model\MetaData\ Files` then the first two queries will not be performed as the metadata cache will be retrieved from storage.

So, already it is becoming obvious that while these queries are fast that there is still opportunity for optimization here. Later we will learn how to cache the first two queries required to build the necessary meta data for a model. While this time saving may not add up to significant amounts of time for a single user, it can become quite a large deal for systems with thousands of users. Now we have the tools to understand and measure these quantities we will defer the solution to a later recipe.

Finally, it is important to note that is fairly difficult to create natural queries that are actually *slow* as we have defined it, and in all likelihood, if this is occurring then it probably will be the result of a SQL join between multiple tables or with a server that is out of memory, or some other, more serious issue.

8
Fine Tuning and Optimizing

In this chapter, we will cover:

- ▶ Handling a database timeout
- ▶ Precompiling Volt templates for increased performance and security
- ▶ Optimizing PHQL queries
- ▶ Caching model metadata and query results for faster performance

Introduction

In this chapter, we will cover some advanced techniques for improving the reliability and scaling of our Phalcon application. We will create a database timeout plugin that will ensure that our long-running processes are able to continue functioning even after exceeding the database connection timeout duration. This will allow us to use Phalcon for long running CLI scripts. Then we will create a multi-module system that uses the CLI environment to first precompile our `Volt` templates to increase performance in our web environment as well as increasing security, by making the `cache` directory read-only for the web server. We will then optimize our PHQL queries by demonstrating three successively faster query implementations and the specific differences between them. Finally, we will use the APC extension to cache model metadata and specific query results to persist beyond the execution of a single process and dramatically speed up our application in the process.

Handling a database timeout

Long running server processes that are accessing the database will run into connection timeout errors if the period of inactivity on the connection is longer than the setting in the database. Although this is typically only an issue with a command line script, in this script we will use a normal MVC web application. We will first demonstrate the issue by allowing the database connection to timeout due to inactivity and then next we will create a solution to this.

Getting ready

This recipe uses the **Phalcon Developer Tools**, which we will use to set up a project skeleton. We will need a database to test our reconnection plugin.

How to do it...

Follow these steps to complete this recipe:

1. We need to have an application skeleton for experimentation. If you already have such an application, you can skip this step. Create a project skeleton using the `simple` template:

   ```
   phalcon project reconnect simple
   ```

2. Now point the web browser at the root directory of the project. There should be a page with `Congratulations!` ..... If we see the `Volt directory can't be written` error message, then the permissions of the `cache` directory need to be changed to allow the web server to write to it.

3. Open up the `app/config/loader.php` file and register the `plugins` directory by adding `$config->application->pluginsDir` to the `registerDirs` command.

4. Create the database, `reconnect`:

   ```
   DROP TABLE IF EXISTS 'records';
   CREATE TABLE 'records' (
     'id' int(11) NOT NULL AUTO_INCREMENT,
     'name' varchar(10) NOT NULL,
     PRIMARY KEY ('id')
   ) ENGINE=InnoDB AUTO_INCREMENT=6 DEFAULT CHARSET=utf8mb4;
   INSERT INTO 'records' VALUES (1,'stuff'),(2,'things'),(3,'John'),(
   4,'cars'),(5,'anything');
   ```

5. We will need to increase the connection wait timeout so open up the `Mysql/MariaDB` configuration file and add the setting `wait_timeout = 5` under the `[mysld]` section. If the `wait_timeout` option already exists then comment that line out and add in our new value. Don't forget to restart the database server:

```
[mysqld]
… # other settings
wait_timeout = 5
```

6. Create the model, `app/models/Records.php`:

```php
<?php

class Records extends Phalcon\Mvc\Model
{
}
```

7. Add the following inside `db` service in the file, `app/config/services.php`, right after the connection object is created:

```php
if (defined('RECONNECT_AFTER_TIMEOUT')) {
    $eventsManager = new Phalcon\Events\Manager();

    $reconnectPlugin = new ReconnectPlugin();
    $reconnectPlugin->initializeConnection($connection);
    $eventsManager->attach('db', $reconnectPlugin);

    //Assign the eventsManager to the db adapter instance
    $connection->setEventsManager($eventsManager);
}
```

8. Create the the reconnect plugin, `app/plugins/ReconnectPlugin.php`:

```php
<?php

class ReconnectPlugin extends Phalcon\Mvc\User\Plugin
{

    public function initializeConnection($connection)
    {
        // Make sure that the query cache is off.
        $connection->query('SET QUERY_CACHE_TYPE = OFF;');

        // Ask the database how many seconds the timeout is set at
        $result = $connection
```

```
                    ->query("SHOW VARIABLES LIKE 'wait_timeout'")
                    ->fetchArray();

            $timeout = (int) $result['Value'];
            if ($timeout > 5) {
                error_log('Hey! We need to set the timeout to five
seconds so that we can test the timeout reconnect.');
            }
            $connection->timeout = $timeout;

            // Set the connection start time and the timeout duration
            $connection->start = time();
        }

    public function beforeQuery(Phalcon\Events\Event $event,
$connection)
        {
            // We want to return if we are running our test
calculation query.
            if ($connection->getSQLStatement() == 'SELECT 0-1-2-3') {
                return;
            }

            // If the connection duration is past the timeout amount
then we will reconnect.
            $activeTimeout = time() - $connection->start;
            if ($activeTimeout > $connection->timeout) {
                error_log("First attempt to reconnect.");
                $connection->connect();
                $connection->start = time();
            }

            try {
                // We'll issue a simply query that doesn't require any
data.
                $result = $connection
                    ->query('SELECT 0-1-2-3')
                    ->fetch();

                // If the result is not correct then we will try to
reconnect again.
```

```php
            if ($result[0] != -6) {
                error_log("Second attempt to reconnect.");
                $connection->connect();
            }
        } catch (\PDOException $e) {

            // If this was unsuccessful then we will try one last
    time to reconnect.
            error_log("Third attempt to reconnect.");
            $connection->connect();
        }
    }
}
```

9. Create the controller, `app/controllers/TimeoutController.php`:

```php
<?php

class TimeoutController extends Phalcon\Mvc\Controller
{
    public function indexAction()
    {
        $this->test();

        $this->response->send();
    }

    public function reconnectAction()
    {
        define('RECONNECT_AFTER_TIMEOUT', true);

        $this->test();

        $this->response->send();
    }

    protected function test()
    {
        try {
            Records::count();

            sleep(6);
```

```
                Records::count();
            } catch (\Exception $e) {
                $this->response->appendContent('<br><p>The reconnect
failed.<br></p>');
                $this->response->appendContent('<p>' .
$e->getMessage() . '</p>');
                return;
            }

            $this->response->appendContent('The timeout reconnection
succeeded.');
        }
    }
```

10. In the browser, go to the following pages:

    ❑ `/timeout`: We will need to wait six seconds and then we should see some error and warning messages along with `The reconnect failed`. If it does not say this then it's likely that the timeout value wasn't properly set in the database server or it was not restarted.

    ❑ `/timeout/reconnect`: We will need to wait six seconds and then we should see a success message `The timeout reconnection succeeded`.

How it works...

In the Mysql configuration there is a setting named `wait_timeout` that determines the number of seconds during which a database server will hold on to an active connection before breaking it. Typically this is set at al value between 300-600 seconds. Our first inclination might be to simply set this value to a much higher value but then we are not actually solving the eventual timeout on a long running CLI script. In this recipe, we set the timeout to a very low value of 5 seconds so that we can test the timeout without needing to wait an absurdly large amount of time.

In our `db` service, we attached our reconnect plugin to the database connection. Then we check to see if the `RECONNECT_AFTER_TIMEOUT` constant is set before adding our plugin. It is not recommended to use this approach in production code as we are only using it here to allow us to test the system with and without the plugin:

```
if (defined('RECONNECT_AFTER_TIMEOUT')) {
    // ...
}
```

Now we perform a typical plugin setup by creating an event manager (or using the default DI one), creating the plugin object, attaching it to the events manager, and then finally calling the `setEventsManager` method on the object that we wish to listen to events on:

```
$eventsManager = new Phalcon\Events\Manager();

$reconnectPlugin = new ReconnectPlugin();
$reconnectPlugin->initializeConnection($connection);
$eventsManager->attach('db', $reconnectPlugin);

//Assign the eventsManager to the db adapter instance
$connection->setEventsManager($eventsManager);
}
```

However, there is one non-typical line here that we must call to allow the reconnect plugin to set up the database connection as follows:

```
$reconnectPlugin->initializeConnection($connection);
```

Now, for the moment, we'll ignore the `ReconnectPlugin` implementation details to see how this plugin will effect our controller code in the `TimeoutController` class.

The first `indexAction` is designed to show how the system will fail without the `ReconnectPlugin`. Take a look at the following code:

```
public function indexAction()
{
    $this->test();

    $this->response->send();
}
```

When we look inside the `test` method we see a simple way to test the timeout. Since we set the MySQL server timeout to only 5 seconds, we can trigger the timeout by simply waiting 6 seconds between our database queries. The following bit of code will trigger warnings and errors:

```
Records::count();
sleep(6);
Records::count();
```

In the `reconnectAction` method, we set the `RECONNECT_AFTER_TIMEOUT` constant so that `ReconnectPlugin` is added to the connection before we call our database queries. This should succeed by reconnecting after the timeout. Take a look at the following screenshot:

```
define('RECONNECT_AFTER_TIMEOUT', true);

$this->test();
```

Finally, we will look at the `ReconnectPlugin` itself. We'll first need to disable the query cache just in case it is on. Take a look at the following code:

```
public function initializeConnection($connection)
{
    // Make sure that the query cache is off.
    $connection->query('SET QUERY_CACHE_TYPE = OFF;');
```

Next we will retrieve the `wait_timeout` value from the database itself rather than assuming the value. We wait six seconds in our controller code and so we need the real timeout value to be less than this amount. Take a look at the following code snippet:

```
    // Ask the database how many seconds the timeout is set at
    $result = $connection
        ->query("SHOW VARIABLES LIKE 'wait_timeout'")
        ->fetchArray();

    $timeout = (int) $result['Value'];
    if ($timeout > 5) {
        error_log('Hey! We need to set the timeout to five seconds so
that we can test the timeout reconnect.');
    }
    $connection->timeout = $timeout;
Finally, we record the starting time by saving it to the connection
object itself.
    // Set the connection start time and the timeout duration
    $connection->start = time();
}
```

In the `beforeQuery` event, we first check to see if we can ignore our test query by checking to see if it is `'SELECT 0-1-2-3'`:

```
public function beforeQuery(Phalcon\Events\Event $event, $connection)
{
```

```
        // We want to return if we are running our test calculation query.
        if ($connection->getSQLStatement() == 'SELECT 0-1-2-3') {
            return;
        }
```

Next we attempt to reconnect if the known timeout duration has been exceeded:

```
        // If the connection duration is past the timeout amount then we
    will reconnect.
        $activeTimeout = time() - $connection->start;
        if ($activeTimeout > $connection->timeout) {
            error_log("First attempt to reconnect.");
            $connection->connect();
            $connection->start = time();
        }
```

Next we will perform a simple query to perform the calculation 0 - 1 - 2 - 3 to see if the database connection is still active. Since this query works only with constants then the database server can process it without accessing any table data. If the result does not equal -6 then we will reconnect again to be sure. Take a look at the following code snippet:

```
        try {
            // We'll issue a simply query that doesn't require any data.
            $result = $connection
                ->query('SELECT 0-1-2-3')
                ->fetch();

            // If the result is not correct then we will try to reconnect
    again.
            if ($result[0] != -6) {
                error_log("Second attempt to reconnect.");
                $connection->connect();
            }
        } catch (\PDOException $e) {

            // If this was unsuccessful then we will try one last time to
    reconnect.
            error_log("Third attempt to reconnect.");
            $connection->connect();
        }
    }
```

Be sure to investigate the web server error log file to see when the connection is timing out. Also be sure to restore the timeout setting to something much more normal.

Precompiling Volt templates for increased performance and security

In this recipe, we will create a multi-module application with both a web and CLI environment. We first use the CLI environment to precompile the `Volt` templates for the web environment while taking care to avoid difficult-to-solve edge cases and then we will use the web environment to displaying our precompiled templates. This approach is useful for increasing the performance of a website while also allowing us to set the permissions of our `Volt` `cache` directory to be unwritable by the web server. This is useful because compiled `Volt` templates are essentially phtml fragments and it is a good idea to never allow the web server to generate executable code.

Getting ready

This recipe uses the **Phalcon Developer Tools**, which we will use to set up a project skeleton. We will not need a database for this recipe. This recipe will make advanced use of Phalcon modules and CLI and web integration.

How to do it...

Follow these steps to complete this recipe:

We need to have a multi-module application skeleton for experimentation. If you already have such an application, you can skip this step. Create a project skeleton using the modules template:

```
phalcon project volt_compile modules
```

1. This recipe is different from all the others because we specifically want to ensure that the web server cannot write to the `Volt` cache directory at `app/cache/volt`. So check that the `cache` directory is read-only for the web server by trying to load the index controller by accessing the root project path in the browser. If the `Congratulations...` message appears then change the permissions of the `Volt` cache directory to prevent the web server from writing there. Then make sure to delete all of the compiled `Volt` templates in the cache directory.

2. Open the `app/config/services.php` files and make the following changes to the `voltShared` service. Add the following to the beginning of the `voltShared` service function:

```
if (php_sapi_name() === "cli") {
    $compileAlways = true;
    $stat = true;
```

```
    } else {
        $compileAlways = false;
        $stat = false;
    }
```

Add the `compileAlways` and `stat` lines to the `$volt->setOptions` call:

```
$volt setOptions([
    // ...
    'compileAlways' => $compileAlways,
    'stat' => $stat,
    // ...
]);
```

3. Create our `Volt` compiler class at `app/common/library/ModuleCompiler.php`:

```php
<?php
namespace Volt_compile;

class ModuleCompiler extends \Phalcon\DI\Injectable
{
    public function __construct()
    {
        if (php_sapi_name() !== "cli") {
            throw new \Exception('The module compiler must be run
from the command line.');
        }
    }

    public function compile($moduleName)
    {
        $moduleClass = '\\' . __NAMESPACE__ . '\\Modules\\' .
ucfirst($moduleName) . '\\Module';
        $module = new $moduleClass();

        // Create a temporary DI and register the module services
to it.
        $diModule = new \Phalcon\DI();
        $module->registerServices($diModule);

        // Get a raw unresolved view function and bind it to our
DI instead of our temporary DI.
        $viewFactory = \Closure::bind($diModule->getRaw('view'),
$this->getDI());
```

```php
        $this->compileVoltDir($viewFactory()->getViewsDir(),
    $viewFactory);
        }

        private function compileVoltDir($path, $viewFactory)
        {
            $dh = opendir($path);
            while (($fileName = readdir($dh)) !== false) {
                if ($fileName == '.' || $fileName == '..') {
                    continue;
                }

                $pathNext = $path . $fileName;
                if (is_dir($pathNext)) {
                    $this->compileVoltDir("$pathNext/", $viewFactory);
                } else {
                    $this->getDI()
                        ->getVoltShared($viewFactory())
                        ->getCompiler()
                        ->compile($pathNext);
                }
            }

            // close the directory handle
            closedir($dh);
        }
    }
```

4. Create the Compiler task at `app/modules/cli/tasks/CompileTask`:

```php
<?php
namespace Volt_compile\Modules\Cli\Tasks;

class CompileTask extends \Phalcon\Cli\Task
{
    public function mainAction()
    {
        $this->incorrectAction();
    }

    public function incorrectAction()
    {
```

```
            $moduleCompiler = new \Volt_compile\ModuleCompiler();
            $moduleCompiler->setDI($this->getDI());

            $moduleCompiler->compile('frontend');

            echo 'Unfortunately there will be issues.';
        }


        public function correctAction()
        {
            $this->fillMissingServices();

            $moduleCompiler = new \Volt_compile\ModuleCompiler();
            $moduleCompiler->setDI($this->getDI());

            $moduleCompiler->compile('frontend');

            echo 'We did it the right way.';
        }


        private function fillMissingServices()
        {
            $config = $this->getDI()
                ->getConfig();

            $diPrimary = $this->getDI();

            $di = new \Phalcon\DI();
            require $config->application->appDir . 'config/services_
web.php';

            foreach ($di->getServices() as $serviceName => $service) {

                // We will fill in any missing service that exists
only for the web services
                // to ensure that Volt will understand DI services.
                if (!$diPrimary->has($serviceName)) {
                    $diPrimary->set($serviceName, function() {});
                }
            }
        }
    }
}
```

5. Add the following line somewhere in the `Volt` view, `app/modules/frontend/views/index/index.volt`:

```
<p>Our session id is <b>{{ session.getId() }}</b></p>
```

6. On the command line change the directories into the root path of this recipe. Run the command:

```
./run compile
```

We should see `Unfortunately there will be issues.`

In the browser, go to the base path of the recipe. We should see a warning and then a fatal error. If it is not visible on the page then it should be present in the web server error log.

7. Go back to the command line and enter:

```
./run compile correct
```

We should see `We did it the right way.` Now in the browser go to the `base` path. We should see that everything is fine and that we can see our browser session ID.

How it works...

We added some optional configuration settings to our `voltShared` service. When `compileAlways` is `true` it requires that every `Volt` template is always compiled. The `stat` option forces a check against the filesystem to see if the file exists. We want to always do the most work in the CLI environment where we will be compiling the templates and in the web environment we want to assume that the `Volt` view already exists in compiled form.

```
if (php_sapi_name() === "cli") {
    $compileAlways = true;
    $stat = true;
} else {
    $compileAlways = false;
    $stat = false;
}
```

We will now look at the `ModuleCompiler` class to see how the compiling is actually performed.

First we simply extend from the `Phalcon\DI\Injectable` class to add typical methods such as `setDI` and `getDI`:

```
class ModuleCompiler extends \Phalcon\DI\Injectable
```

In the `compile` method we first create a variable that contains the module name and then we use that string variable to instantiate the module class:

```
public function compile($moduleName)
{
    $moduleClass = '\\' . __NAMESPACE__ . '\\Modules\\' .
ucfirst($moduleName) . '\\Module';
    $module = new $moduleClass();
```

Then we create a new empty DI object and we register all of the services that are provided by the module (only *frontend* in our case) into the empty DI. There should not be any side effects in this operation as it should only be attaching service functions to the object. Take a look at the following code snippet:

```
// Create a temporary DI and register the module services to it.
$diModule = new \Phalcon\DI();
$module->registerServices($diModule);
```

Next we get the raw `view` service from our temporary DI object and we bind it to our normal project DI object as the `$viewFactory` variable. In this way, we are able to use `$viewFactory` without modifying our normal DI as follows:

```
$viewFactory = \Closure::bind($diModule->getRaw('view'), $this-
>getDI());
```

Finally, we call the recursive `compileVoltDir` method to go through the modules `view` directory to compile each view:

```
$this->compileVoltDir($viewFactory()->getViewsDir(), $viewFactory);
```

The `compileVoltDir` method is just a typical recursive function that operates on each file in the tree.

If the file is a directory then we recurse deeper into the directory as follows:

```
if (is_dir($pathNext)) {
    $this->compileVoltDir("$pathNext/", $viewFactory);
```

Otherwise we call out to the `voltShared` service by passing in a new `Phalcon\Mvc\View` object and then we get direct access to the Volt Compiler and ask it to compile our current `view` template with the `compile` method. Take a look at the following code snippet:

```
} else {
    $this->getDI()
        ->getVoltShared($viewFactory())
        ->getCompiler()
        ->compile($pathNext);
}
```

If we look back on the `Volt` service, we see that it takes a single `$view` parameter, which is used to set up where the template fragments will be compiled to, based upon the `compiledPath` setting as shown in the following code:

```
$di->setShared('voltShared', function($view) {
    ...
    $volt = new VoltEngine($view, $this)
    $volt->setOptions([
        'compiledPath' => ...
```

Now let's look at the `CompileTask` to see how this is run. The first thing that stands out is that there is an `incorrectAction` and `correctAction` method. These two methods are identical except for one key difference in that `correctAction` first calls `fillMissingServices()`.

To understand the difference between these two methods first look at `app/modules/frontend/views/index/index.volt` and notice the part `{{ session.getId() }}` that we added. Now let's see how our two approaches compile it.

To observe the **incorrect** behavior, we simply call `./run compile` and then view the compiled `Volt` file `cache/volt/modules%%frontend%%views%%index%%index.volt.php`. Notice that it says `<?= $session->getId() ?>`.

Now for the **correct** behavior, we call `./run compile correct` and then notice that it is converted to `<?= $this->session->getId() ?>`. So the two compilations are not equivalent.

The difference between the two is due to the differences between the factory default CLI and web dependency injectors. If a service exists in the DI then the Volt Compiler will convert a variable with a service name to `$this->serviceName` and if it cannot match it to a service then it will assume that it is a variable that needs to be attached to the view during execution and it will be converted to `$serviceName`. This difference arises since the CLI compilation step doesn't load all of the same services that the web service does since many of them are not relevant to that environment. So we remedy this by filling in all of the missing services in our CLI environment DI by using the `fillMissingServices` method.

Optimizing PHQL queries

PHQL is by default one of the fastest ORM technologies available in PHP but even so there are still things that need to be understood if one wishes to achieve top efficiency. In this recipe, we will first start with the least efficient approach and then we will progress to two increasingly faster and more memory-efficient approaches. The first stage of this recipe will involve generating database records and their linked records. Once we have created these records then we can perform the three tests to see how they measure up.

Getting ready

This recipe uses the **Phalcon Developer Tools**, which we will use to set up a project skeleton.

We will need a database connection for this recipe.

How to do it...

Follow these steps to complete this recipe:

1. We need to have an application skeleton for experimentation. If you already have such an application, you can skip this step. Create a project skeleton using the `cli` template:

```
phalcon project optimize_phql cli
```

2. Create the database, `optimize_phql`:

```
DROP TABLE IF EXISTS 'links';
CREATE TABLE 'links' (
   'id' int(11) NOT NULL AUTO_INCREMENT,
   'recordsId' int(11) NOT NULL,
   'uniq' varchar(20) NOT NULL,
   PRIMARY KEY ('id')
) ENGINE=InnoDB DEFAULT CHARSET=latin1;

DROP TABLE IF EXISTS 'records';
CREATE TABLE 'records' (
   'id' int(11) NOT NULL AUTO_INCREMENT,
   'uniq' varchar(20) NOT NULL,
   PRIMARY KEY ('id')
) ENGINE=InnoDB DEFAULT CHARSET=latin1;
```

3. Create the model, `app/models/Links.php`:

```php
<?php

class Links extends Phalcon\Mvc\Model
{
}
```

4. Create the model, `app/models/Records.php`:

```php
<?php

class Records extends Phalcon\Mvc\Model
{
    protected function initialize()
    {
        $this->hasMany('id', 'Links', 'recordsId', [
            'alias' => 'Links'
        ]);
    }
}
```

5. Create the task, `app/tasks/FillTask.php`:

```php
<?php

class FillTask extends \Phalcon\Cli\Task
{

    public function mainAction()
    {
        $this->fillRecordsTable(2000, 3);
    }

    private function fillRecordsTable($neededRecords,
$neededLinksPerRecord)
    {
        $recordCount = Records::count();

        $needsToCreateCount = $neededRecords - $recordCount;
        if ($needsToCreateCount == 0) {
            echo "The records were already created.";
            return;
        }

        echo "We need to create $needsToCreateCount records each
with $neededLinksPerRecord links." . PHP_EOL;
        echo "Please wait..." . PHP_EOL;

        for ($i = $recordCount; $i < $neededRecords; $i++) {
            $record = new Records([
                'uniq' => uniqid()
```

```
            ]);
            $record->create();

            for ($j = 0; $j < $neededLinksPerRecord; $j++) {
                $link = new Links([
                    'recordsId' => $record->id,
                    'uniq'      => uniqid()
                ]);
                $link->create();
                unset($link);
            }

            unset($record);
        }

        echo "Records were created." . PHP_EOL;
    }
}
```

6. Create the task, `app/tasks/TestTask.php`:

```php
<?php

class a extends \Phalcon\Cli\Task
{
    public function mainAction()
    {
        $this->efficiency1Action();
    }

    public function efficiency1Action()
    {
        $this->startTime = microtime(true);

        $records = Records::find();
        foreach ($records as $record) {
            echo $record->id . ': ' . $record->uniq . PHP_EOL;

            $links = Links::find("recordsId = {$record->id}");
            foreach ($links as $link) {
                echo "   " . $link->id . ': ' . $link->uniq . PHP_
EOL;
            }
```

```
            }

            $this->printStats();
        }

        public function efficiency2Action()
        {
            $this->startTime = microtime(true);

            $records = Records::find();
            foreach ($records as $record) {
                echo $record->id . ': ' . $record->uniq . PHP_EOL;

                $links = Links::find([
                    "recordsId = :recordsId:",
                    'bind' => [
                        'recordsId' => $record->id
                    ]
                ]);
                foreach ($links as $link) {
                    echo "   " . $link->id . ': ' . $link->uniq . PHP_
EOL;
                }
            }

            $this->printStats();
        }

        public function efficiency3Action()
        {
            $this->startTime = microtime(true);

            // One way to setup a query
            $records = $this->getDI()
                ->getModelsManager()
                ->createQuery("SELECT id, uniq FROM Records")
                ->execute();

            foreach ($records as $record) {
                echo $record->id . ': ' . $record->uniq . PHP_EOL;
```

```
                // A second way to setup a query
                $query = new Phalcon\Mvc\Model\Query("SELECT id, uniq
    FROM Links WHERE recordsId = :recordsId:", $this->getDI());
                $links = $query->execute([
                    'recordsId' => $record->id
                ]);

                foreach ($links as $link) {
                    echo "   " . $link->id . ': ' . $link->uniq . PHP_
    EOL;
                }
            }

            $this->printStats();
        }

        protected function printStats()
        {
            echo PHP_EOL;

            $totalTime =  microtime(true) - $this->startTime;
            $peakMegaBytes = memory_get_peak_usage() / (1024 * 1024);

            echo 'peak memory: ' . round($peakMegaBytes, 3) . " MB" .
    PHP_EOL;
            echo 'total time: ' . round($totalTime, 3) . " seconds.";
        }
    }
```

7. On the command line execute the following command and then wait until the database has been filled.

    ```
    ./run fill
    ```

8. Execute the following tests:

    ❑ `./run test efficiency1`

    ❑ `./run test efficiency2`

    ❑ `./run test efficiency3`

How it works...

We created two models, **Records** and **Links**, and added a relationship from *Records* to *Links* while ignoring the relationship from the other direction since it is not needed for this recipe.

This relationship in *Records* allows us to quickly get all *Links* models that point from Links `recordsId` to Records `id` as take:

```
$this->hasMany('id', 'Links', 'recordsId', [
    'alias' => 'Links'
]);
```

To start our experiment, we first must run the `FillTask::indexAction` with the command `./run fill` and this will create 2,000 Records with three Links attached to each one. We will only quickly go over the code in the `FillTask` since this is handled in great detail in *Chapter 4, Dealing with Data*.

When running `FillTask`, we iterate in a `for` loop to create the necessary number of *Records* entries as shown in the following code snippet:

```
for ($i = $recordCount; $i < $neededRecords; $i++) {
    $record = new Records([
        'uniq' => uniqid()
    ]);
    $record->create();
```

Then we will create and attach three *Links* models to each *Record* as shown in the following code snippet:

```
for ($j = 0; $j < $neededLinksPerRecord; $j++) {
    $link = new Links([
        'recordsId' => $record->id,
        'uniq'      => uniqid()
    ]);
    $link->create();
    unset($link);
}
```

By the end of this, we will have 2,000 *Records* models each with three *Links* models pointed at each `Records` model. This will give us a large enough data set for our experimentation.

Now that we have our data, we will run our first test in `TestTask::efficiency1` by executing `./run test efficiency1`:

```
$records = Records::find();
foreach ($records as $record) {
```

```
        echo $record->id . ': ' . $record->uniq . PHP_EOL;

        $links = Links::find("recordsId = {$record->id}");
        foreach ($links as $link) {
            echo "   " . $link->id . ': ' . $link->uniq . PHP_EOL;
        }
    }
}
```

The problem with `efficiency1` is that we are including the literal values in the PHQL statement and so, each time we make a query, Phalcon will need to create and cache a new PHQL statement.

Now we will look at `TestTask::efficiency2` by executing `./run test efficiency2`:

```
$records = Records::find();
foreach ($records as $record) {
    echo $record->id . ': ' . $record->uniq . PHP_EOL;

    $links = Links::find([
        "recordsId = :recordsId:",
        'bind' => [
            'recordsId' => $record->id
        ]
    ]);
    foreach ($links as $link) {
        echo "   " . $link->id . ': ' . $link->uniq . PHP_EOL;
    }
}
```

We can see that that `efficiency2` code is almost the same as `efficiency1`, the main difference being that the values are bound to the query using the `bind` key and that we use a placeholder, `:recordsId:`, for this value. This increases our performance by quite a bit but we can still do better.

Now we will look at `TestTask::efficiency3` by executing `./run test efficiency3`. The main difference in this approach compared to the previous two is that we are now only retrieving individual fields.

Notice that we are only requesting individual `id` and `uniq` fields instead of asking for `*` (all fields). This allows us to retrieve a `Phalcon\Mvc\Model\Resultset\Complex` object instead of `Phalcon\Mvc\Model\Resultset\Simple` and by doing so we will avoid creating a `Phalcon\Mvc\Model` object for each database row, as shown in the following code snippet:

```
// One way to setup a query
$records = $this->getDI()
```

```
    ->getModelsManager()
    ->createQuery("SELECT id, uniq FROM Records")
    ->execute();
```

Next we will iterate through our `Records` results and perform a query to obtain each related Link. This time we will perform a query by directly creating a `Phalcon\Mvc\Model\Query` instead of obtaining it through the `modelsManager` service. This is just another way to start a query and both approaches will yield the same results.

Notice that this time we are also only asking for individual fields and this will save the processing time of creating full objects when we only need specific values from our results, as shown in the following code snippet:

```
foreach ($records as $record) {
    echo $record->id . ': ' . $record->uniq . PHP_EOL;

    // A second way to setup a query
    $query = new Phalcon\Mvc\Model\Query("SELECT id, uniq FROM Links
WHERE recordsId = :recordsId:", $this->getDI());
    $links = $query->execute([
        'recordsId' => $record->id
    ]);

    foreach ($links as $link) {
        echo "    " . $link->id . ': ' . $link->uniq . PHP_EOL;
    }
}
```

This recipe demonstrates the overhead of a full ORM layer as well as the overhead in creating new queries. While the full ORM layer is valuable and useful it does come with some of its own tradeoffs when dealing with large datasets.

Caching model metadata and query results for faster performance

In this recipe, we will detail how to dramatically increase the performance of our website by caching both the models metadata used in the ORM and also the results of specific queries. These simple Phalcon capabilities will allow for dramatic improvements to our scaling capabilities.

Getting ready

This recipe uses the **Phalcon Developer Tools** for building a project skeleton and it will require a database.

In this recipe, we will need to use the `acpu` PHP extension.

How to do it...

Follow these steps to complete this recipe:

1. We need to have an application skeleton for experimentation. If you already have such an application, you can skip this step. Create a project skeleton using the `simple` template:

   ```
   phalcon project cache_data simple
   ```

2. Create the database, `cache_data`:

   ```
   DROP TABLE IF EXISTS 'links';
   CREATE TABLE 'links' (
      'id' int(11) NOT NULL AUTO_INCREMENT,
      'val' varchar(50) NOT NULL,
      PRIMARY KEY ('id')
   ) ENGINE=InnoDB DEFAULT CHARSET=utf8;

   DROP TABLE IF EXISTS 'records';
   CREATE TABLE 'records' (
      'id' int(11) NOT NULL AUTO_INCREMENT,
      'val' varchar(50) NOT NULL,
      PRIMARY KEY ('id')
   ) ENGINE=InnoDB DEFAULT CHARSET=utf8;

   DROP TABLE IF EXISTS 'records_links';
   CREATE TABLE 'records_links' (
      'id' int(11) NOT NULL AUTO_INCREMENT,
      'recordsId' int(11) NOT NULL,
      'linksId' int(11) NOT NULL,
      PRIMARY KEY ('id')
   ) ENGINE=InnoDB DEFAULT CHARSET=utf8;
   ```

3. Create the model, `app/models/Records.php`:

```php
<?php

class Records extends Phalcon\Mvc\Model
{
    public function initialize()
    {
relation
        $this->hasMany(
            'id',
            'RecordsLinks',
            'linksId'
        );

        $this->hasManyToMany(
            'id',
            'RecordsLinks',
            'recordsId',
            'linksId',
            'Links',
            'id',
            [
                'alias' => 'links',
            ]
        );
    }
}
```

4. Create the model, `app/models/Links.php`:

```php
<?php

class Links extends \Phalcon\Mvc\Model
{
    public function initialize()
    {
        $this->hasManyToMany(
            'id',
            'RecordsLinks',
            'linksId',
            'recordsId',
            'Records',
```

```
                'id',
                [
                  'alias' => 'records',
                ]
            );
        }
    }
```

5. Create the model, `app/models/RecordsLinks.php`:

```php
<?php

class RecordsLinks extends Phalcon\Mvc\Model
{
    public function initialize()
    {
 relation
        $this->belongsTo(
            'linksId',
            'Cache_results\Models\Links',
            'id'
        );
    }
}
```

6. Ensure that our `app/plugins` directory is included in the registered autoloader path. If it isn't then add it to `app/config/loader.php` by adding the directory `$config->application->pluginsDir` to a `registerDirs` call.

7. Add the `modelsCache` service in `app/config/services.php`:

```php
$di->set('modelsCache', function () {
    $frontend = new Phalcon\Cache\Frontend\Data([
        "lifetime" => 86400
    ]);

    $backend = new Phalcon\Cache\Backend\Apc($frontend);

    return $backend;
});
```

8. Add the following to the `db` service in `app/config/services.php`:

```php
$connection->totalQueries = 0;
$databasePlugin = new DatabasePlugin();
$databasePlugin->setDI($this);
```

```php
$eventsManager = $this->getEventsManager();
$eventsManager->attach('db', $databasePlugin);
$connection->setEventsManager($eventsManager);
```

9. Create a database plugin, `app/plugins/DatabasePlugin.php`, for recording the number of queries performed:

```php
<?php

class DatabasePlugin extends \Phalcon\Mvc\User\Plugin
{
    public function afterQuery($event, $connection)
    {
        error_log($connection->getRealSQLStatement());
        $connection->totalQueries++;
    }
}
```

10. Add the controller, `app/controllers/FillController.php`:

```php
<?php

class FillController extends Phalcon\Mvc\Controller
{

    public function indexAction()
    {
        $this->fillRecordsTable(10, 3);
    }

    private function fillRecordsTable($neededRecords,
$neededLinksPerRecord)
    {
        $recordCount = Records::count();

        $needsToCreateCount = $neededRecords - $recordCount;
        if ($needsToCreateCount == 0) {
            echo "The records were already created.";
            return;
        }

        echo "We need to create $needsToCreateCount records each
with $neededLinksPerRecord links." . PHP_EOL;
        echo "Please wait..." . PHP_EOL;
```

```php
        for ($i = $recordCount; $i < $neededRecords; $i++) {
            $record = new Records([
                'val' => uniqid()
            ]);

            $links = [];
            for ($j = 0; $j < $neededLinksPerRecord; $j++) {
                $links[] = new Links([
                    'val' => uniqid()
                ]);
            }
            $record->links = $links;

            $record->save();

            if ($record->getMessages() !== null) {
                foreach ($record->getMessages() as $message) {
                    echo $message->getMessage() . "\n";
                }
            }
        }

        echo "Records were created." . PHP_EOL;
    }
}
```

11. Add the controller, `app/controllers/TestController.php`:

```php
<?php

class TestController extends Phalcon\Mvc\Controller
{
    public function indexAction()
    {
        $this->startTime = microtime(true);

        $records = Records::find();
        foreach ($records as $record) {
            $this->response->appendContent('<p>');
            $this->response->appendContent($record->id . ': ' .
$record->val . '<br>');

            $links = $record->getLinks();
```

```
            foreach ($links as $link) {
                $this->response->appendContent('-- ' . $link->id .
': ' . $link->val . '<br>');
            }

        $this->response->appendContent('</p>');
    }

    $totalTime = microtime(true) - $this->startTime;

    $this->response->appendContent('<div>total time: ' .
round($totalTime, 5) . " seconds.</div>");
    $this->response->appendContent('<div>total queries: ' .
$this->db->totalQueries . "</div>");

    $this->response->send();
}

public function cacheAction()
{
    $this->getDI()->setShared('modelsMetadata', function() {
        return new Phalcon\Mvc\Model\MetaData\Apc([
            "lifetime" => 86400,
            "prefix"   => "cache_data"
        ]);
    });

    $this->startTime = microtime(true);

    $records = Records::find([
        'cache' => [
            'key' => 'all-records',
            'lifetime' => 15
        ]
    ]);
    foreach ($records as $record) {
        $this->response->appendContent('<p>');
        $this->response->appendContent($record->id . ': ' .
$record->val . '<br>');

        $cache = $this->getDI()
            ->getModelsCache();
```

```
            $cacheKey = 'record-links-' . $record->id;
            $links = $cache->get($cacheKey);
            if (!$links) {
                $phql = <<<PHQL
SELECT Links.* FROM Links
JOIN RecordsLinks ON Links.id = RecordsLinks.linksId
JOIN Records ON Records.id = RecordsLinks.recordsId
WHERE Records.id = :recordsId:
PHQL;

                $query = new \Phalcon\Mvc\Model\Query($phql,
$this->getDI());
                $links = $query->execute([
                    'recordsId' => $record->id,
                ]);

                $cache->save($cacheKey, $links);
            }

            foreach ($links as $link) {
                $this->response->appendContent('-- ' . $link->id .
': ' . $link->val . '<br>');
            }

            $this->response->appendContent('</p>');
        }

        $totalTime =  microtime(true) - $this->startTime;

        $this->response->appendContent('<div>total time: ' .
round($totalTime, 8) . " seconds.</div>");
        $this->response->appendContent('<div>total queries: ' .
$this->getDI()->getDb()->totalQueries . "</div>");

        $this->response->send();
    }
}
```

12. In the browser, in the root path of the project, go to the following paths:

   - ❑ `/fill`: to generate the required records
   - ❑ `/test`
   - ❑ `/test/cache`

- ❑ /test/cache
- ❑ /test/cache
- ❑ /test/cache: Visit the page many times

13. After the first visit to /test/cache (for each process), the models metadata and the query results will already be stored in the APC cache and so the total time involved should be dramatically better than /test.

How it works...

In this recipe, we are benefiting from utilizing the APC cache for two different expensive operations. The models metadata cache is an easy fit for caching because it rarely changes except during development when the model schemas are being changed and otherwise they will not change. The models metadata cache performs several data queries as well as needing to process that data and by caching this we can save significant time. Finally, we are caching the results of individual queries and this can be quite a time saver as well but it is not appropriate for queries that could be rapidly changing.

Let's look at our models. In this case we are using a typical hasManyToMany relationship between Links and Records, which uses the RecordsLinks model to join the two together. In this recipe, we are looking to cache expensive queries to demonstrate time savings and so we are using the results of table joins rather than simply retrieving records from a single table.

The first thing that we'll want to do is to populate our database with linked data via the FillController. This is very standard record creation stuff but we do show off how easy it is to have Phalcon do the hard work of creating the intermediate linked table (which is RecordsLinks in our case).

We simply loop through to create the needed number of records while attaching an array of Links to our relationship alias property so that Phalcon can do the tedious relationship work for us.

```
for ($i = $recordCount; $i < $neededRecords; $i++) {
    $record = new Records([
        'val' => uniqid()
    ]);

    $links = [];
    for ($j = 0; $j < $neededLinksPerRecord; $j++) {
        $links[] = new Links([
            'val' => uniqid()
        ]);
    }
```

```
$record->links = $links;

$record->save();
}
```

Now that we have our dataset, we'll look at our `modelsCache` service, which is used for storing results:

First we will create a frontend for our data. In this case, the typical `Data` adapter is what we will only be interacting with our PHP environment:

```
$frontend = new Phalcon\Cache\Frontend\Data([

    "lifetime" => 86400

]);
```

For our backend, we will be using the well-established APC storage mechanism to allow data to persist across PHP processes. This is a very simple and foolproof backend that is easy to work with and doesn't require an additional server technology to use:

```
$backend = new Phalcon\Cache\Backend\Apc($frontend);
```

Alternatively, we could use a **Redis** or **Memcache** backend, which would be more appropriate for a massive scaled out system but has the downside of adding the overhead of TCP/IP communication.

Next we will add a database service plugin that will record all of the queries performed. This is a rather typical plugin setup except that we are hacking in the total queries counter directly onto the connection itself as follows:

```
$connection->totalQueries = 0;
$databasePlugin = new DatabasePlugin();
// ...
```

Now we will test the completion time for iterating through each Record and outputting each `Records` related `Links`. Let's first look at an abbreviated version of the uncached `indexAction` method. In this method, we have removed the lines that output text to only focus on the loops and queries as, shown in the following code snippet:

```
public function indexAction()
{
    $this->startTime = microtime(true);

    $records = Records::find();
    foreach ($records as $record) {
```

```
        $links = $record->getLinks();

        foreach ($links as $link) {
            // Output
        }
    }

    $totalTime =  microtime(true) - $this->startTime;
}
```

Now let's look at the fully cached version of that method. Notice that, at the very top, we are first redefining the typical `modelsMetadata` service to store the data using the APC persistent mechanism. Although it works out perfectly for our example it is not recommended to ever define services within a controller like this because, when the program execution reaches this point in the code, we have not yet called out to database for our models metadata as shown in the following code snippet:

```
public function cacheAction()
{
    $this->getDI()->setShared('modelsMetadata', function () {
        return new Phalcon\Mvc\Model\MetaData\Apc([
            "lifetime" => 86400,
            "prefix"    => "cache_data"
        ]);
    });

    $this->startTime = microtime(true);

    $records = Records::find([
        'cache' => [
            'key' => 'all-records',
            'lifetime' => 15
        ]
    ]);
    foreach ($records as $record) {
        $links = $record->getLinks([
            'cache' => [
                'key' => 'record-links-' . $record->id,
                'lifetime' => 100
            ]
        ]);
    }

    $totalTime =  microtime(true) - $this->startTime;
}
```

Now the first time that the `cacheAction` method is called (through the `/test/cache` path), the amount of time needed should be roughly equal to that of the cached version. However, any subsequent request should be take a dramatically reduced amount of time for some non-trivial time and CPU savings. However, there are multiple PHP processes and each of them will need to be warmed up when using the APC cache.

9
High Performance Applications with Phalcon

In this chapter, we will cover:

- ▶ Introduction to asynchronous work by using Beanstalk
- ▶ Implementing a three-level cache to increase performance
- ▶ Cache view fragments or full pages in Phalcon
- ▶ Implementing your own cache adapters
- ▶ Cache data to reduce access to database systems
- ▶ Creating a PHP extension using Zephir
- ▶ Extending Phalcon using Zephir

Introduction

One of the most important architecture solutions of every large project is asynchronous (background) processing. Since the amounts of information to be processed in a certain moment increase, as well as the popularity of Internet resources, it is evident that tasks cannot be accomplished in real-time and in one stack. It slows down for sure the work of the remaining parts of the application. Actually, all tasks in the call stack just join the queue and are accomplished sequentially. Such an approach negatively affects application performance, as well as the general impression of the application users.

In general, when working on any application which has become critical, it is a fact that dividing the services, where possible into synchronous and asynchronous, is a winning strategy in the application's scalability.

In this chapter, we will consider the development basics of asynchronous task execution in Phalcon by using the lightweight queue manager, **Beanstalk**. The Phalcon framework team, as well as its active community, are intensively developing the course of the work with queues. So, it is safe to say that when you are reading these words, the Phalcon kernel-level support in Beanstalk will be improved and the number of available ways of working with Beanstalk will be increased. As this book is being prepared, the Phalcon queue client can implement only the base features set provided by Beanstalk. Nevertheless, this is quite sufficient to allow you to create full-range applications with queue implementation.

It is evident that things that are changed rarely must be cached in every rapid-growing project. This is the case with views too. It is not infrequent that there are some views in a project, that do not need to be rendered all the time, so Phalcon, is aiming to be the fastest framework in every aspect, and gives you an opportunity to avoid rendering views when there is no need. The framework can cache what you need, whether this is a view or only a part of one. Certainly, you can work with this cache as with any other cache; in particular, you can get cached views, remove them from the cache, and put them into a cache with a random key for a certain time. In this chapter, we will consider the main principles and approaches in caching views and their snippets.

In this chapter, you will also learn how to create your own extensions using the **Zephir** language. Zephir is the high-level language developed for the easy creation of any PHP extension. This is its main intended use and it is the sole up-to-date programming language created with this express purpose. The Phalcon framework team works hard so that this language can continue to be a relevant self-sufficient tool. Thanks to the open development concept, the project gets regular feedbacks from users concerning its improvement, as well as debugging patches. We will get a view of the whole cycle of all the necessary steps that you must go through to get a ready-to-use PHP extension.

As stated before, you can create PHP extensions of any level of difficulty using Zephir. Those extensions can communicate together. For example, you can declare the dependence of one extension on the other and use the outsourced classes provided by third parties in your extension. It is quite convenient, considering the fact that you will not have to implement any new functionality that has already been implemented in another application.

Without question, one of the most resource-intensive spheres in the framework realm is ORM. To reduce the load on the database, as well as the time of code execution, to some extent, it is reasonable to cache data that is rarely clanged. Phalcon provides you with a unified caching interface in the context of using different adapters. In this chapter, we will consider the main principles of using a cache when working with the database, as well as ways of using different adapters.

Additionally, in this chapter, we will get a view of creating a custom caching adapters.

Introduction to asynchronous work by using Beanstalk

Modern Internet applications abound with tasks that should be done asynchronously. There are heavy tasks such as multimedia content converting, mailing, work with external resources, and so on. However, some less resource-intensive tasks should be accomplished asynchronously too. Imagine a situation when the task is to implement click-rate tracking. It looks like the following: the project sends mails to a group of users, and you need to know who has gone to the site through the link in the mail. Along with immediate chart creating, you need to store all historical user information, including his or her click through. The user opens the mail in his or her mail client and goes through a link like this `http://{your-host-here}?uid=123`. After the user has got to the site you can identify the user exactly by using a `GET` parameter such as `uid`. In a similar fashion, you can add more useful information into the link to identify the mail which was sent, the date of sending, calculate the CTR related to this user, and display all this information in the charts. As you will appreciate, this stack of small tasks will turn into a serious problem for your application if the click through increases. It is possible that your users will just wait, or view a white screen instead of your distinctive design, until all marketing and analytical tasks are accomplished and the queue is released. That is how synchronous processes run.

In this recipe, we will consider a slightly easier task. However, it will demonstrate the principle of working with queues in Phalcon perfectly. We will try to explore the topic of asynchronous task accomplishment. But we will not go into the matter of general application configuring, database creating, and so on.

Imagine the following task. You have a short link service. The user can visit our web resource, put a long URL into the input field, and get a generated short URL. Hereafter, the service can store and display the following information per request—the short URL click-rate, the date of every click, the date of link generation, and so on. You can take this a step further and put forward a case that it will be convenient to store information related to the user agent including the language, the version, the name of the browser, the engine, and so on. But we will not be distracted by the application. Let's focus on the principle of working with queues.

It is evident that while those URLs increase in number in our site, the click-rate will increase too. You need to update the information in two tables after every short URL click. To improve the application performance, as well as shorten the time needed to redirect the user to the long URL, we will update the information in the background.

Getting ready

To successfully implement this recipe, we will need a working application that will need to be able to receive and handle requests. You can use an application skeleton created with Phalcon Devtools. If you have one already, you can use it.

Additionally, we will need a database to store the links and related data. For this recipe, we will use MySQL but you can use any database you see fit. For a different RDBMS, you will need to adapt the relevant parts of the recipe to your needs.

Finally, you will need to have a beanstalkd daemon installed and running. The installation of beanstalkd varies depending on the operating system of your computer. Since this is outside the scope of this recipe, we will not cover it. However there are some reference links at the end of the recipe that could help.

How to do it...

Follow these steps to complete this recipe:

1. First you will need an application set up. We will use a boilerplate application created by Phalcon Devtools. If you already have an application ready, you can use that, or create it in any other way you see fit. Create the application using the following command:

   ```
   phalcon project links simple
   ```

2. We now need to configure our application. The database needs to be set up, We will use a user named `root` without a password:

   ```
   'database' => [
           'adapter'      => 'Mysql',
           'host'         => '127.0.0.1',
           'username'     => 'root',
           'password'     => '',
           'dbname'       => 'links',
           'charset'      => 'utf8',
           'port'         => 3306
   ],
   ```

3. Then add a section to your application configuration, which stores the configuration for Beanstalk:

```
'queue' => [
    'host' => '127.0.0.1',
    'port' => 11300
],
```

4. Now we need to configure the `queue` client. Open your `bootstrap` file and add the following Beanstalk configuration into it:

```
$di->setShared('queue', function () use ($config) {
    return new Phalcon\Queue\Beanstalk(
        $config->get('queue')->toArray()
    );
});
```

5. The last part of the configuration is to route all requests to a single controller—`IndexController`:

```
$di->setShared('router', function () {
    $router = new Phalcon\Mvc\Router();

    $router->add(
      '/([\w]{1,12})',
      [
        'controller' => 'index',
        'action'     => 'index',
        'code'       => 1,
      ]
    );


    return $router;
});
```

6. Note that the configuration parameters for the database and other parts can be different in your installation. If you are not able to install beanstalkd or a RDBMS yourself, there are plenty of instructional articles on the Internet.

7. We will also need to create all the tables in our database. We will not focus on database normalization since this is not in the scope of this recipe. We will run the following script in our database:

```sql
CREATE TABLE 'users' (
    'id' INT UNSIGNED NOT NULL AUTO_INCREMENT,
    'name' VARCHAR(72) DEFAULT NULL,
    'email' VARCHAR(70) DEFAULT NULL,
    'last_ip' INT UNSIGNED DEFAULT NULL,
    'last_visit'  TIMESTAMP DEFAULT NULL,
    'created_at' TIMESTAMP NOT NULL DEFAULT CURRENT_TIMESTAMP,
    'updated_at' TIMESTAMP NOT NULL DEFAULT CURRENT_TIMESTAMP,
    PRIMARY KEY ('id'),
    KEY 'email' ('email')
) ENGINE=InnoDB DEFAULT CHARSET=utf8;


CREATE TABLE 'links' (
    'id' BIGINT UNSIGNED NOT NULL AUTO_INCREMENT,
    'user_id' INT UNSIGNED NOT NULL,
    'long_url' VARCHAR(255) NOT NULL,
    'short_code' VARCHAR(12) NOT NULL,
    'last_visit'  TIMESTAMP DEFAULT NULL,
    'created_at' TIMESTAMP NOT NULL DEFAULT CURRENT_TIMESTAMP,
    PRIMARY KEY ('id'),
    KEY 'link_user_id' ('user_id'),
    KEY 'link_short_code' ('short_code')
) ENGINE=InnoDB DEFAULT CHARSET=utf8;


CREATE TABLE 'clicks' (
    'id' BIGINT UNSIGNED NOT NULL AUTO_INCREMENT,
    'link_id' BIGINT UNSIGNED NOT NULL,
    'click_date' TIMESTAMP NOT NULL DEFAULT CURRENT_TIMESTAMP,
    PRIMARY KEY ('id')
) ENGINE=InnoDB DEFAULT CHARSET=utf8;
```

8. The mechanism or the algorithm to create the short link for each URL is beyond the scope of this recipe, so we will skip that step. We will add some data in the database to use it in this recipe. Imagine that we already have a user who has created two short links:

```
INSERT INTO 'users' ('id', 'name', 'email', 'created_at',
'updated_at') VALUES
    (1, 'John', 'john@doe.com', NOW(), NOW());


INSERT INTO 'links' ('id','user_id', 'long_url', 'short_code')
VALUES
    (688765, 1, 'https://www.igvita.com/2010/05/20/scalable-work-
queues-with-beanstalk/', '6wwj'),
    (688766, 1, 'https://docs.phalconphp.com/en/latest/reference/
queue.html', '6wwk');
```

9. Next we need to create the relevant models in our application:

```php
class Users extends Phalcon\Mvc\Model
{
    public function initialize()
    {
        $this->hasMany('id', 'Links', 'user_id');
    }
}


class Links extends Phalcon\Mvc\Model
{
    public function initialize()
    {
        $this->belongsTo('user_id', 'Users', 'id');
        $this->hasMany('id', 'Clicks', 'link_id');
    }
}


class Clicks extends Phalcon\Mvc\Model
{
    public function initialize()
    {
        $this->belongsTo('link_id', 'Links', 'id');
    }
}
```

10. Now it is time for the Controllers. Modify the `IndexController` as follows:

```
class IndexController extends ControllerBase
{
  public function indexAction()
  {
    $code = $this->dispatcher->getParam('code');
    $link = Links::findFirstByShortCode($code);

    $queue = $this->di->getShared('queue');
    $queue->put([
        'code' => $code,
        'date' => date('Y-m-d H:i:s')
    ]);

    return $this->response->redirect(
        $link->long_url,
        true
    );
  }
}
```

11. Now, let us create a simple worker which will handle the `queue`. Create in the project root a directory named `scripts`, and a file named `process-links.php` in it, with the following code:

```
define('APP_PATH', realpath('..'));

// Read the configuration, auto-loader and services
$config = include APP_PATH . "/app/config/config.php";
include APP_PATH . "/app/config/loader.php";
include APP_PATH . "/app/config/services.php";

$queue = $di->getShared('queue');

while (($job = $queue->peekReady()) !== false) {
  $message = $job->getBody();
  $code    = $message['code'];
  $date    = $message['date'];

  $link = Links::findFirstByShortCode($code);
  $link->last_visit = $date;
```

```
$click = new Clicks();
$click->click_date = $date;
$click->link = $link;

if ($click->save()) {
  echo 'The visit was successfully updated.', PHP_EOL;
} else {
  // put here job to the fail_queue
}

$job->delete();
}
```

12. Now, try to click on the links we have created at the beginning of this recipe. Open the link `http://{your-host-here}/6wwj` in your browser, then open `http://{your-host-here}/6wwk`. You will be redirected to the original URLs.

13. Finally, it is time to test our worker. Open your Terminal and go to the `scripts` directory. Execute the file as follows:

    php process-links.php

14. You will see two messages informing you that logging is successful.

How it works...

Writing this recipe, we have intentionally simplified the code and left out everything that could divert our focus from queues. In particular, check for the original link existence, the behavior in case of an error, error handling in the worker, and so on. Our goal is to show how to manage working with queues in Phalcon.

Essentially, we have created a fully functional application, able to record short link clicks. Of course, in order for the application to be production-ready, you will need to implement functionality such as user registration, personal accounts, statistics, and so on. Those will be handled in other recipes.

We added some simple logic in the controller. The short URL will be resolved to the original one and the request will be redirected. Since we are using queues, the response to the user will be almost instant while the queue will handle additional tasks pertaining to link tracking and so on.

The worker receives tasks from the queue (if any are waiting). Following that, the worker will perform all the actions and the task will be removed from the queue, avoiding duplicate execution of the tasks.

The common practice is to remove the task from the queue regardless of the result of the task execution. If we leave the task in the queue until it is processed then the following might happen—the task executes correctly and then it is removed from the queue; or the task encountered an error and is not removed from the queue. The next time the runner runs to pick the next task in the queue, it will be the same one and a new error will be thrown. This will easily saturate the queue causing critical failures and memory will be depleted. This is a common mistake that programmers make when dealing with queues.

A safer approach is to remove the task from the queue as soon as it is received and then execute it. If it fails, we can either reschedule it, adding it again in the queue, and/or inform the developers about the error.

There's more...

For more detailed information about compiling and building the Beanstalk queue manager, please see `http://kr.github.io/beanstalkd/`.

Detailed information on the `Phalcon\Queue\Beanstalk` component can be found at `https://docs.phalconphp.com/en/latest/reference/queue.html`.

Implementing a three-level cache to increase performance

Phalcon offers developers the option to use multi-level caches. With the help of a multi-level cache, you can create a very flexible caching logic, caching different pieces of information of your application to different adapters with different lifetimes. You can then retrieve this information beginning with the fastest (as the adapters were registered) and finishing with the slowest until the lifetime expires.

In this recipe, you will learn how to use multi-level caches in your application and see that the configuration and the usage of such caches does not differ from one adapter to another.

Getting ready

To successfully implement this recipe, we will need a working application, which will need to be able to receive and handle requests. You can use an application skeleton created with Phalcon Devtools. If you have one already, you can use it.

In this recipe, we will showcase multi-level caching by using different adapters that could be depending on PHP extensions. For example, and the adapter `Phalcon\Cache\Backend\Apc` requires the PHP extension `apc` (apcu), the adapter `Phalcon\Cache\Backend\Libmemcached` requires the PHP extension `memcached` as well as the `Memcached` server installed. If you are unable to install any of the dependencies for the adapters used in this recipe, you can replace them with others that your system supports. However, we recommend these installations so that you can follow the recipe steps closely.

It should be noted that we have intentionally not used adapters that are either out of date or not recommended, such as `Phalcon\Cache\Backend\Memcache` in this recipe. This is due to the fact that it is very difficult to meet the dependencies of these adapters. For instance, at the time of writing, the `memcache` extension (not to be confused with the `memcached` extension) has not been ported to PHP 7.

How to do it...

Follow these steps to complete this recipe:

1. First we will need an application. We will use a boilerplate application created by Phalcon Devtools. If you already have an application ready, you can use that, or create it in any other way you see fit. Create the application using the following command:

   ```
   phalcon project store simple
   ```

2. We will then need to implement the caching service in such a way that it can use multi-level caching. Different adapters require different configurations. To keep things tidy, we create an area in our configuration, so as to keep all the caching options together. Open your application configuration file and add the following sections in it. We will need them later in this recipe:

   ```
   'cache' => [
       'apc' => [
           'prefix'  => 'cache.',
       ],
       'libmemcached' => [
           'servers'  => [
               'host'   => 'localhost',
               'port'   => 11211,
               'weight' => 1,
           ],
           'client' => [
               \Memcached::OPT_HASH => Memcached::HASH_MD5,
               \Memcached::OPT_PREFIX_KEY => 'cache.',
   ```

```
            ],
        ],
        'file' => [
            'prefix'   => 'cache.',
            'cacheDir' => APP_PATH . '/app/cache/',
        ],
    ]
```

3. We now need to register our cache service. Open your `bootstrap` file and add the cache service as shown in the following code:

```
use Phalcon\Cache\Multiple;
use Phalcon\Cache\Backend\Apc as ApcCache;
use Phalcon\Cache\Backend\File as FileCache;
use Phalcon\Cache\Frontend\Data as DataFrontend;
use Phalcon\Cache\Backend\Libmemcached as MemcachedCache;

$di->set('cache', function () use ($config) {
    return new Multiple(
        [
            new ApcCache(
                new DataFrontend(['lifetime' => 3600]),
                $config->get('cache')->apc->toArray()
            ),
            new MemcachedCache(
                new DataFrontend(['lifetime' => 86400]),
                $config->get('cache')->libmemcached->toArray()
            ),
            new FileCache(
                new DataFrontend(['lifetime' => 604800]),
                $config->get('cache')->file->toArray()
            )
        ]
    );
});
```

4. That is all what you need to do to use multi-level caching. The multi-level cache service (`Phalcon\Cache\Multiple`) can now be accessed from our DI container from anywhere in our application:

```
$cache = $this->di->get('cache');
$cache->save('some-key', $someData);
```

How it works...

Configuring and registering a multi-level caching service is no different than configuring and registering any cache adapter on its own.

We have created an instance of `Phalcon\Cache\Multiple` in the DI container and added all the needed adapters to it. You can add as many adapters as needed for your project. The adapters could be different in type but also of the same type serving different purposes. Phalcon does not restrict the number of adapters used, although developers should consider memory consumption when using adapters that use memory.

By using this implementation, you will be able to distribute the load of your project units evenly throughout your application. Note that you can also register the service `modelsCache` in the same way, which will be used by the ORM to cache `resultsets`, or you can register a custom service for your specific application needs.

There's more...

Additional information about caching in Phalcon can be found at: `https://docs.phalconphp.com/en/latest/reference/cache.html`

Cache view fragments or full pages in Phalcon

When developing sites of any type, dynamic or static, certain parts of specific pages rarely change. The `Phalcon\Mvc\View` component provides the necessary functionality to cache those parts or even the whole page rendered, thus speeding up your application.

In this recipe, we will learn the main principles of view caching.

Getting ready

To successfully implement this recipe, we will need a working application which will need to be able to receive and handle requests. You can use an application skeleton created with Phalcon Devtools. If you have one already, you can use it.

We will use the file `cache` to demonstrate the caching mechanism. However, you can use any cache adapter you want, depending on your needs and preference.

How to do it...

Follow these steps to complete this recipe:

1. First you will need an application set up. We will use a boilerplate application created by Phalcon Devtools. If you already have an application ready, you can use that, or create one in any other way you see fit. Create the application using the following command:

   `phalcon project store simple`

2. To demonstrate how caching can speed up your application under heavy loads, we will simulate resource intensive processes. After you have created your project, open the `IndexController` and modify the `indexAction` as follows:

   ```
   public function indexAction()
   {
       sleep(10);
   }
   ```

3. Open the page in your browser by visiting `http://{your-host-here}`. You will notice that it takes around 10 seconds for the page to load. We have successfully simulated a resource-intensive page. Now add the following line before the sleep function:

   ```
   $this->view->cache(true);
   ```

4. Refresh the page. If you have used a new application for this recipe, you will see the following error message:

   `Service 'viewCache' wasn't found in the dependency injection container`

5. The error message is self-explanatory, so we will add the `viewCache` service into our `bootstrap` file. Create a directory for the cached data `app/cache/data` and add the required service into the DI container:

   ```
   use Phalcon\Cache\Frontend\Output as OutputFrontend;
   use Phalcon\Cache\Backend\File as FileBackend;

   $di->set('viewCache', function () {
       $cache = new FileBackend(
           new OutputFrontend(['lifetime' => 86400]),
           ['cacheDir' => APP_PATH . '/app/cache/data/']
       );

       return $cache;
   });
   ```

6. As stated previously, we are using a file cache adapter for this recipe. After you have added the `viewCache` service in the DI container, refresh the page. You will notice that the error message no longer appears. Additionally, you can check the `app/cache/data` folder to make sure that the relevant cache file has been created successfully.

7. Open the newly created file with an editor of your choice, and you will notice that it contains the same HTML code as your page.

8. Now, refresh the page several times. You will notice that the page is still loading slowly. Let us fix that. Open the `IndexController` and modify the `indexAction` as follows:

```
public function indexAction()
{
    $cacheKey = md5(
            json_encode([__CLASS__, __FUNCTION__])
    );

    if (!$this->view->getCache()->exists($cacheKey)) {
        sleep(10);
    }

    $this->view->cache(
        [
                'key' => $cacheKey,
                'lifetime' => 1200,
        ]
    );
}
```

Refresh the page several times again. You will notice that the resource-intensive action happens only during the first page load. The following page loads render very fast.

How it works...

As you can see, caching content is very simple; there are no complex tasks required to achieve it.

The first thing you have to note is that you always need a caching service to cache views. When the `Phalcon\Mvc\View` component has to cache something it will request a cache service from the service container. This service is called `viewCache`. This is why in our recipe we saw the relevant error message (if you have used a new application skeleton without that service being registered).

There are two important requirements for the `viewCache`. First, the `viewCache` service must always be registered as not shared. Second, the Frontend Cache must always be of `Phalcon\Cache\Frontend\Output`. Following these requirements is important to ensure trouble free setup and use of the `viewCache`.

Once we had added the cache service in the DI container, we did not do anything special. The method call, `$this->view->cache(true)`, instructs the service that we will be using it with the default configuration. If the parameters of the `cache()` function are `true`, the service will use `md5` as the function to create the `cache` key, using the controller and view names in the format `controller/view`. This ensures uniqueness in the `cache` files. The cache lifetime will be the same as our setting when we created the service.

To avoid unnecessary rendering of the same content all the time, we have used a conditional to check if the cache exists and used it if it does. Your conditional will vary of course depending on your implementation. We have also created a unique key for our cache entries, to avoid collisions and stored the contents for an hour. Note that the lifetime for each `cache` file was set by the lifetime argument in the associative array. This is how we override the default cache lifetime defined in the service registration (`bootstrap` file).

We can also pass the service that will handle the caching as the third parameter of the `cache()` method. This is especially helpful when you need to implement different caching logic based on incoming data. The custom cache service can be accessed when using the `service` key. We do this as follows:

```
$this->view->cache(
    [
        "service"  => "myCache",
        "lifetime" => 86400,
        "key"      => "resume-cache"
    ]
);
```

We specify the service name here, which was used in the DI container earlier for its registration.

There's more...

For more information about the `Phalcon\Mvc\View` component and caching, please refer to `https://docs.phalconphp.com/en/latest/reference/views.html`.

Implementing your own cache adapters

If your project requirements necessitate handling large amounts of data, the most common RDBMs will not be able to handle the load. Additionally, if your requirements are high performance, scalability, and no down time, then your choices for data storing are limited. We encourage you to check **Aerospike**, because it meets all these requirements. The question then concentrates on implementation. How can we implement Aerospike seamlessly in our project, as if it is a Phalcon core cache component?

In this recipe, we will implement the Aerospike adapter. With it you will be able to use the Aerospike database as a cache for your application.

Phalcon provides an interface for backend caching adapters. All we need to do is implement our functionality for Aerospike in a class implementing the `Phalcon\Cache\BackendInterface`. This interface allows us to use any custom class that implements it in Phalcon as if we were using one of the existing cache adapters.

Getting ready

You will of course need an instance of the Aerospike server to implement this recipe. Additionally the php client for Aerospike will be used to communicate with the server. References for these can be found at the end of this recipe.

How to do it...

Follow these steps to complete this recipe:

1. First you need to create a class skeleton with all necessary methods. We must implement all methods specified in the interface `Phalcon\Cache\BackendInterface` as follows:

   ```
   namespace Phalcon\Cache\Backend;

   use Phalcon\Cache\Backend;
   use Phalcon\Cache\Exception;
   use Phalcon\Cache\FrontendInterface;
   use Phalcon\Cache\BackendInterface;

   class Aerospike extends Backend implements BackendInterface
   {
   ```

```php
    public function __construct(FrontendInterface $frontend, array
$options)
    {

    }

    public function get($keyName, $lifetime = null)
    {
        // ...
    }

    public function save($keyName = null, $content = null,
$lifetime = null, $stopBuffer = true)
    {
        // ...
    }

    public function delete($keyName)
    {
        // ...
    }

    public function exists($keyName = null, $lifetime = null)
    {
        // ...
    }

    public function queryKeys($prefix = null)
    {
        // ...
    }
}
```

2. We have not declared the methods implemented in the base class `Phalcon\Cache\Backend`. We will only need to implement five methods in our class. We will also need to pass the Aerospike client in the adapter, so that our cache adapter can communicate with the Aerospike server. There are many ways of implementing this, but for this recipe we will just pass the client in the constructor to simplify things. Change the class constructor as follows:

```php
protected $db;
protected $namespace = 'test';
protected $set = 'cache';
```

```php
public function __construct(FrontendInterface $frontend, array
$options)
{
    if (empty($options['db']) || !$options['db'] instanceof \
Aerospike) {
        throw new Exception(
            'Parameter "db" is required and it must be an instance
of \Aerospike'
        );
    }

    $this->db = $options['db'];

    if (!$this->db->isConnected()) {
        throw new Exception(
            sprintf(
                "Aerospike failed to connect [%s]: %s",
                $this->db->errorno(),
                $this->db->error()
            )
        );
    }

    parent::__construct($frontend, $options);
}
```

3. Now we need to implement the most commonly used methods of our adapter—getting and saving data. The `save` method then becomes:

```php
public function save($keyName = null, $content = null, $lifetime =
null, $stopBuffer = true)
{
    if ($keyName === null) {
        $prefixedKey = $this->_lastKey;
    } else {
        $prefixedKey = $this->_prefix . $keyName;
    }

    if (!$prefixedKey) {
        throw new Exception('The cache must be started first');
    }
```

```php
        if (null === $content) {
            $cachedContent = $this->_frontend->getContent();
        } else {
            $cachedContent = $content;
        }

        if (null === $lifetime) {
            $lifetime = $this->_lastLifetime;

            if (null === $lifetime) {
                $lifetime = $this->_frontend->getLifetime();
            }
        }

        $aKey = $this->buildKey($prefixedKey);

        if (is_numeric($cachedContent)) {
            $bins = ['value' => $cachedContent];
        } else {
            $bins = ['value' => $this->_frontend-
>beforeStore($cachedContent)];
        }

        $status = $this->db->put(
            $aKey,
            $bins,
            $lifetime,
            [\Aerospike::OPT_POLICY_KEY => \Aerospike::POLICY_KEY_
SEND]
        );

        if (\Aerospike::OK != $status) {
            throw new Exception(
                sprintf('Failed storing data in Aerospike: %s', $this-
>db->error()),
                $this->db->errorno()
            );
        }

        if (true === $stopBuffer) {
            $this->_frontend->stop();
        }
```

```
        if (true === $this->_frontend->isBuffering()) {
            echo $cachedContent;
        }

        $this->_started = false;
    }
```

4. And the `get` method becomes:

```
public function get($keyName, $lifetime = null)
{
    $prefixedKey    = $this->_prefix . $keyName;
    $aKey           = $this->buildKey($prefixedKey);
    $this->_lastKey = $prefixedKey;

    $status = $this->db->get($aKey, $cache);

    if ($status != \Aerospike::OK) {
        return null;
    }

    $cachedContent = $cache['bins']['value'];

    if (is_numeric($cachedContent)) {
        return $cachedContent;
    }

    return $this->_frontend->afterRetrieve($cachedContent);
}
```

5. As you can see, the implementation is pretty simple. The methods we need to concentrate on now are `delete`, `exists`, and `queryKeys`, implemented as follows:

```
public function delete($keyName)
{
    $prefixedKey = $this->_prefix . $keyName;
    $aKey = $this->buildKey($prefixedKey);
    $this->_lastKey = $prefixedKey;

    $status = $this->db->remove($aKey);

    return $status == \Aerospike::OK;
}
```

```php
    public function exists($keyName = null, $lifetime = null)
    {
        if ($keyName === null) {
            $prefixedKey = $this->_lastKey;
        } else {
            $prefixedKey = $this->_prefix . $keyName;
        }

        if (!$prefixedKey) {
            return false;
        }

        $aKey = $this->buildKey($prefixedKey);
        $status = $this->db->get($aKey, $cache);

        return $status == \Aerospike::OK;
    }

    public function queryKeys($prefix = null)
    {
        if (!$prefix) {
            $prefix = $this->_prefix;
        } else {
            $prefix = $this->_prefix . $prefix;
        }

        $keys = [];
        $prefix = $this->_prefix;

        $callback = function ($record) use (&$keys, $prefix, $prefix)
        {
            $key = $record['key']['key'];

            if (empty($prefix) || 0 === strpos($key, $prefix))
            {
                $keys[] = preg_replace(
                    sprintf('#^%s(.+)#u', preg_quote($prefix)),
                    '$1',
                    $key
                );
            }
        };
```

```
    $this->db->scan($this->namespace, $this->set, $callback);

    return $keys;
}
```

6. Finally, we need a method that can create unique keys so that we can identify our data in the Aerospike database. We do this by creating a new method as follows:

```
protected function buildKey($key)
{
    return $this->db->initKey(
        $this->namespace,
        $this->set,
        $key
    );
}
```

7. It is now time for tests. To run the first test, we need the necessary dependencies. For that we will just use the `FactoryDefault` DI, which automatically registers certain services. Create the following test adjusting the `include_once` call with the path of your Aerospike installation:

```
use Phalcon\Tag;
use Phalcon\Di\FactoryDefault;
use Phalcon\Cache\Frontend\Output as FrontOutput;
use Phalcon\Cache\Backend\Aerospike as BackAerospike;

include_once 'Aerospike.php';

$di = new FactoryDefault;

// Create an Output frontend. Cache the files for 2 days
$frontCache = new FrontOutput(['lifetime' => 172800]);

$aerospike = new Aerospike(['hosts' => [['addr' => 'aerospike',
'port' => 3000]]]);

// Create the component that will cache from the "Output" to a
"Aerospike" backend
$cache = new BackAerospike($frontCache, ['db' => $aerospike]);

// Get/Set the cache file to my-cache-key
$content = $cache->start("some-cache-key");
```

```php
// If $content is null then the content will be generated for the
cache
if (null === $content) {
    // Print date and time
    echo date('r') . "\n";

    // Generate a link to the sign-up action
    echo Tag::linkTo(['user/signup', 'Sign Up', 'class' =>
'signup-button']) . "\n";

    // Store the output into the cache file
    $cache->save();
} else {
    // Echo the cached output
    echo $content;
}
```

8. Running the test should show that the time and date remain in line with the result returned, which means that the data is retrieved from our cache. We have just created a Phalcon-ready cache adapter with an initial test.

How it works...

Our recipe is a simple interface implementation. Due to the clear interface provided by Phalcon, implementing a custom cache adapter was really easy. You can use this recipe as a guide to implement your own cache adapters, using any number of storage options for your cache. This simplicity and extendibility is what we love in Phalcon!

We have completed this recipe in a relatively short time. We created a new class that implements the Phalcon\Cache\BackendInterface and then populated/created all the necessary methods for our adapter. The implementation was mostly focused on the use of the Aerospike PHP client.

There's more...

Installation instructions and other resources for the Aerospike server and PHP client can be found at: http://www.aerospike.com/

Additionally, you can find more information about caching adapter implementations in the Phalcon Incubator GitHub repository at: https://github.com/phalcon/incubator/tree/master/Library/Phalcon/Cache/Backend

Cache data to reduce access to database systems

One of the most resource-intensive areas of any framework is the database. It is associated with the complexity of connection and communication processes to be executed by PHP by every database query to get the required data. So, it is reasonable to cache data that changes rarely, thereby reducing database load as well as code execution time. In doing so, the identical code will not be executed twice or more times. Phalcon provides you with a unified caching interface in the context of using various adapters. In this chapter, we will consider the main principles of caching by working with a database, as well as the applicability of different adapters.

Getting ready

To successfully implement this recipe, we will need a working application, which will need to be able to receive and handle requests. You can use an application skeleton created with Phalcon Devtools. If you have one already, you can use it.

Additionally, we need a DBMS to store different link information. We will use MySQL in our example, but you can choose any other which you are used to. Of course, if you use any other DBMS you need to adapt those parts of the recipe related to the differences in the DBMS.

In this recipe, we will use different adapters to learn the unified caching interface. It is evident that we shall provide the adapters, which we will use, with the dependencies they need. For example, you need to have Memcached Server installed and started for the adapter Phalcon\Cache\Backend\Libmemcached.

How to do it...

Follow these steps to complete this recipe:

1. First you will need an application setup. We will use a boilerplate application created by Phalcon Devtools. If you already have an application ready, you can use that, or create it in any other way you see fit. Create the application using the following command:

   ```
   phalcon project cache simple
   ```

2. After the application skeleton has been created, we need to edit the configuration accordingly. First we will need a database connection. Open the configuration file and make the necessary changes to the database section. We will use a user `root` without a password. Your configuration might vary so you will need to adjust the recipe according to your needs:

```
'database' => [
        'adapter'      => 'Mysql',
        'host'         => '127.0.0.1',
        'username'     => 'root',
        'password'     => '',
        'dbname'       => 'cachedb',
        'charset'      => 'utf8',
        'port'         => 3306
],
```

3. Create a companies table and populate it with sample data:

```
CREATE TABLE 'companies' (
    'id' int(10) unsigned NOT NULL AUTO_INCREMENT,
    'name' varchar(70) COLLATE utf8_unicode_ci NOT NULL,
    'telephone' varchar(30) COLLATE utf8_unicode_ci NOT NULL,
    'address' varchar(40) COLLATE utf8_unicode_ci NOT NULL,
    'city' varchar(40) COLLATE utf8_unicode_ci NOT NULL,
    PRIMARY KEY ('id')
) ENGINE=InnoDB DEFAULT CHARSET=utf8 COLLATE=utf8_unicode_ci;


INSERT INTO 'companies' VALUES
    (1,'Acme','31566564','Address','Hello'),
    (2,'Acme Inc','+44 564612345','Guildhall, PO Box 270,
London','London');
```

4. Next, create the `Companies` Phalcon model with the following code:

```
class Companies extends \Phalcon\Mvc\Model
{
    public $id;
    public $name;
    public $telephone;
    public $address;
    public $city;
}
```

5. Open the `IndexController` and modify the `indexAction` as follows:

```
public function indexAction()
{
    $this->view->setVar(
        'companies',
        Companies::find(['order' => 'id'])
    );
}
```

6. For the presentation layer, we will need to modify the relevant view. Open the `views/index/index.volt` file and modify the code as shown in the following code snippet:

```
<h1>Companies</h1>

<table class="table">
    <thead>
        <tr>
            <th>#</th>
            <th>Name</th>
            <th>Telephone</th>
            <th>Address</th>
            <th>City</th>
        </tr>
    </thead>
    <tbody>
        {% for index, company in companies %}
            <tr>
                <td>{{ company.id }}</td>
                <td>{{ company.name }}</td>
                <td>{{ company.telephone }}</td>
                <td>{{ company.address }}</td>
                <td>{{ company.city }}</td>
            </tr>
        {% endfor %}
    </tbody>
</table>
```

7. Open `http://{your-host-here}` in your browser and you will see a list of companies.

8. Our next step is to enable a `logger` service so that we can check what happens when the page refreshes. We will need to set up the `logger` service in our `bootstrap` file by pasting the following code. If you already have a `logger` service setup, you can skip this step:

```
use Phalcon\Logger\Adapter\File as Logger;

$di->setShared('logger', function () use ($config) {
    return new Logger(
        $config->application->logsDir . 'application.log'
    );
});
```

9. We now need to change the configuration so that our logger service can log queries in the relevant file. Open the configuration file and make the necessary adjustments as shown in the following code snippet:

```
defined('APP_PATH') || define('APP_PATH', realpath('.'));

use Phalcon\Config;

return new Config([
    'database' => [
        'adapter'      => 'Mysql',
        'host'         => 'localhost',
        'username'     => 'root',
        'password'     => '',
        'dbname'       => 'cachedb',
        'charset'      => 'utf8',
    ],
    'application' => [
        'controllersDir' => APP_PATH . '/app/controllers/',
        'modelsDir'      => APP_PATH . '/app/models/',
        'migrationsDir'  => APP_PATH . '/app/migrations/',
        'viewsDir'       => APP_PATH . '/app/views/',
        'pluginsDir'     => APP_PATH . '/app/plugins/',
        'libraryDir'     => APP_PATH . '/app/library/',
        'cacheDir'       => APP_PATH . '/cache/',
        'logsDir'        => APP_PATH . '/logs/',
        'baseUri'        => '/',
    ]
]);
```

10. If the folders cache and logs do not exist, you will need to create them and ensure that they are writable by the web server user.

11. We now need to adjust our database service (db). Open the bootstrap file and adjust the service for the database as follows, so that we can log every query:

```
use Phalcon\Events\Manager as EventsManager;

$eventsManager = new EventsManager();

$di->setShared('db', function () use ($config, $eventsManager,
$di) {
    $dbConfig = $config->database->toArray();
    $adapter = $dbConfig['adapter'];
    unset($dbConfig['adapter']);

    $class = 'Phalcon\Db\Adapter\Pdo\\' . $adapter;
    $connection = new $class($dbConfig);

    $eventsManager->attach(
        'db',
        function ($event, $connection) use ($di) {
            if ($event->getType() == 'afterQuery') {
                $logger = $di->get('logger');
                $logger->debug(
                    $connection->getSQLStatement()
                );
            }
        }
    );

    $connection->setEventsManager($eventsManager);

    return $connection;
});
```

12. We now need to refresh the page. The list of companies should show up again. We will need to also monitor the log file (use the tail -f command). Each time the page refreshes, we will see the list of companies on screen as well as the query run in the log file.

13. Introducing database caching is very simple. Open the bootstrap file and add the modelsCache service as shown in the following code snippet:

```
use Phalcon\Cache\Frontend\Data as FrontendData;
use Phalcon\Cache\Backend\Libmemcached as BackendMemcached;
```

```
$di->set('modelsCache', function () {
  $cache = new BackendMemcached(
    new FrontendData(['lifetime' => 172800]),
    [
      'servers' => [
        [
          'host'   => 'memcached',
          'port'   => 11211,
          'weight' => 1
        ],
      ],
      'client' => [
        Memcached::OPT_HASH => Memcached::HASH_MD5,
      ]
    ]
  );

  return $cache;
});
```

14. Modify the `indexAction` as shown in the following code snippet:

```
public function indexAction()
{
    $this->view->setVar(
        'companies',
        Companies::find(
            [
                'order' => 'id',
                'cache' => ['key' => 'all-companies'],
            ]
        )
    );
}
```

15. Refresh the page several times and keep an eye on the `log` file created by the logger. You will notice that there is only one query to get the company data, and it happened during the first refresh. For any subsequent page load, the data is retrieved from the cache.

16. Let us see what is in the cache. Open the Terminal and run the command using telnet:

```
telnet 172.20.0.8 11211
Trying 172.20.0.8...
Connected to 172.20.0.8.
Escape character is '^]'.
get all-companies
```

17. You will see something like this (the output is reduced):

```
get all-companies
VALUE all-companies 0 1001
C:34:"Phalcon\Mvc\Model\Resultset\Simple":953:{...}
END
```

18. We will now try a different adapter to check our recipe:

```
use Phalcon\Cache\Backend\File as BackendFile;

$di->set('modelsCache', function () use ($config) {
    $cache = new BackendFile(
        new FrontendData(['lifetime' => 86400]),
        [
            'cacheDir' => $config->application->cacheDir,
        ]
    );

    return $cache;
});
```

19. Refresh the page several times again. Look in the query, and you will again notice that the database query occurred only once, during the first refresh. Any subsequent page loads used the cache to return the result set.

20. Finally, open the file `cache/all-companies` in the text editor of your choice. You will notice that the file contents show a serialized object just like the output we saw for the adapter `Phalcon\Cache\Backend\Libmemcached`.

How it works...

At the beginning of this recipe, we deployed the test application and configured it with database connection parameters as well as logs and cache folders.

Why is the **Phalcon Backend Cache** interface important and what does it mean to your application? Clearly, when developing your application you need to disable the cache, to ensure that your data is always fresh and to avoid mistakes by seeing cached versus actual data.

At times you might not need to use cache or use only the file `cache` so as to check what data is cached by inspecting the `cache` files in the filesystem. In all those situations, a careful implementation in the `bootstrap` class will allow you to register or not the cache and enable or disable it at will with simple configuration changes.

You can configure your caching implementation to be as flexible as you need it to be. For instance, a cache adapter could be defined in a configuration file and therefore you will not need to edit your main `bootstrap` class, which is essential especially in a production environment.

Defining different configuration environments is usually enough for most applications, one for development and one for production. Using those different environments, we can set up different parameters for our caching strategy, for instance a different lifetime for the cached objects.

If you wish to cache the returned data regardless of the adapter used (or use the cache service), you can use the cache parameter array in a model and cache the result set for five minutes as follows:

```
Companies::find([
  'cache' => [
    'key'      => 'my-cache',
    'lifetime' => 300
  ]
]);
```

You can even use a custom adapter provided, it implements the relevant cache backend interface as follows:

```
Companies::find([
  'order' => 'id',
  'cache' => 'myCustomCache',
]);
```

In the previous snippet, we need to have the `myCustomCache` service registered in the DI container. You can do it all without giving a thought to how your caching service is actually configured and what adapter is specified there. You have done it once and in one place. If you need to change this you can do it just as easily. Due to caching driver unification you can use any available driver or your own without worrying about any additional work on adapting the specifications.

There's more...

More detailed information about ORM in Phalcon, as well as different ways of data caching, can be found at: `https://docs.phalconphp.com/en/latest/reference/models-cache.html`

Creating a PHP extension using Zephir

From Phalcon 2.0 onwards, the framework is developed mainly using the Zephir language. Zephir is a language created by the Phalcon team, in order to ease the development of PHP extensions, and without the need to know C. The full refactoring of the framework, rewriting it from C to Zephir, has proven to be a daunting task and Zephir managed to pass with flying colors. The main goal was to ensure that the language was capable of creating PHP extensions for any purpose. The benefit of using this approach is that developers can now contribute to the framework without the need to know C, using a language that resembles Javascript or PHP and is thus easier to learn and use.

In this recipe, we will discuss the main principles of creating PHP extensions with Zephir. With the help of this recipe, you will discover how easy it is to learn and program in Zephir and, moreover, you will could find it easier to contribute to Phalcon with your ideas and bug fixes.

Getting ready

To successfully implement this recipe, you will need the latest version of Zephir installed on your computer. You can get the latest version from GitHub using `Git`. Using `Git` is not in the scope of this recipe, so we will not extend on that. You will also need a basic understanding and usage of the Linux operating system as well as being confident in working with the command line. Finally, you will need to have `sudo` or `root` access. If you do not have that, you will need to contact your system administrator.

To build an extension for PHP and to use Zephir to compile it, you will need to have the following packages installed:

- `gcc >= 4.x or clang >= 3.x`
- `re2c >= 0.13`

- ▸ gnu make >= 3.81
- ▸ autoconf >= 2.31
- ▸ automake >= 1.14
- ▸ libpcre3
- ▸ PHP development headers and tools

If you are using the **Ubuntu** operating system you can install these packages by issuing the following command (for different Linux flavors the command will vary depending on your package manager):

```
sudo apt-get update
sudo apt-get install git gcc make re2c php5 php5-json php5-dev libpcre3-
dev
```

We are using PHP 5 for the preceding commands. You will need to change the package names accordingly if you are using PHP 7. Additionally, the previous command is for Ubuntu 14.04.5. For different versions, you will have to check the package names and modify the previous command accordingly. There are resource links at the end of this recipe that will further help you to get answers to questions regarding packages and Zephir.

How to do it...

Follow these steps to complete this recipe:

1. Get the latest Zephir version by cloning the repository from GitHub:

   ```
   git clone git@github.com:phalcon/zephir.git
   ```

2. Go to the newly created folder `zephir` and install Zephir globally using the following command:

   ```
   ./install -c
   ```

3. Check whether Zephir was correctly installed and available from any folder by issuing the following command:

   ```
   zephir help
   ```

4. We will assume that we will create the new application under the /home/user/my-extension folder.

5. Now change to the folder where you will create the extension:

   ```
   cd /home/my-extension
   ```

6. The first thing you need to do is initialize the project by creating a project skeleton for the extension. Run the following command in the Terminal. Note, we tell Zephir about the desired namespace (Support) by passing it as the second parameter:

    ```
    zephir init support
    ```

7. Once that is completed, you will have a structure as follows:

    ```
    support/
    ├── ext
    │       └── kernel
    │                   └── extended
    └── support
    ```

8. The `ext` directory will be used by the compiler to create the extension. Zephir will generate C code, which will be placed there as well as necessary system files and libraries. We will focus on the `support/support` folder. You will create the necessary classes for the extension in this folder. Create a file called `support/support/arr.zep` and paste the following code into it:

    ```
    namespace Support;

    class Arr
    {
      public static function path(var ary, var path, var def = null,
    var delim = null) -> var
        {
        var keys, key, k, values, value, v, node, exists;

        if typeof ary != "array" {
          return def;
        }

        if typeof path == "array" {
          let keys = path;

        } else {
          if fetch node, ary[path] {
            return node;
          }

          if typeof delim != "string" {
            let delim = ".";
          }
    ```

```
          let path = ltrim(path, delim . " ");
          let path = rtrim(path, delim . " *");
          let keys = explode(delim, path);
        }

      do {
        let key = array_shift(keys);


        if ctype_digit(key) {
          let key = (int) key;
        }

        if fetch exists, ary[key] {
          if !empty keys {
            if typeof exists == "array" {
              let ary = exists;
            } else {
              break;
            }
          } else {
            return exists;
          }
        } else {
          if key == "*" {
            let values = [];

            for k, v in ary {
              let value = self::path(v, implode(".", keys));

              if value {
                let values[] = value;
              }
            }

            if !empty values {
              return values;
            } else {
              break;
            }
          } else {
            break;
```

```
        }
      }

    } while (keys);

    return def;
  }
}
```

9. We now need to build the project into an extension. Our project has only one class, `Support\Arr`, with one method, path. To compile the project we only need the following command:

    `zephir build`

10. If there are no typos or other errors, Zephir will display a success message as well as instructions to enable the extension. For our recipe, we are using PHP 5 in Ubuntu Linux 14.4.05. For this setup, PHP is located under the `/etc/php5` folder. Your setup might differ depending on your Linux distribution and version, and therefore the location of PHP will be different. You will need to adjust the instructions accordingly. We will now create a new configuration file to enable our extension:

    `sudo nano /etc/php5/cli/conf.d/50-support.ini`

11. Next, paste the following line into it:

    `extension=support.so`

12. To check if our extension has been loaded, we issue the following command:

    `php -m | grep support`

13. If the word support is displayed on the screen, we have just compiled and loaded our first extension successfully! Now let's test our extension. Create a file called `test.php` in a folder of your choice and paste the following content in it:

    ```php
    use Support\Arr;

    $array = 'string';

    // Get the value from non-array
    assert(Arr::path($array, 'foo', 'bar') === 'bar');

    $array = [
      'foo' => [
        'bar' => 'baz',
      ]
    ];
    ```

```php
// Get the value of $array['foo']
assert(Arr::path($array, 'foo') === ['bar' => 'baz']);

// Get the value of $array['foo']['bar']
assert(Arr::path($array, 'foo.bar') === 'baz');

$array = [
  'theme' => [
    'phalcomat' => [
      'color' => 'orange'
    ],
    'zyxep' => [
      'color' => 'turquoise'
    ],
  ]
];

$actual = Arr::path($array, 'theme.*');
$expect = ['phalcomat' => ['color' => 'orange'], 'zyxep' =>
['color' => 'turquoise']];

// Get the values of "*" in theme
assert($actual === $expect);

$array = [
  'theme' => [
    'button' => [
      'color' => '#f6f3e8',
      'background-color' => '#428bca',
    ],
    'link' => [
      'color' => '#118f9e',
      'background-color' => '#fff',
    ],
  ]
];


$actual = Arr::path($array, 'theme.*.color');
$expect = ['#f6f3e8', '#118f9e'];
```

```
// Get the values of "color" in theme
assert($actual === $expect);

// Get the values of "color" in theme
$colors = Arr::path($array, ['theme', '*', 'color']);

var_dump($colors);
```

14. Execute the test script as follows:

```
php test.php
```

15. You should be able to see the following:

```
array(2) {
  [0] =>
  string(7) "#f6f3e8"
  [1] =>
  string(7) "#118f9e"
}
```

How it works...

We have managed to create a very simple PHP extension without the need to know C by using Zephir. This is pretty revolutionary and opens the door to a wide variety of implementations. Zephir is not PHP, although its syntax resembles it. It does however offer a lot of functionality that could allow the implementation of any number of extensions. The Phalcon team is convinced that the future of PHP extensions lies in Zephir's popularity and feature set. Zephir is in constant development and more and more features are introduced in every release.

There's more...

For more information about installing Zephir in Windows see the documentation at: https://github.com/phalcon/zephir/blob/master/WINDOWS.md

For information related to the Zephir language refer to the detailed documentation at: http://docs.zephir-lang.com

Additionally, you can try to find solutions for non-common tasks on the Zephir forum at: https://forum.zephir-lang.com

Extending Phalcon using Zephir

In this recipe, we will learn how to use Phalcon classes and components in your PHP extension written in Zephir. We will create additional functionality custom to our extension with the use of Zephir and Phalcon, thus extending the Phalcon framework! Using Phalcon classes in Zephir has been a difficult task with minimal success for a long time, but recently the Phalcon team and the community found a solution and implemented it in the language.

Getting ready

To successfully implement this recipe, you will need the latest version of Zephir installed on your computer. You can get the latest version from GitHub using Git. Using Git is not in the scope of this recipe so we will not extend on that. You will also need a basic understanding of the Linux operating system as well as being confident in working with the command line. Finally, you will need to have `sudo` or `root` access. If you do not have that, you will need to contact your system administrator.

To build an extension for PHP and to use Zephir to compile it, you will need to have the following packages installed:

- gcc >= 4.x or clang >= 3.x
- re2c >= 0.13
- gnu make >= 3.81
- autoconf >= 2.31
- automake >= 1.14
- libpcre3
- PHP development headers and tools

If you are using the Ubuntu operating system you can install these packages by issuing the following command (for different Linux flavors the command will vary depending on your package manager):

```
sudo apt-get update
sudo apt-get install git gcc make re2c php5 php5-json php5-dev
libpcre3-dev
```

We are using PHP 5 for the preceding commands. You will need to change the package names accordingly if you are using PHP 7. Additionally, the previous command is for Ubuntu 14.04.5. For different versions, you will have to check the package names and modify the previous command accordingly. There are resource links at the end of this recipe that will further help you get answers to questions regarding packages and Zephir.

How to do it...

Follow these steps to complete this recipe:

1. The first step is to get the Phalcon project code. For the purposes of this recipe, we will use the `3.0.x` branch, but your source version might vary. You will need to adjust the following command accordingly if that is the case. Clone the repository as follows:

   ```
   git clone https://github.com/phalcon/cphalcon.git -b 3.0.x
   ```

2. Get the latest Zephir version just by cloning it from GitHub:

   ```
   git clone git@github.com:phalcon/zephir.git
   ```

3. Go to the newly created folder `zephir` and install Zephir globally using the following command:

   ```
   ./install -c
   ```

4. Check if Zephir is accessible from any directory, by using the following command:

   ```
   zephir help
   ```

5. Next we need to build the Phalcon source classes, so that Zephir will be able to understand and use them. We do this by exporting the classes and symbols using the following command:

   ```
   zephir build —export-classes
   ```

6. Now, go to the directory where you will create the skeleton for your extension, and run the following command. Note, we tell Zephir about the desired namespace (`ExtraDebug`) by passing it as the second parameter:

   ```
   zephir init ExtraDebug
   ```

7. After creating the needed structure of directories, create the file `extradebug/extradebug/debug.zep` and paste the following code:

   ```
   namespace ExtraDebug;

   use Phalcon\Version;

   class Debug extends \Phalcon\Debug
   {

       public function getVersion()
       {
           var version;
   ```

```
let version = Version::get() . "-debug";

return version;
    }
}
```

8. Then edit `extradebug/config.json` and add the following at the end of the file:

```
"external-dependencies": {
        "phalcon": "/path/to/the/phalcon/repo/which/you/have/just/
cloned"
}
```

9. Now we will compile the extension. Make sure that you are at the root of the `extradebug` folder and execute the following command:

   `zephir build`

10. If there are no typos or other errors, Zephir will display a success message as well as instructions to enable the extension. For our recipe, we are using PHP 5 in Ubuntu Linux 14.4.05. For this setup, PHP is located under the `/etc/php5` folder. Your setup might differ depending on your Linux distribution and version, and therefore the location of PHP will be different. You will need to adjust the instructions accordingly. We will now create a new configuration file to enable our extension:

    `sudo nano /etc/php5/cli/conf.d/999-extradebug .ini`

11. Then, place the following configuration parameter into it:

    `extension=extradebug.so`

12. Now let's check if the extension has been loaded:

    `php -m | grep extradebug`

13. If the word `extradebug` is displayed on the screen, we have just compiled and loaded our first extension, extending Phalcon successfully! Now let's test our extension. Execute the following command:

    `php -r 'echo (new ExtraDebug\Debug)->getVersion()."\n";'`

14. You should be able to see something like this:

    `3.0.2-debug`

How it works...

Creating an extension that uses Phalcon PHP is not a difficult task. We cloned the relevant repositories and exported the classes/symbols from Phalcon so that Zephir can use them as a known shared library.

We wrote the code for our test extension and *instructed* Zephir to use the Phalcon classes by setting up the external-dependencies section in the configuration. This instructed Zephir on how to use the Phalcon classes and load them as necessary. This strategy allows for internal static analysis taking into account external classes as well as other optimizations such as constant propagation and method caches, to name a few.

Note that extensions that depend on symbols exported by other extensions must be loaded after their dependencies:

```
extension=phalcon.so
```

```
extension=extradebug.so
```

To avoid editing the file `/etc/php5/cli/conf.d/phalcon.ini` we have created `/etc/php5/cli/conf.d/999-extradebug.ini`, specifying a large number as a prefix. This trick works in most Unix-like systems and defines the extension loading order.

This process works for all extensions created with Zephir but will not work for non- Zephir created extensions.

There's more...

For more information about installing Zephir in Windows see the documentation at: `https://github.com/phalcon/zephir/blob/master/WINDOWS.md`

For information related to the Zephir language refer to the detailed documentation at: `http://docs.zephir-lang.com`

Additionally, you can try to find solutions for unconventional tasks on the Zephir forum at: `https://forum.zephir-lang.com`

See also

The *Creating a PHP extension using Zephir* recipe, in this chapter

10

Securing Your Applications

In this chapter, we will cover:

- ▶ Securing data by encrypting it
- ▶ Securing passwords with hashing
- ▶ Preventing cross-site scripting (XSS) attacks
- ▶ Preventing cross-site request forgery (CSRF) attacks
- ▶ Implementing alternative access control lists
- ▶ Using OAuth for account authorization

Introduction

Phalcon offers a wealth of built-in classes and interfaces for hardening your application. These classes can be used and extended to fit many scenarios and to create custom solutions. Phalcon Incubator can help with this as it provides alternative classes to the built-in ones. Sometimes these Incubator solutions turn out to be very popular and are then included in the next Phalcon release.

With our first usage of the Incubator, we will implement the Database **Access Control List** (**ACL**) class from Incubator to keep our ACL data stored within the database. This is a more realistic usage of an ACL than using the bare-bones ACL class, since it can easily be modified for custom use while also potentially allowing users to modify settings via a web interface.

Next we will implement password hashing with the built-in `Phalcon\Security`. This will allow us to use a very simple interface for protected passwords that was designed to evolve to meet our future security needs.

There are a wide range of applications that are based upon the displaying of user-generated data, and without a strict focus on security, this will open up trivial **cross-site scripting** (**XSS**) security vulnerabilities in an application. Fortunately, the solution for this serious problem is rather simple and so we will explore a simple technique for preventing XSS attacks by using `Phalcon\Security`.

The next attack type that we will cover occurs when the server is accepting user input. The problem arises when another website makes a request to our application. Since this request is coming from the user's browser it appears as though the user initiated the action from within our system and so malicious sign-ins and comment postings can be made against our user's wishes. The solution for this **cross-site request forgery** (**CSRF**) attack is to use a single use nonce token in all of our forms. This ensures that the request came from within our site and not from outside of it. We will explore a solution for this by using `Phalcon\Security`.

Following are the source for more resources:

▸ Cryptographic Nonce: `https://en.wikipedia.org/wiki/Cryptographic_nonce`

▸ OAuth Authentication: `https://en.wikipedia.org/wiki/OAuth`

Securing data with encryption

In this recipe, we will create a solution for encrypting and decrypting data. This could be useful for creating a storage vault website that allows users to securely store their data in such a way that even the admins cannot access it or it could also be used to securely store valuable data on a remote machine. This recipe will use a reversible process so that the data can be decrypted after being encrypted. Although it is not necessary to understand the miraculous math involved with this process it is vital to understand one critical concept: Don't lose the encryption key or give anyone access to it. Other than that big one, it's all just good times.

Getting ready...

This recipe uses the Phalcon Developer Tools which we will use to setup a project skeleton.

How to do it...

Follow these steps to complete this recipe:

1. We need to have an application skeleton for experimentation. If you already have such an application, you can skip this step. Create a project skeleton using the `cli` template:

```
phalcon project encrypt_data cli
```

2. Add the following encryption key setting to your configuration file at `app/config/config.php`:

```
'security' => [
    // Change Key
    'key' => '%31.1e$i86e$f!8jz'
]
```

3. Create a `crypt` service in `app/config/services.php`:

```
$di->setShared('crypt', function () {
    $config = $this->getConfig();

    $crypt = new Phalcon\Crypt();
    $crypt->setKey($config->security->key);

    return $crypt;
});
```

4. Create the task, `app/tasks/SecureTask.php`:

```php
<?php

class SecureTask extends Phalcon\Cli\Task
{
    public function encryptAction($args)
    {
        if (count($args) < 2) {
            error_log('Encryption requires an input and output
file parameter.');
            exit(1);
        }

        $inputFile = $args[0];
        $outputFile = $args[1];

        $input = file_get_contents($inputFile);
        if ($input === false) {
            error_log('The source data file could not be read.');
            return;
        }

        $output = $this->getDI()
            ->getCrypt()
            ->encryptBase64($input);
```

```
        if (file_put_contents($outputFile, $output) === false) {
            error_log('The encrypted data could not be written.');
            return;
        }
    }

    public function decryptAction($args)
    {
        if (count($args) < 2) {
            error_log('Decryption requires an input and output
file parameter.');
            exit(1);
        }

        $inputFile = $args[0];
        $outputFile = $args[1];

        $input = file_get_contents($inputFile);
        if ($input === false) {
            error_log('The encrypted file could not be read.');
            return;
        }

        $output = $this->getDI()
            ->getCrypt()
            ->decryptBase64($input);

        if (file_put_contents($outputFile, $output) === false) {
            error_log('The decrypted data could not be written.');
            return;
        }
    }
}
```

5. Create a test data file in the root of the `project` directory named `data.txt` and put some interesting text in there, such as `This is important data!`.

6. Run the following command:

   `./run secure encrypt data.txt enc.txt`

7. There should now be an `enc.txt` file that contains some scrambled data. Run the following command:

   `./run secure decrypt enc.txt dec.txt`

   The `dec.txt` file should contain our original data.

How it works...

The math behind this recipe is incredibly complex, but from just an API viewpoint it is exceedingly simple. First let's look at the `SecureTask` class. We'll skip over the basic argument checking routines as they are typical and self-explanatory.

First we need to retrieve the data from the filesystem. While there are more complicated and flexible stream-based methods, the following approach is quite nice due to its simplicity:

```
$input = file_get_contents($inputFile);
```

Next use our `crypt` service to encrypt the data using a `base64` number system:

```
$output = $this->getDI()
    ->getCrypt()
    ->encryptBase64($input);
```

Finally, we save the encrypted data to disk with the following:

```
file_put_contents($outputFile, $output)
```

The decryption process is almost the same and so I'll abbreviate the entire method into just three calls. We can easily see that we are simply reading the file, using the `crypt` service to decrypt it and then saving it to the filesystem:

```
$input = file_get_contents($inputFile);

$output = $this->getDI()
    ->getCrypt()
    ->decryptBase64($input);

file_put_contents($outputFile, $output)
```

So it's as easy as that. Note that in our recipe, we are only working with text data, and with more complicated approaches, we could read the data in binary format and operate on it in batches while streaming it back out to the filesystem.

Securing passwords with hashing

In this recipe, we will create a solution for protecting passwords from data security breaches by using cryptographic one-way irreversible hashing. Using this technique will make it so that if anyone is ever able to penetrate the security of the website to steal the user's passwords, the data will be useless for signing into a user's profile or for using on other websites. While it may sound like we are resigning ourselves to defeat from the very start this is in fact not the best way to think about this issue.

We must do many things to protect our system and users, and each additional step simply builds our overall protection to contain a security breach from completely compromising all aspects of the system. Users may use the same password on multiple sites and this will allow us to protect their other accounts. Additionally, hashing the user passwords is a very simple step and without this step, any security audit of any value would most certainly give a system an instant fail if it did not use this industry standard protection.

Getting ready

This recipe uses Phalcon Developer Tools, which we will use to set up a project skeleton.

This recipe requires the **mbstring (multi-byte string)** PHP extension to be installed in the web environment.

How to do it...

Follow these steps to complete this recipe:

1. We need to have an application skeleton for experimentation. If you already have such an application, you can skip this step. Create a project skeleton using the `simple` template:

   ```
   phalcon project secure_password simple
   ```

2. Now point the web browser at the root directory of the project. There should be a page with `Congratulations!` ..... If we see the `Volt directory can't be written` error message, then permissions of the `cache` directory need to be changed to allow the web server to write to it.

3. Create the database, `secure_password`:

   ```
   DROP TABLE IF EXISTS 'users';
   CREATE TABLE 'users' (
       'id' int(11) NOT NULL AUTO_INCREMENT,
       'username' varchar(30) NOT NULL,
       'password' varchar(80) NOT NULL,
       PRIMARY KEY ('id')
   ) ENGINE=InnoDB DEFAULT CHARSET=utf8;
   ```

4. Add the following password setting to the application configuration at `app/config/config.php`:

```php
'application' => [
    // ...
    'password' => [
        'minLen' => 4,
        'maxLen' => 12
    ]
],
```

5. Create the model, `app/models/Users.php`:

```php
<?php

class Users extends Phalcon\Mvc\Model
{
    public function beforeValidationOnCreate()
    {
        if (!$this->hashPassword()) {
            return false;
        }
    }

    public function beforeValidationOnUpdate()
    {
        if ($this->hasChanged('password')) {
            if (!$this->hashPassword()) {
                return false;
            }
        }
    }

    protected function hashPassword()
    {
        $configPassword = $this->getDI()
            ->getConfig()
            ->application->password;
```

```php
        // The "mbstring" extension must be installed to provide
this function.
        $length = mb_strlen($this->password);
        if ($length < 4 || $length > 12) {
            $this->appendMessage(new Phalcon\Mvc\Model\
Message('Invalid password length', 'password', 'InvalidValue'));
            return false;
        }

        $this->password = $this->getDI()
            ->getSecurity()
            ->hash($this->password);

        return true;
    }

    public function validation()
    {
        $validator = new Phalcon\Validation();

        $validator->add('username', new Phalcon\Validation\
Validator\Uniqueness([
            'message' => 'The username already exists.'
        ]));

        return $this->validate($validator);
    }

    public function initialize(){
        $this->keepSnapshots(true);
    }
}
```

6. Create the controller, `app/controllers/UsersController.php`:

```php
<?php

class UsersController extends Phalcon\Mvc\Controller
{
    public function indexAction()
    {

    }
```

```php
public function createAction()
{
    $username = $this->request->getPost('username', 'string');
    $password = $this->request->getPost('password', 'string');

    $user = new Users([
        'username' => $username,
        'password' => $password
    ]);
    if(!$user->create()) {
        $this->flash->error($user->getMessages()[0]);
        return;
    }

    $this->flash->success('User created');
}

public function changePasswordAction()
{
    $username = $this->request->getPost('username', 'string');
    $password = $this->request->getPost('password', 'string');

    $user = Users::findFirstByUsername($username);
    if (!$user) {
        $this->flash->error('The user could not be found.');
        return;
    }

    $user->password = $password;
    if(!$user->save()) {
        $this->flash->error($user->getMessages()[0]);
        return;
    }

    $this->flash->success('Password Changed successfully.');
}

public function signinAction()
{
    $username = $this->request->getPost('username', 'string');
    $password = $this->request->getPost('password', 'string');
```

```
        $user = Users::findFirstByUsername($username);
        if (!$user) {
            $this->flash->error('The user could not be found.');
            return;
        }

        if (!$this->security->checkHash($password, $user-
>password)) {
            $this->flash->error('Invalid password.');
            return;
        }

        $this->flash->success('Signed in successfully.');
    }
}
```

7. Create the `Volt` view, `app/views/users/index.volt`:

```
<h3>Create</h3>
<form method="post">
  <input type="text" name="username" placeholder="username"/>
  <input type="password" name="password" placeholder="password"/>
  <input type="submit" formaction="{{ url('users/create') }}"
value="Create User"/>
</form>

<h3>Signin</h3>
<form method="post">
  <input type="text" name="username" placeholder="username"/>
  <input type="password" name="password" placeholder="password"/>
  <input type="submit" formaction="{{ url('users/signin') }}"
value="Sign User"/>
</form>

<h3>Change Password</h3>
<form method="post">
  <input type="text" name="username" placeholder="username"/>
  <input type="password" name="password" placeholder="password"/>
  <input type="submit" formaction="{{ url('users/changePassword')
}}" value="Change Password"/>
</form>
```

8. In the browser, go to the path, /users, from the root folder. Create a user by entering the username and password, and clicking the **Create a User** button. Next, go back to the /users path and sign into the system under the **Signin** section. If that worked then go back and try to enter in the incorrect password to see that it fails. Then go back to the /users path and change the users password under the **Change Password** section. After that, click back and try to sign in again with the new password.

How it works...

First we'll start out by looking at the Users model.

In this model, we've defined two event methods, beforeValidationOnCreate and beforeValidationOnUpdate, which are part of the dispatch cycle and are called respectively during a model creation and on updating.

With the model creation, we want to always hash the user password; if there is a problem with the password then we want to abort the model creation by returning false. Take a look at the following code:

```
public function beforeValidationOnCreate()
{
    if (!$this->hashPassword()) {
        return false;
    }
}
```

With model updates, we only want to hash the password if the value changed from when it was taken from the database, as shown in the following code snippet:

```
public function beforeValidationOnUpdate()
{
    if ($this->hasChanged('password')) {
        if (!$this->hashPassword()) {
            return false;
        }
    }
}
```

However, by default, our models will be incapable of knowing if their properties changed from the original database value, and so we must enable property snapshots in the initialize event, as shown in the following code:

```
public function initialize(){
    $this->keepSnapshots(true);
}
```

Our `hashPassword` method acts as a sort of validator that also transforms the data before storing the password field in the database. By using this approach, we ensure that the password will always be hashed each time that it is set.

Here we are checking that the password is of the correct length and if it is not then we append a new `Message` object to the model so that we can determine the reason for the model creation or update failure. Also, we must return `false` to halt the model dispatch cycle, as shown in the following code:

```
$length = mb_strlen($this->password);
if ($length < 4 || $length > 12) {
    $this->appendMessage(new Phalcon\Mvc\Model\Message('Invalid
password length', 'password', 'InvalidValue'));
    return false;
}
```

Finally, we use the security service to hash the password:

```
$this->password = $this->getDI()
    ->getSecurity()
    ->hash($this->password);
```

Now we'll look at the `UsersController`, and since we have pushed so much of the business logic into the `Users` model, the controller becomes fairly simple.

First we'll abbreviate the `createAction` method to remove error handling, to just show the important parts, as shown in the following code snippet:

```
$user = new Users([
    'username' => $username,
    'password' => $password
]);
$user->create();
```

It's very simple, actually. We pass in the full password value and the model does the hashing for us.

Now let's look at and abbreviate the `changePasswordAction` method to only show the essential parts:

```
$user = Users::findFirstByUsername($username);
$user->password = $password;
$user->save();
```

Again, it's very simple due to the business logic being in the model.

Now we'll finish by looking at the partially abbreviated `signinAction` method:

```
$user = Users::findFirstByUsername($username);

if (!$this->security->checkHash($password, $user->password)) {
    $this->flash->error('Invalid password.');
    return;
}

$this->flash->success('Signed in successfully.');
```

The important part of this method is the `checkHash` method on the security service. What this does is to hash the raw password from user input and compare it with an already hashed password stored in the `Users` record. Since we are able to make use of the hashed password without knowing its original value, we have proven that storing the original value is only a security risk without benefits.

Preventing Cross-site scripting (XSS) attacks

In this recipe, we will demonstrate simple techniques for stopping XSS attacks. These attacks are the result of trusting user input directly in the output of either CSS, JavaScript, or HTML. Although these values are typically stored and then later retrieved from the database, we don't actually need to use a database to illustrate these attacks. This recipe is rather simple, in that in our controller, we have stored snippets of code that, when used directly in our Volt views, will cause the browser to run our malicious JavaScript code. Today we are hackers.

Getting ready...

This recipe uses Phalcon Developer Tools, which we will use to set up a project skeleton, Database access is not required.

How to do it...

Follow these steps to complete this recipe:

1. We need to have an application skeleton for experimentation. If you already have such an application, you can skip this step. Create a project skeleton using the `simple` template:

   ```
   phalcon project xss_protection simple
   ```

2. Now point the web browser at the root directory of the project. There should be a page with Congratulations! ..... If we see the Volt directory can't be written error message then permissions of the cache directory need to be changed to allow the web server to write to it.

3. Create the controller, app/controllers/HackedController.php:

```php
<?php

class HackedController extends Phalcon\Mvc\Controller
{
    protected function onConstruct()
    {
        $this->hack = "<script>confirm('Transfer $10,000 to
Nigeria for miracle hair treatment.')</script>";
    }

    public function htmlAction()
    {
        $this->view->setVars([
            'isSecure' => $this->request->getQuery('secure') ===
'yes',
            'post'     => $this->hack
        ]);
    }

    public function javascriptAction()
    {
        $this->view->setVars([
            'isSecure' => $this->request->getQuery('secure') ===
'yes',
            'title'    => "';</script>{$this->hack}<script>var
blah='"
        ]);
    }

    public function cssAction()
    {
        $this->view->setVars([
            'isSecure' => $this->request->getQuery('secure') ===
'yes',
            'style'    => "\"> {$this->hack} <p id=\""
        ]);
    }
}
```

4. Create the view, `app/views/hacked/css.volt`:

```
{% if isSecure %}
  <p style="{{ style | escape_css }}">The world is a big place</p>
{% else %}
  <p style="{{ style }}">The world is a big place</p>
{% endif %}
```

5. Create the view, `app/views/hacked/html.volt`:

```
{% if isSecure %}
  You were protected from XSS with proper escaping.
  <p>{{ post | escape }}</p>
{% else %}
  You were just hacked with XSS!
  <p>{{ post }}</p>
{% endif %}
```

6. Create the view, `app/views/hacked/javascript.volt`:

```
{% if isSecure %}
  You were protected from XSS with proper escaping.
  <script>
    window.title = '{{ title | escape_js}}'
  </script>
{% else %}
  You were just hacked with XSS!
  <script>
    window.title = '{{ title }}'
  </script>
{% endif %}
```

7. In the browser, go to the following paths from the root path of the project:

```
/hacked/css
/hacked/css?secure=yes
/hacked/html
/hacked/html?secure=yes
/hacked/javascript
/hacked/javascript?secure=yes
```

   ❑ For each path, without the secure query variable a rather interesting message should appear and when `?secure=yes` is added it should escape the specially crafted escaped characters that caused the XSS attack.

How it works...

In the `HackedController` class, we are storing a malicious JavaScript segment in the `onConstruct` event that we will use later in the `htmlAction`, `javascriptAction`, and `cssAction` methods. In each of these three `action` methods, we simple pass the `isSecure` value into the view based upon the secure HTTP query variable, and then we insert our hack wrapped in various control characters designed to break out of each of the three environments (script, style, and HTML). In this instance, the script is merely a popup, but it could be something much worse like actually calling out to a remote site and executing foreign JavaScript right within the context of our website. The sky is the limit for this sort of attack and once something can be run then anything is possible.

Preventing Cross-Site Request Forgery (CSRF) attacks

CSRF attacks are a very old class of vulnerability that must be addressed for proper security. The issue arises when a website uses JavaScript to make a request to a second website and the second website is unable to know if the user made that request themselves through an action on their own website or through another website. If there is no protection for this fraudulent request then a second website can perform actions such as attempting to sign in for the user, or if the user is already signed in then requesting sensitive API data, parsing it, and then retransmitting it. In this recipe, we will detail some methods for securing this security vulnerability.

Getting ready...

This recipe uses Phalcon Developer Tools, which we will use to set up a project skeleton.

How to do it...

Follow these steps to complete this recipe:

1. We need to have an application skeleton for experimentation. If you already have such an application, you can skip this step. Create a project skeleton using the `simple` template:

   ```
   phalcon project csrf_protection simple
   ```

2. Now point the web browser at the root directory of the project. There should be a page with `Congratulations!` ..... If we see the `Volt directory can't be written` error message, then permissions of the `cache` directory need to be changed to allow the web server to write to it.

3. Create the controller, `app/controllers/ControllerBase.php`, to be used as the base controller for all other `controllers`. In the simple dev tools template, this class should already exist and so in that case simply add the `beforeExecuteRoute` method to the class:

```php
<?php

use Phalcon\Mvc\Controller;

abstract class ControllerBase extends Controller
{
    public function beforeExecuteRoute($dispatcher)
    {
        $this->response->setHeader('X-Frame-Options',
'SAMEORIGIN');
    }
}
```

4. Create the controller, `app/controllers/SigninController.php`:

```php
<?php

class SigninController extends ControllerBase
{
    public function indexAction()
    {
        if ($this->request->isPost()) {
            if ($this->security->checkToken()) {
                $this->flash->success('Succesfully signed in.');
            } else {
                $this->flash->error('CSRF token did not match.');
            }
        }
    }
}
```

5. Create the view, `app/views/signin/index.volt`:

```
<h3>CSRF example</h3>

<div>
  <form method="post">
    <input type="text" name="email" placeholder="email"
value=""/>
```

```
    <input type="hidden" name="{{ security.getTokenKey() }}"
value="{{ security.getToken() }}"/>
    <input type="submit" formaction="{{ url('signin') }}"
value="Sign In"/>
  </form>
</div>

<div>
  {{content()}}
</div>
```

6. In the browser, go to the root of the project path and open up two identical windows to the path /signin. Now go back to the first window and click **Sign In**. It's not necessary to fill in the e-mail text box as that is only used to fill out the page. It should say CSRF token did not match. Now, immediately click the **Sign In** button again and it should say Successfully signed in.

How it works...

When we load the signin/index.volt view it makes a call to security.getTokenKey() and security.getToken(), which will then store these values in the PHP session as $PHALCON/CSRF/KEY$ and $PHALCON/CSRF$. Each time the signin page is accessed it generates new session values.

If we look at the sign-in controller then we see that it calls the checkToken method on the security service. This checks to make sure that the security token key and value that were provided in the sign-in form match the values stored in the session variables, as shown in the following code:

```
if ($this->security->checkToken()) {
    $this->flash->success('Succesfully signed in.');
} else {
    $this->flash->error('CSRF token did not match.');
}
```

However, there is one exceedingly common and also difficult to solve pitfall when the browser tries to access missing files, which will return a 404 error, such as a favicon or CSS. The problem is that missing files are interpreted as a path for the index.php entry point and so this will cause our application to run the dispatch loop two or more times and, as a result, the first call to getTokeyKey() will receive and then remove the key stored in the $_SESSION. Once the second dispatch loop runs there will no longer be a key in the session, which will cause the CSRF check to fail.

Additionally, as another form of protection, we are making each response send back an HTTP header that tells the browser that our page should never be embedded within another page's iframe as this could open up additional security vulnerabilities. Take a look at the following code:

```
public function beforeExecuteRoute($dispatcher)
{
    $this->response->setHeader('X-Frame-Options', 'SAMEORIGIN');
}
```

In this recipe, we are using an event in our base controller, but this could also be performed by attaching a plugin to the dispatcher that listens for this same event. There is often more than one way to do things in Phalcon. Examples of how to set up a dispatcher plugin can be found in many other recipes in this book, as well as the Phalcon documentation.

Implementing alternative access control lists

In this recipe, we will learn how to extend the base Phalcon ACL with a more feature-rich version from Phalcon Incubator. This powerful ACL class has built-in support for PDO databases and can even directly add, delete, and modify the database to construct the ACL data through its API. This recipe is a bit different in that we will only be importing the structure of the database without any specific entries to describe the permissions. We will fill this data by first running a CLI task to generate our permissions using the Incubator ACL class and then we will test them using the web environment.

Following is the source for more resources:

> ▸ `https://docs.phalconphp.com/en/latest/reference/acl.html`

Getting ready...

This recipe uses Phalcon Developer Tools, which we will use to set up a project skeleton, as well as Composer for installing the Phalcon Incubator resources.

We will need a database connection for this recipe.

We need to install Composer to be able to install the officially supported Phalcon Incubator repository. The open-source Composer tool may be obtained at: `https://getcomposer.org/`

How to do it...

Follow these steps to complete this recipe:

1. We need to have an application skeleton for experimentation. If you already have such an application, you can skip this step. Create a project skeleton using the `modules` template:

   ```
   phalcon project access_list modules
   ```

2. Now point the web browser at the root directory of the project. There should be a page with `Congratulations!` ..... If we see the `Volt directory can't be written` error message, then permissions of the `cache` directory need to be changed to allow the web server to write to it.

3. Install the Phalcon Incubator resources with the following:

   ```
   composer require phalcon/incubator
   ```

4. Add the following line to the end of the loader `config` at `app/config/loader.php` to integrate the Incubator package:

   ```
   require BASE_PATH . '/vendor/autoload.php';
   ```

5. Create the database, `access_list`, and then set the database settings in `app/config/config.php`:

   ```
   CREATE TABLE 'roles' (
     'name' VARCHAR(32) NOT NULL,
     'description' TEXT,
     PRIMARY KEY('name')
   );

   CREATE TABLE 'access_list' (
     'roles_name' VARCHAR(32) NOT NULL,
     'resources_name' VARCHAR(32) NOT NULL,
     'access_name' VARCHAR(32) NOT NULL,
     'allowed' INT(3) NOT NULL,
     PRIMARY KEY('roles_name', 'resources_name', 'access_name')
   );

   CREATE TABLE 'resources' (
     'name' VARCHAR(32) NOT NULL,
     'description' TEXT,
     PRIMARY KEY('name')
   );
   ```

```
CREATE TABLE 'resources_accesses' (
  'resources_name' VARCHAR(32) NOT NULL,
  'access_name' VARCHAR(32) NOT NULL,
  PRIMARY KEY('resources_name', 'access_name')
);

CREATE TABLE 'roles_inherits' (
  'roles_name' VARCHAR(32) NOT NULL,
  'roles_inherit' VARCHAR(32) NOT NULL,
  PRIMARY KEY(roles_name, roles_inherit)
);
```

6. Add the ACL service to app/config/services.php:

```
$di->setShared('acl', function() {
    $acl = new Phalcon\Acl\Adapter\Database([
        'db'                => $this->getDb(),
        'roles'             => 'roles',
        'rolesInherits'     => 'roles_inherits',
        'resources'         => 'resources',
        'resourcesAccesses' => 'resources_accesses',
        'accessList'        => 'access_list'
    ]);

    $acl->setDefaultAction(Phalcon\Acl::DENY);

    return $acl;
});
```

7. Add the security plugin to the dispatcher service by changing it to the following in app/config/services_web.php:

```
$di->setShared('dispatcher', function() {
    $dispatcher = new Dispatcher();
    $dispatcher->setDefaultNamespace('Access_list\Modules\
Frontend\Controllers');

    $eventsManager = $this->getEventsManager();

    $securityPlugin = new Access_list\SecurityPlugin();
    $securityPlugin->setDI($this);

    $eventsManager->attach('dispatch', $securityPlugin);

    $dispatcher->setEventsManager($eventsManager);
```

```
        return $dispatcher;
});
```

8. Create a security plugin, `app/common/library/SecurityPlugin.php`:

```php
<?php
namespace Access_list;

class SecurityPlugin extends \Phalcon\Mvc\User\Plugin
{
    public function beforeExecuteRoute(\Phalcon\Events\Event
$event, \Phalcon\Mvc\Dispatcher $dispatcher)
    {
        $acl = $this->getDI()
            ->getAcl();
        $request = $this->getDI()
            ->getRequest();
        $router = $this->getDI()
            ->getRouter();

        $role = ($request->hasQuery('role')) ? $request-
>getQuery('role') : 'Anonymous';
        $controllerName = $dispatcher->getControllerName();
        $actionName = $dispatcher->getActionName();
        $moduleName = $router->getModuleName();

        $resourceName = "$moduleName::$controllerName";

        if (!$acl->isAllowed($role, $resourceName, $actionName)) {
            echo "Not allowed!";
            exit;
        }
    }
}
```

9. Create a CLI environment task for building the ACL with `app/modules/cli/tasks/BuildTask.php`:

```php
<?php
namespace Access_list\Modules\Cli\Tasks;

class BuildTask extends \Phalcon\Cli\Task
{
    public function mainAction()
    {
```

```php
        $acl = $this->getDI()
            ->getAcl();

        $acl->addRole(new \Phalcon\Acl\Role('Admin'));
        $acl->addRole(new \Phalcon\Acl\Role('User'));
        $acl->addRole(new \Phalcon\Acl\Role('Anonymous'));

        $acl->addResource('frontend::index', ['index']);
        $acl->addResource('frontend::products', ['index',
'change', 'add', 'cart']);

        $acl->allow('Admin', 'frontend::products', '*');
        $acl->allow('Admin', 'frontend::index', '*');

        $acl->allow('User', 'frontend::products', ['index',
'cart']);
        $acl->allow('User', 'frontend::index', '*');

        $acl->allow('Anonymous', 'frontend::index', '*');
    }
}
```

10. Create a test controller for the ACL with `app/modules/frontend/controllers/ProductsController.php`:

```php
<?php
namespace Access_list\Modules\Frontend\Controllers;

class ProductsController extends \Phalcon\Mvc\Controller
{
    public function indexAction()
    {
        return 'Accessed Products Index';
    }

    public function changeAction()
    {
        return 'Accessed Products Change';
    }

    public function addAction()
    {
        return 'Accessed Products Add';
    }
```

```
        public function cartAction()
        {
            return 'Accessed Products Cart';
        }
    }
```

11. In the browser, go to the base path of the project. We should see `Not allowed!`. If there is an error message then try setting the `cache/volt` directory to be writable by the web server.

12. On the command line, change to the `project` directory and create the ACL entries by executing the following command:

    `./run build`

13. In the browser, go to the following paths from the base of the project. Let's see if we can guess each result before proceeding to the next *How it works* section. Remember that the default routing scheme is set up so that if the controller or action are not specified, they each default to `index`:

    `/`

    `/index/index?role=blahblah`

    `/products`

    `/products?role=user`

    `/products/add?role=user`

    `/products/add?role=admin`

How it works...

First let's start by being very clear about a serious security-related shortcut that we took in this recipe where for simplicity's sake we use the HTTP query variable *role* to specify which ACL role we will be using for a request. In a normal production application, this ACL setup would be accompanied by a fully featured authorization system and without that, our ACL system can never be secure. Now, with this understanding, we will allow ourselves this shortcut to be able to specifically look at just the ACL.

Let's look at our ACL service. Now, as is typical for all resources in Phalcon, we are providing access to our ACL through the DI service. This is useful because the ACL object depends upon the db service, and so by making this service shared we can get the benefits of a singleton object while also handling the dependencies. Take a look at the following code snippet:

```
$di->setShared('acl', function() {
    $acl = new Phalcon\Acl\Adapter\Database([
        'db'                    => $this->getDb(),
        // ...
});
```

Notice how we pass in each table to be used in our database ACL. This allows us the flexibility to name our tables anything:

```
'roles'             => 'roles',
'rolesInherits'     => 'roles_inherits',
'resources'         => 'resources',
'resourcesAccesses' => 'resources_accesses',
'accessList'        => 'access_list'
```

Notice how we are skipping the use of models for our ACL and we are going with direct table access as performed inside the ACL. Phalcon allows this kind of flexibility and performance. Remember that full use of the ORM layer adds performance penalties, and in our case we specifically want to go through the API that our ACL class provides.

Next we have perhaps the most important line of all. This sets the default action of our ACL to deny permission unless there is a specific rule that grants the permission, as shown in the following code snippet:

```
$acl->setDefaultAction(Phalcon\Acl::DENY);
```

We will now look at `app/modules/cli/tasks/BuildTask.php`, which we use to construct our ACL rules. In our ACL, there are three specific types of entries that we create: roles, resources, and grants.

Roles are simply classifications of users. Here we are creating a super user, a normal user, and a user who has yet to authenticate:

```
$acl->addRole(new \Phalcon\Acl\Role('Admin'));
$acl->addRole(new \Phalcon\Acl\Role('User'));

$acl->addRole(new \Phalcon\Acl\Role('Anonymous'));
```

Next we will add our resources. In this recipe, we are using both the module and controller names together to create our resource name, as this allows our application to work with multiple web modules, with the second argument being the list of actions to support, as shown in the following code snippet:

```
$acl->addResource('frontend::index', ['index']);
$acl->addResource('frontend::products', ['index', 'change', 'add',
'cart']);
```

Finally, we grant each role access to specific resources.

In the case of the `Admin` user, we are giving access to all resource-action pairs in the `IndexController` and `ProductsController`, as shown in following:

```
$acl->allow('Admin', 'frontend::products', '*');
$acl->allow('Admin', 'frontend::index', '*');
```

For the `User` user, we are granting some permissions but being careful not to give access to the ability to `add` and `change` Product items:

```
$acl->allow('User', 'frontend::products', ['index', 'cart']);
$acl->allow('User', 'frontend::index', '*');
```

Finally, the `Anonymous` user only gains access to the index page:

```
$acl->allow('Anonymous', 'frontend::index', '*');
```

Next let's look at the security plugin that we attached to our dispatcher. Here, we are implementing the event, `beforeExecuteRoute`, because this event is capable of canceling the dispatch process if our ACL conditions are not met, as shown in the following:

```
public function beforeExecuteRoute(\Phalcon\Events\Event $event, \
Phalcon\Mvc\Dispatcher $dispatcher)
```

Here, we are after four important bits of information: the role, controller, action, and module name. Remember that we defined the ACL resource names as the module name together with the controller name. As explained earlier, we are taking a shortcut here with the role by allowing the user to directly enter it from the HTTP query variable, `role`. In a normal system, the role name would be controlled by an authentication service and stored as a PHP session variable, as shown in the following code snippet:

```
$role = ($request->hasQuery('role')) ? $request->getQuery('role') :
'Anonymous';
$controllerName = $dispatcher->getControllerName();
$actionName = $dispatcher->getActionName();
$moduleName = $router->getModuleName();

$resourceName = "$moduleName::$controllerName";
```

Finally, if the current role does not have access to the resource then we will exit the request. More advanced use cases would instead use the `Dispatcher::forward` method to stop the execution of the current controller-action route and to continue to another controller-action such as to display a permission-denied notice, as shown in the following:

```
if (!$acl->isAllowed($role, $resourceName, $actionName)) {
    echo "Not allowed!";
    exit;
}
```

Using OAuth for account authorization

OAuth is a powerful and easy to use authentication system that allows a user to sign into a website through the credentials of a third-party site. This reduces the burden of needing to remember passwords and it can be more convenient as well by allowing sign in with a single click. In this recipe, we will create a system that allows automatic account creation and sign in through a user's Google account.

Getting ready...

This recipe uses Phalcon Developer Tools for creating a project skeleton and Composer for installing third-party libraries. Additionally, since this recipe uses Google as the authentication service, we will need to create and configure a Google account for use with the OAuth.

This recipe has a very delicate setup due to the conditions of the Google OAuth API.

This recipe requires the PHP **curl** extension to be installed.

How to do it...

Follow these steps to complete this recipe:

1. We need to have an application skeleton for experimentation. If we already have such an application, we can skip this step. Create a project skeleton using the `simple` template:

   ```
   phalcon project oauth_signin simple
   ```

2. Use Composer to install third-party packages for OAuth authentication. Run these commands in the base path of the `project` folder:

   ```
   composer require league/oauth2-client
   composer require league/oauth2-google
   ```

3. Make sure that the loader config contains the library path by adding it to the `registerDirs` call:

   `$config->application->libraryDir,`

4. Set up the Composer third-party packages by adding the following to the end of the loader config in the file, `app/config/loader.php`:

   ```
   include BASE_PATH . '/vendor/autoload.php';
   ```

5. Create the `oauth_signin` database:

```
DROP TABLE IF EXISTS 'users';
CREATE TABLE 'users' (
   'id' int(11) NOT NULL AUTO_INCREMENT,
   'email' varchar(100) CHARACTER SET utf8 COLLATE utf8_bin NOT
NULL,
   PRIMARY KEY ('id')
) ENGINE=InnoDB DEFAULT CHARSET=utf8;
```

6. Set the database name in `app/config/config.php`. Change the `dbname` to `oauth_signin` and username and password to their correct values.

7. Create the model, `app/models/Users.php`:

```php
<?php

class Users extends Phalcon\Mvc\Model
{
}
```

8. We need to generate a Google OAuth credential. Unfortunately, even though we are only working locally, the hostname that points to the web server will need to be a valid domain name (not localhost) for it to be accepted by the Google OAuth API setup. Fortunately, it is not necessary to actually purchase a domain name for local use because we can instead fool the computer by using the operating system's hosts file. The first thing is to pick a domain name for use with the project, and we will refer to this as `DOMAIN.com` so that anywhere we see this, we will instead substitute it for the chosen domain name. We can accomplish this by modifying the hosts file of the operating system. On Windows this file is located at `C:\Windows\System32\drivers\etc` and on OSX and Linux it is located at `/etc/hosts`. While using administrator permissions, modify the hosts file by adding the following:

```
127.0.0.1  DOMAIN.com
```

9. Go to `https://console.developers.google.com` and do the following:
   - Create a project called `Phalcon Book`:

❑ Click the **Library**, left-side tab and search for **Google+ API**, and click the
ENABLE button:

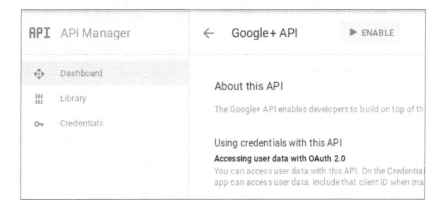

❑ Click the **Credentials** left-hand tab and click **Create credentials**, and then
Oauth client ID:

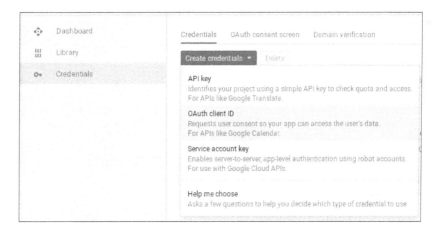

❑ Finally, create and save the credential by filling in the values as they appear.
Make sure that the domain `phalcon-book.com` is the same domain that
you used for this recipe and that the path from the webspace matches
your system. For example, your path might be missing the `chapter_10`
path prefix or it might have an additional path, depending on how you
are organizing your projects. Unfortunately, there is no way to completely
generalize and it needs to exactly match with what you supply in the Google
form.

> ❑ In other words, the **Authorized JavaScript origins** should look like **http://DOMAIN.com** and the **Authorized redirect URIs** should look like **http://DOMAIN.com/PREFIX_PATH/oauth_signin/session/oauth/google/**. Replace the DOMAIN.com with whatever locally defined hostname you have set up. On my machine, I used phalcon-book.com but you can use whatever you want as long as you added the domain to your hosts file:

❏   After creating the credential a popup should appear that says **OAuth client**.
Copy the client ID and client secret for use in the next step:

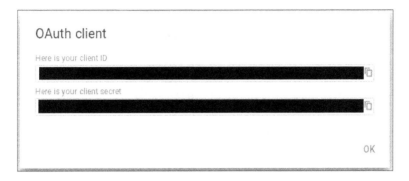

10. Add the following `services` key to the config file located at `app/config/config.`
`php`, while filling in the `clientId` and `clientSecret` with the values from the
last step:

```
'services' => [
    'google' => [
        'clientId'     => 'put client ID here',
        'clientSecret' => 'put client secret here.'
    ]
],
```

11. Create the `auth` and `oauthProviderGoogle` services in the `app/config/`
`services.php` file:

```
$di->setShared('auth', function() {
    $auth = new Auth();
    $auth->setDI($this);
    return $auth;
});

$di->setShared('oauthProviderGoogle', function() {
    $configProvider = $this->getConfig()
        ->services->google;

    $relativePath = $this->getUrl()
        ->get('session/oauth/google/');

    $redirectUri = 'http://' . $_SERVER['HTTP_HOST'] .
$relativePath;
    $hostedDomain = 'http://' . $_SERVER['HTTP_HOST'];
```

```
        return new League\OAuth2\Client\Provider\Google([
            'clientId'     => $configProvider->clientId,
            'clientSecret' => $configProvider->clientSecret,
            'redirectUri'  => $redirectUri,
            'hostedDomain' => $hostedDomain
        ]);
    });
```

12. Create the controller, app/controllers/SessionController.php:

```php
<?php

class SessionController extends Phalcon\Mvc\Controller
{
    public function indexAction()
    {
    }

    public function oauthRedirectAction()
    {
        $provider = $this->dispatcher->getParam(0);
        if (!isset($provider)) {
            error_log('The provider name is not set.');
            return false;
        }

        $authUrl = $this->getDI()
            ->getAuth()
            ->getAuthorizationUrl($provider);

        $this->response->redirect($authUrl, true);
        $this->response->send();
        return false;

    }

    public function oauthAction()
    {
        $provider = $this->dispatcher->getParam(0);
        $code = $this->request->get('code');
        if (empty($code)) {
```

```
                $this->flash->error('The OAuth provider information is
    invalid.');
                return false;
            }

            $ownerDetails = $this->auth->checkOauth($provider, $code);

            $email = $ownerDetails->getEmail();

            $user = Users::findFirstByEmail($email);
            if ($user) {
                $this->flash->success("User with email '$email' signed
    in successfully.");
            } else {
                $user = new Users();
                $user->email = $email;
                $user->save();
                $this->flash->success("Successfully created user with
    email: '$email'.");
            }
        }
    }
```

13. Create the `app/library/Auth.php`:

```php
<?php

class Auth extends Phalcon\DI\Injectable
{
    public function checkOauth($providerName, $code)
    {
        switch ($providerName) {
            case 'google':
                $provider = $this->getDI()
                    ->getOauthProviderGoogle();
                break;
            default:
                throw new AuthException('Invalid oauth provider');
                break;
        }

        $token = $provider->getAccessToken('authorization_code', [
            'code' => $code
        ]);
```

```
        // We got an access token, let's now get the owner details
        return $provider->getResourceOwner($token);
    }

    public function getAuthorizationUrl($providerName)
    {
        switch ($providerName) {
            case 'google':
                $authUrl = $this->getDI()
                    ->getOauthProviderGoogle()
                    ->getAuthorizationUrl();
                break;
            default:
                throw new AuthException('Invalid oauth
provider.');
                break;
        }

        return $authUrl;
    }
}
```

14. Create the view, `app/views/session/index.volt`:

```
<a href="{{ url('session/oauthRedirect/google') }}">Signin with Google</a>
```

15. Go to the following pages in the root path of the project:

   ❑ Go to the page `/session` and click **Signin with Google**. Then proceed to sign in normally with Google and it should redirect us back to our website with the message `Successfully created user with email: 'YOUR_EMAIL@gmail.com'`.

   ❑ Go to the page `/session` and click **Signin with Google**, and it should immediately redirect us back to our website with the message `User with email 'YOUR_EMAIL@gmail.com' signed in successfully`.

How it works...

OAuth works using exchanges of cryptographic tokens. When the user first clicks the `session/oauthRedirect/google` link the dispatcher sends an execution to the `Session Controller::oauthRedirectAction` method where we first obtain the authorization URL through the `auth` service:

```
$authUrl = $this->getDI()
    ->getAuth()
    ->getAuthorizationUrl($provider);
```

If we then look into the `Auth::getAuthorizationUrl` method, we find that we are obtaining the authorization URL from our Google OAuth provider service:

```
$authUrl = $this->getDI()
    ->getOauthProviderGoogle()
    ->getAuthorizationUrl();
```

When we look in the `oauthProviderGoogle` service we see that we are calling out to a third-party `League` package, which we installed earlier using Composer. This OAuth provider class accepts our Client ID and Client Secret, which it will use to authenticate with the Google servers. Additionally, we need to supply a `redirectUri` and `hostedDomain` that must match the ones that we provided Google. This helps to seal up any edge-case mischief that a hacker could use to infiltrate a system, as shown in the following code snippet:

```
return new League\OAuth2\Client\Provider\Google([
    'clientId'     => $configProvider->clientId,
    'clientSecret' => $configProvider->clientSecret,
    'redirectUri'  => $redirectUri,
    'hostedDomain' => $hostedDomain
]);
```

Now that we have access to our OAuth provider service we will go back to where this started in `SessionController::oauthRedirectAction`, where we finally send an HTTP header redirected to the user to send them over to the Google servers for authentication. Note that the authorization URL contains secure tokens that were just obtained through communication from our server and Google's server. Take a look at the following code snippet:

```
$this->response->redirect($authUrl, true);
$this->response->send();
return false;
```

At this point we have temporarily lost control of the web request and it is now up to Google to do its part and send the user back to the URI we specified. So our web server waits for the user to authenticate and when Google sends the user back the router should send the user to the `SessionController::oauthAction` action. Next we use our `auth` service to check the `code` that Google sent pack in a query variable:

```
$provider = $this->dispatcher->getParam(0);
$code = $this->request->get('code');

$ownerDetails = $this->auth->checkOauth($provider, $code);
```

So now let's jump into the `Auth::checkOauth` method to see what happens there. First we use our `oauthProviderGoogle` to once again reach out to Google to see if the `code` that the user's browser just supplied agrees with Google's assessment of the situation:

```
$token = $provider->getAccessToken('authorization_code', [
    'code' => $code
]);
```

After Google has agreed about the situation, we would like to get further details about the user, and so we reach out to Google once again to get additional data, which this is why we needed to enable the Google+ API. So then we return an owner-details object, as shown in the following code snippet:

```
// We got an access token, let's now get the owner details
return $provider->getResourceOwner($token);
```

Now, going back to our `SessionController::oauthAction` method, we access the e-mail address and if a user already exists with this address, then we will sign them in If not, then we will create a new user:

```
$email = $ownerDetails->getEmail();

$user = Users::findFirstByEmail($email);
if ($user) {
    $this->flash->success("User with email '$email' signed in
successfully.");
} else {
    $user = new Users();
    $user->email = $email;
    $user->save();
    $this->flash->success("Successfully created user with email:
'$email'.");
}
```

Note that there are many ways to use OAuth and each provider can either use the most generic of configurations or, in the case of Google, they can have their own specific configurations and additional features.

Index

D

data
securing, with encryption 328-331
database timeout
handling 248-255
data caching
for reducing access, to database
systems 307-315
Debug component 221
default routing strategy
for controllers 54-56
dependencies
registering, in effective way 171-174
Dependency Injection Container (DIC)
about **27**
reference 175
using, on different scopes 175-177
Dependency Injection (DI) 12, 169
dispatching loop
reference 62
DRY (Don't Repeat Yourself) 53, 148

E

encryption
data, securing with 328-331
event driven programming
about 170, 178-182
reference 184
Events Manager
about 178
reference 184

F

features, query builder
reference 104
Firebug
reference 224
Firelogger
reference 224
flexible key-value action parameter pairs
using 60-62

H

handy persistence
for controllers, and components 200-205
hashing
passwords, securing with 331-338
Heredoc string format 111
**HMVC (Hierarchical Model View
Controller) 57**
HTML fragments
for AJAX-based applications 142-148
HTTP Request 28
HTTP Response 28

I

implementation
best location, selecting for 32-35
improved exception reporting 222-224
information repositories
models, using as 124-132
in-memory session handlers
using 195-200
Integrated Development Environment (IDE)
about 1, 2
ways, to enable Phalcon API autocompletion,
in NetBeans 3
ways, to enable Phalcon API autocompletion,
in PhpStorm 3
ways, to enable Volt syntax highlighting, in
NetBeans 3
ways, to enable Volt syntax highlighting, in
PhpStorm 3

J

Jinja template engine 142
jQuery 147

L

layout structure
splitting 148-151
Lazy Initialization
about 14
reference 19

M

Memcache 279
middleware
  reference 52
middleware, adding between Phalcon and app
  about 44
  critical errors, logging 44-46
  description and keywords meta tags,
    modifying depending on route 47, 48
  pages, caching to reduce processing 50, 51
  site status reports, receiving 48, 49
  user, redirecting to login screen 51, 52
model metadata
  caching, for faster performance 270-281
models
  fetching, from raw SQL queries 113-121
  naming conventions, applying to 92-94
  presenting 154-161
  relationships, defining between 96-99
  storing, across multiple databases 132-139
  using, as information repositories 124-132
mod-rewrite rules 23
multiple controllers
  request, handling along 57-59
multiple databases
  models, storing across 132-139

N

naming conventions
  applying, to models 92-94

O

OAuth
  about 353
  reference 328
  using, for account authorization 353-362
online cache
  reference 205
ORM, in Phalcon
  reference 315
ORM (Object Relational Model) 238

P

passwords
  securing, with hashing 331-339
PCRE format
  about 194
  reference 195
PDO, in PHP
  reference 44
Phalcon
  about 1
  extending, Zephir used 322-325
Phalcon Backend Cache interface 314
Phalcon Developer Tools 55, 171, 192
Phalcon Developer Tools installation
  reference 40
Phalcon DI documentation
  reference 177
Phalcon Incubator 17
Phalcon Incubator GitHub repository
  reference 306
Phalcon installation notes
  reference 23
Phalcon\Mvc\Micro application type
  reference 52
Phalcon\Mvc\View component
  reference 298
PHP extension
  creating, Zephir used 315-321
PHP-FPM configuration directives
  reference 23
PHQL (Phalcon Query Language)
  capabilities 104-112
PHQL queries
  optimizing 262-269
PSR-0 standard
  about 14
  reference 19
PSR-4 standard 14

Q

query builder
  using, for complex yet fluent model
    querying 100-104
query results
  caching, for faster performance 270-281

R

Ratchet
  reference 87
Ratchet Websocket server
  creating 78-86
raw SQL queries
  models, fetching from 113-121
RDBMS
  using 121-124
React PHP
  reference 87
reconnection feature 74
Redis 195, **279**
redis-cli 196
relationships
  defining, between models 95-99
request
  handling, along multiple controllers 57-59
request entry point
  setting up 7-13, 19-22
request life cycle
  about 2, 23-27
  working 27-29
route test suite
  creating 227-232
routine tasks
  automating 36-40
routing documentation
  reference 195

S

Scaffold
  reference 44
scaffold command 143
scopes
  DI container, using on 175-177
server messages
  logging, to browser console 224-226
server-sent events
  reference 77
server-sent message server
  creating 75-78
Service Locator 169

session adapter configuration
  reference 200
Singletons 177
slow queries
  detecting 238-245
Sublime Text
  syntax highlighting 4
synchronous processes 285

T

telnet 196
TextMate
  syntax highlighting 4
three-level cache
  implementing, for increasing
    performance 292-295
transaction mechanisms
  availability, checking 206
  working 206-211
transactions
  reference 212

U

unsuccessful requests
  making fail, softly 69-74
UUIDs (Universally Unique Identifiers) 125

V

validation changes, Phalcon blog
  reference 191
validations
  centralizing, for rock solid
    business rules 184-191
  reference 192
view fragments
  caching 295-297
view snippets
  reusing 162-165
Vökuró
  about 178
  reference 184
Volt engine 192